BEASTLY MORALITY

Beastly Morality

Animals as Ethical Agents

Edited by JONATHAN K. CRANE

Columbia University Press
New York

Columbia University Press
Publishers Since 1893
New York   Chichester, West Sussex
cup.columbia.edu
Copyright © 2016 Columbia University Press
All rights reserved

Library of Congress Cataloging-in-Publication Data
Beastly morality : animals as ethical agents / edited by Jonathan K. Crane.
pages cm
Includes bibliographical references and index.
ISBN 978-0-231-17416-9 (cloth : alk. paper) — ISBN 978-0-231-17417-6
(pbk. : alk. paper) — ISBN 978-0-231-54053-7 (e-book)
1. Animals (Philosophy)   2. Agent (Philosophy)   3. Conduct of life.   4. Ethics.
I. Crane, Jonathan K. (Jonathan Kadane), editor.
B105.A55B43 2015
179'.3—dc23
2015009579

⊗

Columbia University Press books are printed on permanent and durable acid-free paper.
This book is printed on paper with recycled content.
Printed in the United States of America

c 10 9 8 7 6 5 4 3 2 1
p 10 9 8 7 6 5 4 3 2 1

COVER DESIGN: Milenda Nan Ok Lee

COVER IMAGE: Courtesy Myrtle Beach Safari. Bubbles the elephant
and Bella the dog share one of the amazing animal friendships
that have developed at Myrtle Beach Safari in South Carolina.

References to websites (URLs) were accurate at the time of writing. Neither the author
nor Columbia University Press is responsible for URLs that may have expired or changed
since the manuscript was prepared.

For Nadav, Amitai, and Rafael

What we need now . . . is a philosophy that does not discriminate between different species, one that addresses each being on an individual basis.

—JAMES RACHELS

Contents

Acknowledgments

IN THE FIRST FACULTY MEETING I attended at Emory University's Center for Ethics, we were invited to share our research interests. One scholar—Lori Marino, a cetologist and professor of psychology—mentioned her varied and profound projects in animal studies, including animal mentation and psychology. Intrigued, I approached her to learn more, and those conversations led us to develop a new cotaught course, Animal Ethics, combining psychology, ethology, philosophy, religion, anthropology, history, and more—to spur rethinking about how we humans conceive the very category of "animal." The years of teaching that course with Lori, as well as the decades of working alongside Aaron S. Gross, a brilliant scholar of religion and animal studies and founder of the animal-advocacy organization Farm Forward, and the seeming lack of a venue devoted to animal ethics broadly construed inspired me to organize a symposium in which myriad disciplines would be welcome to offer fresh thoughts about animals. The first Animal Ethics Workshop, in 2012, was without theme and gathered only local scholars. To be sure, the scholarship was excellent, and the energy was as palpable as the interest in deepening and expanding the conversation. Emboldened, I composed a theme for the next year's conference—exploring the question of *Beastly Morality*—and advertised more strategically. Proposals streamed in from around the world, and I invited what I thought were the best dozen to present at a one-day conference. That day's conversation in 2013 brought together an internationally and disciplinarily diverse scholarly community. When Frans de Waal asked in his plenary presentation who among those present worked with actual animals, the silence was both telling and unsurprising. The resounding quiet eloquently articulated the increasing need for scholars throughout the academy who work in, on, and with animals to speak with and to one another. For how could the field of animal studies be a field if its ostensible contributors do not interact? To at least approximate this more ideal and mixed conversation, I sought out a few more ethologists to contribute to this otherwise humanities-rich collection.

Gratitude is thus due to the scholars who contributed to that conference and this volume. They worked and reworked their pieces to make even more compelling arguments on whether, whence, and whither animal morality. I also appreciate the support of Wendy Lochner at Columbia University Press for honing and improving the project, as well as the responses of the anonymous reviewers. Those conferences and this book would not have come into being were it not for the unwavering support of Paul Root Wolpe, the director of the Center for Ethics. Thanks are also extended to Kristina Johnson, who diligently worked on the manuscript and kept my loose ends tidy. I am grateful to the Department of Religion at Emory University, the Judith London Evans Director's Fund of Emory University's Tam Institute for Jewish Studies, and the Center for Ethics for their critical support completing this volume.

Thanks are also due to colleagues in the Society of Jewish Ethics and the American Academy of Religion who offered suggestions and encouragement throughout this endeavor. I am grateful for the many scholars at Emory University who contributed to and took interest in this project. Of course, included in this group of supporters is my greatest thinking partner, provocateur, and muse, Lindy Miller, whose insights and challenges inspire me no end.

Thinking about animals, and animal morality in particular, is no easy task; to be sure, more needs to be done. I hereby acknowledge and thank that future conversation for enriching us all.

Introduction

One Beastly Morality

A TWISTING TALE

Jonathan K. Crane

THE 2013 DOCUMENTARY *BLACKFISH* EXPOSES the dramatic story of Tilikum, a massive orca whale captured for the sole purpose of performing for human audiences, first at SeaLand in British Columbia and then at SeaWorld in Florida. Ripped from his natural oceanic environment, trapped in confinement pens, subjected to hours, years even, of grueling training—is it any wonder he exhibited psychological trauma? Should we be shocked that Tilikum, a killer whale, killed and injured many humans over several decades of being confined to relatively tiny swimming pools and trained to do what humans wanted him to do—not what he wanted to do? Professional trainers who worked with Tilikum and other orca whales concur with cetologists: we should not.

Such giant creatures of the deep are not just highly intelligent. They are unique individuals whose identities are bound up with their freedom of movement, communicating with their pods, learning and teaching collaborative behaviors, and participating in and contributing to their underwater cultures. The tenderness for which they are renowned is evident when they are encountered in the wild, in environments where they can exercise control and can escape if need be. Lacking both autonomy and social and environmental stimuli, captured orcas experience stress. For years Tilikum suffered such stress, but after an incident eight years after his capture in 1983, he nonetheless chose to abide by the rules and regulations his human captors imposed upon him. After more years of such treatment and of holding himself in check, Tilikum again chose to act out lethally by killing a second human.

Though *Blackfish* explicitly and strongly critiques the animal-captivity industry (which would rather be known as the animal-entertainment industry), it raises a host of other questions about how we humans can and perhaps should view these—and many other—animals.[1] To be sure, the documentary challenges us to rethink what animal welfare means in practical terms. Moreover, it pushes us to revisit our commitment to viewing nonhuman animals as objects of human moral concern in the first place. And, more profoundly, it points to the possibility and even reality that nonhuman animals, especially such intelligent ones as killer whales, function with what appears to be an internal sense of appropriateness— that is, with notions of good and bad: ideas of morality. It is precisely these deeper possibilities that this present volume fleshes out.

COILS

Long have we humans assumed nonhuman animals to be lowly creatures of scant intelligence whose sentience consists only in base and impulsive reactions. For millennia this mind-set has justified human use and abuse of animals. It justified both preferential treatment of *Homo sapiens* and smug indifference to the plight of beasts. Philosophies, theologies, and eventually modern sciences colluded to reinforce this comforting perspective. An ancient example is the Great Chain of Being or *Scala Natura*, which depicted a tiered model of entities: soil and rock at the bottom, above which would be plants, then animals, then humans, and over us would be angels and ultimately gods/God.[2] This model ascended as theoretical truth even while people scrambled to find concrete evidence to support it. Its hierarchical construction of the world conveniently reinforced human supremacy. Few challenged the fact that its maker was humankind, the species ranked just shy of the ethereal angels, who also could do little wrong.

In recent centuries Cartesian thought further severed any ties between the ways humans think about themselves and the ways they consider nonhuman animals. Indeed, Descartes viewed animals primarily (if not completely) as automatons, flesh and viscera responding to stimuli with little if any cognitive activity.[3] For him, bestial nature shared nothing meaningful with human nature beyond the organic. Taking his cue from Plato, he viewed the mind—and his definition of intelligence in particular—as what mattered; ephemeral materiality be damned. Animals, mindless critters that they are, ghost in and away from the terrestrial scene without significance or trace. In this worldview, affording them much attention is a colossal waste of time and energy. Atop the plateau of organic existence are those thinking creatures we recognize as ourselves; all other creatures scrabble mindlessly below. What matters morally is the intelligent crest of creation, not its lower masses.

Crevices have appeared in this conceptual edifice, however.

In just the past couple of centuries and especially the last few decades, much work has been done to reshape our thinking about nonhuman animals. New perspectives have challenged the idea of them as unintelligent—and thus senseless—beasts to which most anything can be done with impunity. Animals are no longer viewed merely as animated organic stuff whose value rests exclusively on whether they benefit humanity. Rather, with Jeremy Bentham's not novel, yet provocative claim that animals suffer—indeed, that they *feel*—nonhuman animals can now be seen as suffering creatures. In this way, animals evolved in our thought from mindless beast machines to suffering machines, à la Descartes's *bête machine*. For some, this evolution in thought—that other creatures suffer, too—admittedly changed little in how they treated animals or viewed themselves.

For many others, however, Bentham's claim that suffering should be the measure of moral significance opened their eyes to a world overflowing with all sorts of pain and, more astonishingly and uncomfortably, a world flooded with moral obligations. Given the assumption that suffering is bad and even reprehensible in certain circumstances, the logic goes that suffering should be avoided or at least mitigated. Action is owed on the sufferer's behalf. This means that the sufferer is not just an object of concern but an object of *moral* concern, and that category now included animals.

However disquieting this new vision of human responsibility for animals may have been, its reflexive quality proved even more disturbing. For this line of thinking reflected back to us our own image as en-suffering agents. Quite frequently, we humans were the ones causing these other creatures copious amounts of heinous harm. From confining them for entertainment to fattening them up for eating, from experimenting upon and inside them for biomedical and other industrial goals to exterminating them for hides or horns or out of disgust, from chaining them to do difficult labor to destroying their natural habitats for human purposes—the examples are too numerous to list exhaustively.

We still continue to justify, explain away, and reinscribe some of those harms. For example, we eat (of) them, so we need to husband and hoard them. We wear them, so we need to skin them, etc. By contrast, we forced ourselves to jettison some habits because we could not find reasonable ways to justify the suffering they cause: cockfighting, for example. Many other habits, however, we labored to regulate, and thereby justified causing (some) nonhuman animals (some) harm (some of the time): for example, regulating hunting and fishing locales and seasons, not to mention animals in the food industry as a whole. In only a few instances did we abandon practices wholesale because we could no longer stomach understanding ourselves as agents who do such things to sufferable others (say, exterminating certain iconic species like the American bison).

By admitting that animals suffer, we reflected our moral gaze back upon ourselves. Who were *we* to do such things? In time and through much political hand-wringing and industrial resistance, increasing numbers of species came into view as objects of moral concern: food-stock animals, companion animals, entertainment animals, captivity animals (e.g., in zoos and safari parks), endangered species in their natural biological niches, and more. Time and again various kinds of suffering were identified and categorized, horror and outrage were expressed, and mitigations and sometimes solutions were offered. These solutions, however, were of a certain sort. If animal conditions could be improved or if animal abuse could be abated, use of nonhuman animals could continue; their use could receive reasonable and reasoned justifications. Many figured that the use of animals should be protected by law and custom. Such thoughts, concerns, investigations, and instruments began to coalesce into what today is known as animal welfare.

Animal welfare, while revolutionary in many aspects, nonetheless maintains its ultimate gaze on the human animal, not the nonhuman animal. Insofar as it perceives nonhuman animals as objects of moral concern, it challenges humans to consider them so. Put differently, the final audience of animal welfare and the ultimate object of its concern is we humans. Animal welfare unwittingly, and in some instances conscientiously, reinscribes nonhuman animals as a distinct (and denigrated) other: they remain the passive objects of pitying, paternalizing people. We change our attitudes and behaviors toward certain classes of animals not because of the animals as such but because we humans (or at least some of us) cannot sustain self-understandings that include such atrocious treatment and use of them. Treat them nicely, animal welfarists insist, because they are objects of our moral concern. Why? Because our own moral integrity is at stake. The reflexive gaze seals itself back upon the viewer, keeping the nonhuman animal beyond our actual view, at a distance, a remove so far that they all but fade from the conversation. Though treated a bit better because of animal-welfarist efforts, the animal as such nonetheless remains ostracized, because the ultimate object of moral concern is ourselves.

No less a philosopher than Immanuel Kant endorses this coiling perspective. In his view, we humans are duty-bound to treat animals with a modicum of kindness precisely because such behavior toward them shapes how we treat one another:

> Thus, if a dog has served his master long and faithfully, his service, on the analogy of human service, deserves reward, and when the dog has grown too old to serve, his master ought to keep him until he dies. Such action helps to support us in our duties towards human beings. . . . We have duties towards the animals because thus we cultivate the corresponding duties toward human beings. . . . [Man] must practice kindness towards animals, for he who is cruel to animals becomes hard also in his dealings with men.[4]

We should treat animals nicely not because the animals need, want, or inherently deserve our kindness but because we need to practice being kind, especially to our conspecifics.

Kant is not alone in holding this attitude. An earlier champion of caring for animals precisely because it is ultimately good for humans is the *Sefer ha-Chinuch*, a thirteenth-century Jewish work enumerating the 613 commandments hidden in the Bible. Rule 596 requires humans to be kind to animals so that our souls acquire a propensity to treat fellow humans kindly. A century earlier, the great twelfth-century Egyptian physician, philosopher, and legal scholar Moses Maimonides teaches the inverse. We are forbidden from eating a limb torn from an animal because it would instill in us cruelty.[5] Behaving cruelly toward animals trains us to be nasty to one another.

Such philosophical and theological perspectives focus the human moral gaze primarily, if not solely, upon the human. Insofar as such views may look at animals, they do so only to search for refraction or reflection. For them, human nature and stature are what matter. Animals per se remain paradoxically tangible and palpable, yet morally invisible or at most relatively unimportant.

That philosophers and theologians contemplated the animal through the lens of the human is not surprising.[6] What is perhaps surprising is that scientists who study animals did so as well. Though naturalists fixed their scholarly gazes on nonhuman animals, they nonetheless did so primarily to discern something about that wily and curious creature *Homo sapiens*. Take the great Austrian psychological biologist Konrad Lorenz as an example. His famous mid-twentieth-century work on nonhuman species' aggressiveness and cooperativeness, *On Aggression*, was geared to clarify why it is that we humans so abuse and torture one another. Lorenz's reflexive investigations were not unusual in the field of ethology, the discipline of studying animal behavior under natural conditions. His graduate fellow and eventual colleague Niko Tinbergen, the Dutch ornithologist at Oxford University, developed a fourfold investigative scheme (ontogeny, phylogeny, mechanism, adaptation) that he then applied to human problems such as autism. While certainly these and many other ethologists study animals because of their fascination with them, their investigations of animal behavior were nonetheless motivated in part by deep-seated concerns about human nature and behavior.

Yet as the field of ethology matured and its professionalization expanded across the continents, its focus shifted away from *Homo sapiens* and reoriented around its primary target: nonhuman animals. The question What did animals do? became the field's central question, irrespective of human analogues. The study of animal behavior in their natural habitats as well as in manufactured laboratory settings became de rigueur. In this way behavioral ecology, the discernment and explanation of species-typical behavior, arose to constitute modern ethology.

The scientific study of animals in and of themselves has shed many of its reflexive concerns. A burgeoning discourse is available on animal behavior, animal psychology, animal cognition, animal culture, and more—all without reference to humanity. This is not to say that all contemporary ethological studies ignore humankind altogether. Indeed, much literature is produced and translated into popular works, such as *Blackfish*, that highlight humankind's impact upon animals, especially animals within and extracted from their natural habitats.[7] A vast and growing literature is also based upon invasive studies of animals—studies in which humans have interfered with their "subjects" by invading the animals' bodies and brains, manufacturing unnatural environments, or genetically engineering the animals. Such studies raise interesting (and troubling) questions about the extent to which the animals studied in this way are truly "themselves," behaving as they would "naturally," and to what extent they are human constructs—constructed and constricted to produce what humans want to observe. However powerful invasive animal studies may be, they remain scientifically, philosophically, legally, theologically, and morally suspect.

That said, if the ethological gaze upon animals is now more or less focused upon animals qua animals, what might this mean? On the one hand, humankind is rightfully dislocated from the center of these scientific investigations so that other creatures can be seen in and of themselves. On the other hand, it could also indicate an increasing severance of the intimate interdependencies between nonhuman animals and humans. For example, consider a recent International Ethological Conference of the Association for the Study of Animal Behavior in August 2013—the largest conference in the field, with eight hundred participants from around the world. Of the thirty-three symposium-style conversations, three addressed animal welfare (a fourth looked at which kinds of death are good for animals). That is, just a tiny fraction of this five-day gathering of the globe's greatest ethologists explicitly explored humankind's influence on animals. By contrast, many projects scattered throughout the conference's other symposia and presentations developed ethological explanations of human evolution. Such fascination with the animal foundations of human nature and capacity bespeaks a kind of narcissism that is hard to shake off. Ethology, supposedly the study of nonhuman animals, seems to be stubbornly concerned with learning about other creatures simply to learn more about ourselves.

To be sure, this is not to say the whole field of ethology and other kinds of animal studies coil their curiosity and creative energies back upon humankind to the exclusion of appreciating other species in and of themselves. Rather, it is to point to a profound dynamic—the constant struggle between studying animals for our benefit and studying them for their own.

This tension is not unique to ethology, of course. Many other disciplines wrestle with the impulse to study animals for the purpose of elucidating human peculiarities and specialness. Philosophy, theology, sociology, ecology, literature, and law, to name but a few fields, also evidence this struggle. These disciplines have long looked upon animals for cues and clues about humankind's nature and self-ascribed superiority, and this impulse continues unabated today. A few popular scholars illustrate this point nicely. Alasdair MacIntyre's *Dependent Rational Animals* works through animals and animality to reinforce his contention that virtues are critical for humans and human nature. Kelly Oliver's *Animal Lessons* echoes this philosophical impulse: animals teach us how to be human, a claim that human ecologist Paul Shepard supports in his *The Others: How Animals Made Us Human*. Such a list can easily go on.

However thin this sampling may seem, it nonetheless indicates the difficulty of appreciating animals in and of themselves, without automatic recourse to or reflection back upon humankind. It also raises a serious question about the very possibility of appreciating animals as such. Might it be possible to look upon nonhuman animals as something more significant than mere objects of human moral concern or as stepping-stones to greater self-understanding or as evidence of human specialness? If so, how?

RECOILING

This volume suggests—and hopefully demonstrates—that looking upon nonhuman animals and appreciating them in their own right is more than a mere possibility. Many of the essays included here argue that this is something that *should* be done. Why? Because increasing evidence from a variety of fields shows that many nonhuman animals look upon themselves and others this way. Tilikum and other orca whales are easy examples to consider. Data are quickly accumulating that show that nonhuman animals are sentient, thinking, self-recognizing, and other-concerned creatures. Such data are certainly biological and behavioral—that is, objectively observable. Yet philosophical, legal, and theological arguments are also emerging along the same lines, expressing a profound recoiling against the narcissism innate to most human attitudes toward—and treatment and assessment of—nonhuman animals.

There is, it seems fair to say, a growing skepticism and even rejection of the human wont to persistently see nonhuman animals as wholly nonmoral creatures, as beings whose apparent kindness is accidental and surprising or, as already noted, as creatures whose fundamental purpose is in part to elucidate how we humans can be better at being human, if not humane. This spiraling anthropocentrism that has long reigned in animal studies is increasingly found wanting, if not suffocating. Its underlying presumption that *Homo sapiens* is the only moral species fails in the face of an honest assessment of recent history and contemporary science. We kill and abuse ourselves in disturbing ways and at alarming rates despite and perhaps because of our presumptive and exclusive morality.

One reason this presumption has endured for so long has to do with the definitional project of constructing categories. Humans have been the ones who created the concepts of personhood, consciousness, morality, and the like. Convinced that we are ab initio special, we humans defined these and related concepts in such ways that only we—or, to be even more historically precise, that only *some* of us (e.g., men, city dwellers, whites, Christians, landowners, etc.)—are the rightful members of these categories. In this way we narrowed the scope of moral citizenship to a single creature: the human. Morality conveniently coiled upon itself, as if to soothe its sole member.

This structure certainly made it expedient to dismiss nonhuman animals from morality and other categories. It also enabled us to excuse or rather excommunicate from the protected environs of "the moral" those fellow humans who failed to (or allegedly failed to) uphold or demonstrate the demands morality makes upon its citizens. Those reprobates and barbarians were to be stripped of their membership in the sacred community of the moral; throughout history they were not just evicted but often hunted and exterminated. The impulse to caricature human outsiders as outside human civilization and beyond human moral concern rendered them not just as other than human but less than human. As philosopher Sam Keen shows in *Faces of the Enemy*, the twentieth century especially drips with the blood of those who were deemed—rightly or wrongly—unworthy to be members of human (moral) communities, who were cast visually, culturally, and legally as grotesque creatures and beasts, vermin and insects to be eradicated.

Yet the very fact that some humans could be excluded from the state of morality (a.k.a. humanity) suggests that morality's borders are more porous than hitherto imagined. If egress is possible and even necessary in some instances, ingress should be possible—necessary, even—as well. This opens the question of whether other creatures with nonhuman features could be welcome within the realm of morality.

In *The Philosophy of Animal Minds*, edited by Robert Lurz, philosophers wrestle with this question. Many argue that, contrary to claims of human exceptionalism, many nonhuman animals also are self-conscious and self-aware, manifest theory of mind (perceiving the world through another's eyes or experiences), and demonstrate sophisticated prosocial behaviors and empathic responses to others, as well as other dimensions of what we otherwise consider constituent dimensions of human morality.[8] If this is so, to be philosophically consistent we must also consider certain animals and species to be moral, albeit with different sets of salient moral impulses and considerations.

Many of these philosophical arguments rely upon the mounting evidence that ethologists are uncovering about animal behavior and thought. It is well known now that primates, cetaceans, elephants, dogs, some birds, and a few other species readily and regularly demonstrate moral intellection and behavior. Studies now show that even rats behave prosocially toward distressed conspecifics without any training or external reward.[9]

Just as some philosophers are making novel arguments about animal morality, scholars of religion are also uncovering sources embedded within religious traditions that speak to these observed and argued realities. Classic sacred texts, religious myths, lore, and even, in some instances, religious law are found to contain theologically grounded reasons to view nonhuman animals as more than just suffering creatures, as more than thoughtless automata. They speak of nonhuman animals as intelligent creatures, sensitive and responsive to their own and others' suffering and communicative in their unique ways. Certainly these diverse religious sources exclaim ancient and enduring admiration of nonhuman animals. They also express anxiety about claiming human specialness. Since some of these sources threaten the long-held theological assumption of human uniqueness and elevated status, it is understandable that religious discourse about the religio-moral status of nonhuman animals has been marginalized in animal studies, not to mention in religious studies. Indeed, bringing these ethological, philosophical, and religious voices out from the sidelines and into the mainstream conversation—as we do here—is not an inconsequential move. It could very well challenge how and what we humans think and believe about nonhuman animals and, eventually— if we allow it—even about ourselves.

UNSPOOLING

If the boundary of "the moral" is more porous than previously conceived and egress and ingress are possible, this is not to say that no boundary at all exists. Nor does it mean that the boundary is so thin that something is either inside or outside that category. Rather, the boundary has some depth, and crossing its threshold is a conceptual, often arduous journey.

Some things are patently and reasonably held to be beyond "the moral": basic elements like mercury and rubidium, for example, are matter without morality. Their moral significance is, for all intents and purposes, close to nil; they exist beyond the moral border. Other things, like plants and the biosphere generally, however, are more difficult to exclude wholesale from the realm of "the moral." Increasing awareness of the importance of the biosphere to sustain life impresses upon many humans the need to see it as morally significant. And some animals, like pets, food animals, and even show animals, have become so useful and cherished that they, too, are increasingly viewed as morally significant. In this fashion certain creatures and features of the world have come to be situated in the liminal space between the amoral and the moral. They populate the category of *objects of moral concern*; they have moral significance, albeit variable.

Expanding the classes eligible for moral concern has long been fraught with challenges. This is particularly evident when we consider how tightly the realm of "the moral" was defined by and confined to certain classes of humans. For example, some people found it repugnant to consider people who looked different or were of a different gender or class or terrain or language or religion or what have you as meritorious of moral concern at all. They would rather exclude those fellow *Homo sapiens* from this sacred class than admit them alongside themselves. Especially since the Enlightenment, this xenophobic pastime has been increasingly disputed. With the French Revolution, huge swaths of humanity were suddenly viewed by the state as morally significant, indeed so significant as to merit individual recognition instead of subsumption into a class or community. The emancipation of slaves in the United States marked another major expansion of who qualifies for admittance into the realm of moral concern. (It took another hundred years, however, before African Americans were granted equal citizenship.) The suffrage movement for women's enfranchisement that swept across Europe and the United States in the early part of the twentieth century and the resistance to it also illustrate the struggles many had when considering arguments to expand the qualifications for inclusion in the realm of moral concern beyond male genitalia. Recent decades have seen continuing calls for the LGBT community to be admitted to the category of the moral, as well as undocumented immigrants and the religiously persecuted, among others.

Once an individual or class is admitted to the realm of objects of moral concern, it becomes increasingly difficult or costly to treat them with impunity. Certain protections are extended to them, perhaps even privileges and, in some instances, rights. Still, those who populate this nebulous realm are not in the same position as those squarely situated within what is considered to be "the moral." Their stature remains "less than," and their freedoms are circumscribed.

Something curious happens, though, in regard to those who are entered into this realm. People—the creatures who created the realm in the first place—perforce must consider those objects of moral concern differently than objects that are beyond that category. Whereas people consider the amoral realm predominantly in terms of quantity, when objects of moral concern are contemplated, dimensions of quality come to the fore. Quality (of life, existence)—an ambiguous concept, to be sure—becomes an inescapable feature that people must contend with as they go about thinking of and interacting with objects of moral concern. This is because objects of moral concern warrant at least a basic quality (of existence, life), and that minimum requires protection and, perhaps, nourishment. It is for this reason that some people balk at expanding the membership in this realm: it is a costly move insofar as it requires people to expend mental and perhaps physical and fiscal resources caring for and about those entities. They would rather hoard such attention only for themselves and those already subsumed into the class of objects of moral concern and refuse to admit new members.

Since quality becomes an intelligible concept only vis-à-vis the class of objects of moral concern, it simultaneously carries with it another thread, the thread of individuation. The appropriate quality of life or existence for one object of moral concern may or may not be the same for another object of moral concern. Difference, and substantive difference at that, appears with (that is, as an intelligible concept in and of itself) and within this realm. Objects beyond the moral boundary are coupled together, aggregated into undifferentiated masses. One carbon molecule is no different from another, for all intents and purposes; they may rightfully be treated and thought of as the same, as fungible. Inside the moral boundary, however, it is necessary to untie these individual differences, and in so doing, biographies spill and spool out.

An example from literature illustrates well how biography becomes discernible once an entity passes into and through the moral boundary. Red Peter, the *Hominidae* hero of Franz Kafka's brilliant short story "A Report for an Academy" (1917), explains to the anonymous gathering of purported scholars his tumultuous tumble from animality into humanity. This at times humiliating experience reinforced for all and sundry that his unique life is as biographical as anyone else's in that auditorium. Indeed, his story expresses the undeniable truth that certain animals, at least, view themselves as creatures with distinct identities, replete with histories and hopes, burdened with memories and emotions. Red Peter concludes his lecture by admitting that he cannot bear looking at the half-trained female chimpanzee waiting for him in the evenings because he is the only one who can recognize in her "the madness of a bewildered trained animal." That he cannot bear witnessing her suffering bespeaks something revolutionary: Peter, an ape, sees in his fellow *Hominidae* a suffering that ought not be. He wishes things were otherwise—that she did not suffer so, or that he was not exposed to her suffering, or that he was not sensitive to her suffering; regardless of what he means by this, it is crystal clear that he wants circumstances to be different for them both. Just before shuffling away from the podium, Red Peter reminds the audience that he seeks no human judgment; he only wants to expand knowledge.

The force of the story of Red Peter demonstrates that some nonhuman objects of moral concern are endowed with more than mere biology; theirs is a biographical existence, a tapestry of unique experiences and expectations. More, Red Peter articulates that he sees fellow members of this nebulous class as benumbed suffering creatures, so inured to their conditions that they seem duped if not doped. This incredible sensitivity to the (deleterious) well-being of his fellow creatures, this yearning for their suffering to end, points to something even more powerful than biography: it evidences that he, at least, can think otherwise. Through Kafka's deft pen, Red Peter envisions an alternate existence in which he and she would not be so confined to their silly roles and subject to heteronomous rules. It is this ability—albeit literally imagined—to think otherwise, and to labor for it, however inefficiently, that demonstrates the capacity to choose between reinforcing suffering and releasing suffering and to behave accordingly. Kafka's vision of an animal contemplating and actively searching for an alternate present condition and different future eloquently depicts features of what can be understood as moral agency.

A century later, could it be that thinking about and pursuing a circumstance different from the current one is what Tilikum, a real animal, did? Consider this: early in his captivity he aggressed against his human captors, killing one and maiming others. They responded by shutting down that initial facility and shipping him to another, larger one. Is it inconceivable that from this he learned that aggressing against the humans he most frequently encountered would produce an alternate, perhaps marginally better circumstance for himself? Given the ample evidence of orca memory in general, it would be difficult to deny him this lesson learned. Conversely, and ironically, what is surprising from *Blackfish* is that the humans who claim to own Tilikum consistently refuse to recognize him as a creature whose sense of self is no less complicated, drawn out, and developed than their own. It is they who fail to envision an alternate circumstance in which his quality of existence would meet the needs of his unique biography, not just his biology. It is the humans who fail to learn, not the whale.

I highlight these brief illustrations from literature and reality to suggest that at least some nonhuman animals can conceive of alternate realities, desire them, and act in ways that perhaps might produce them. In so doing they measure their options vis-à-vis certain standards, much as we humans do. Many humans operate consequentially with a preconceived notion of a desired end or with a preferred interest that is to be maximized. Some animals do this as well. If consequentialism can be deemed a reasonable form of moral reasoning and moral agency for humans, it would be unreasonable to deny this kind of reasoning—and agency—to animals manifesting such intellection.

Many humans also base their decisions on some kind of rule or principle. Some of these foundations are endogenous, like Kant's notions of autonomy; others are exogenous, like the revelations and authorities of certain religious traditions. Cultures also accrue rules and ways of thinking about the world that their members embody and practice. Some nonhuman species, especially long-lived social ones, also operate within cultures that have developed unique patterns of considering problems and enacting solutions. Deviants exist, of course, though they are often ostracized from the group that adheres to the culture's rules. Since deontology is considered a reasonable form of moral reasoning and moral agency among humans, it would be inconsistent to deny this kind of moral reasoning and action to those species who manifest it.

There are other ways of thinking and acting morally, to be sure. Consider the virtue of empathy as an example. Whatever else it may be, empathy includes a gesture that ruptures the ego by going beyond its normal numbing narcissism. This mental and physical movement turns the ego's attention from self to other. Parents attending to the existential cries of infants manifest this primal connection in which the other's well-being takes precedence over the ego's.[10] Every civilization, if it is to be one, incorporates and cultivates through its customs and traditions high esteem for such care, and conversely, eschews compromising others' abilities to self-care. In their simplest forms these instructions are known as the Golden Rule.

Human beings nearly everywhere and at every time identified the Golden Rule as necessary for human flourishing. They embedded it within their religious traditions, they extolled its features within their philosophies, and even made it mandatory in some legal jurisdictions. Still, not all Golden Rules are alike; two kinds emerged over time. The negative version instructs restraint; the positive encourages intervention. One sets a baseline of at least not causing harm; the other points toward aspirational or idealized beneficent behavior. While examples of these rules abound, too many to list exhaustively, let these versions suffice for our purpose here: "What is hateful to you do not do to another" and "Love another as yourself."

Both versions insist on caring for others, whether through acts of omission, such as not injuring, or through acts of commission, by actively intervening. Yet while these Golden Rules encourage an agent to care for an other, they do not require abandoning self-concern altogether. The purposeful displacement of concern away from the ego nonetheless remains partly self-referential. Both the negative and the positive versions invoke the ego as the fundamental measure against which behaviors are to be evaluated. Whatever is hateful *to me* I should refrain from doing to another; what is beneficial *to me* I should perform for another. The self is never completely obliterated by the Golden Rule, however much some religious traditions might teach contrariwise.

In this way the Golden Rule subtly presumes that each member of a group is endowed with unique notions of what is hateful and beneficial. Each member has a different idea of what constitutes flourishing. At least, this is especially true for the positive—interventionist—version of the rule. Across civilizations, a general consensus could be ascertained regarding the negative version that instills restraint from harming others. This could be considered a common moral ground. Nevertheless, it is certainly possible for individuals to suppress their distinctive ideas of flourishing so as to abide by a group's conceptualization, just as it is for individuals and groups to disagree about the features of flourishing. Unanimity is not a prerequisite for either version of the Golden Rule to function. Rather, the

Golden Rule operates with the assumption that the ego is a moral agent no less and no more than the other egos surrounding it.

It is here that another step can be made through the boundary between the amoral and the moral. Human conceptualizations of flourishing—of morality—are notoriously diverse. What one person or civilization considers upstanding, another condemns. If human notions of morality defy unanimity or consistency, holding all humans accountable to a single or idealized morality seems both unreasonable and untenable. Human civilization writ large must permit moral diversity. Certainly this does not mean allowing chaos; that would be maladaptive, evolutionarily speaking. It means that the realm of "the moral" is more diverse, more pliable than some might want to admit.

Insofar as all humans cannot rightfully be beholden to a singular notion and manifestation of morality, expecting nonhuman animals to abide by or manifest a particular morality that humans erect as the "correct" one is all the more specious. Nonhuman-animal morality—whatever that is— must by definition be nonhuman in both concept and behavior. Consider: the impulse among some humans to describe nonhuman animals hunting among themselves as immoral is an example of the imposition of human constructs onto other species. It could very well be that some nonhuman animals and species consider hunting to be necessary for their survival and thus a good in and of itself; for them, it cannot be immoral but rather the very instantiation of morality. Similarly, the human wont to declare certain observed behavior (e.g., grooming) among nonhuman animals as amoral, as without any moral valence whatsoever, again imposes human values and concepts unnecessarily upon other species. As we shall see in subsequent essays in this volume, grooming is a morally significant behavior among some species. Given the diversity of the notions and manifestations of morality among *Homo sapiens*, it stands to reason that morality differs across species and perhaps even among conspecifics.

This line of reasoning leads me to propose viewing some nonhuman animals and species as not merely objects of moral concern but moral agents whose notions and manifestations of morality admittedly differ from humankind's. This is not to say that no nonhuman morality can be comparable or analogous to human morality. Rather, it is to say that a Venn diagram of morality, humanity, and nonhuman animals is more complicated than was sketched out in previous centuries.[11] Earlier depictions portrayed the realms of the moral and of humankind as coterminous, with nonhuman animals being completely separate. History over-flows with human egression from the realm of the moral, puncturing that simple binary and anthropocentric picture. Evidence and arguments now pile up to paint a different picture in which the realm of nonhuman animals overlaps with morality, much as morality overlaps with but is not confined to humanity.

Today, moral agency is no longer unquestionably a feature belonging solely to humankind. There are serious arguments to the effect that we should recognize corporations as moral agents, for example, and that ar-tificial intelligences are reaching levels of complexity that likewise demand recognition. Of course, these may be beholden to notions of morality with dimensions that are not exactly the same as the notions of morality by which human beings are to abide. If businesses and artificial intel-ligences can be understood as moral agents operating with or measured by a distinct set of moral concepts, it is at least conceptually plausible for other nonhuman creatures to be viewed as moral agents operating with their own distinct sets of morality.

THREADS

Ethology, etymologically speaking, is the study of ethos or character; it is the science of ethics. Insofar as the direct focus of ethology is nonhuman species, one would think that ethology is (or should have been) the study of nonhuman morality and moral agency. Even though the modern disci-pline of ethology is not exclusively devoted to the study of animal moral-ity, an argument could be made that it has ancient roots that encourage such a focus.

Humans have long looked at and to nonhuman creatures for notions of morality. That ancient sufferer, Job, advises, "But ask the beasts, and they will teach you; the birds of the sky, they will tell you, or speak to the earth, it will teach you; the fish of the sea, they will inform you. Who among all these does not know that the hand of Adonai has done this? In [God's] hands is every living soul and the breath of all humanity."[12] For Job and many others, the denizens of the natural world are endowed with certain knowledge—the knowledge that each and every creature, even those wily humans, is necessarily within God's grasp. The point is that however much some humans consider themselves radically free, unbound even by rules of nature, they suffer existential delusions. Because they flagrantly deny their embeddedness and dependency, they will ultimately find themselves os-tracized by their communities and the biosphere, unable to endure, much less flourish. True wisdom, Job seems to say, is found by observing the natural world without preconceived notions. One who watches carefully can discover morality's myriad manifestations.

The essays included in *Beastly Morality* watch closely, offering many perspectives, which nonetheless, as Matthew Calarco rightfully notes, cannot be exhaustive.[13] Emerging from such fields as ethology, philosophy, religious studies, sociology, and law, these essays weave together multiple disciplines to create rich tapestries of evidence and argument. Some strongly advocate appreciating nonhuman animals exclusive of any reflexive impulse, without seeking recourse to analogous human intellection, behavior, or notion of morality. Others, by contrast, contend that it is possible to view both simultaneously, that we can look upon nonhuman animals as such and upon humankind as such and see both as moral agents, albeit in different hues. All, however, explore the possibility—or reality—that nonhuman animals are not just objects of moral concern; some are moral actors.

There is good reason for weaving together these disparate fields. Animal studies generally is a composite exploration that draws from multiple fields; it cannot rightfully be called a circumscribed discipline as, say, chemistry or mathematics might be. Rather, animal studies draws on history, anthropology, economics, philosophy, religious studies, political science, law, biology, psychology, and others. The field's diversity reflects the complexity of the subject matter. Not all perspectives are represented in this volume, however. This is in part because scholars in some of these fields have yet to develop robust arguments or discover evidence pertaining to the questions this volume explores. On the other hand, the fields included point to the fact that animal studies is not all of one cloth, that animal welfare is not its exclusive or primary concern.

To make the case—or at least to raise the question—that some nonhuman animals can rightfully be considered moral agents and not just objects of moral concern, *Beastly Morality* knits together three broad and overlapping threads: ethology, philosophy, and religion. These disciplines consider animals from quite distinct vantage points. Ethology, for example, observes animals, often in their natural habitats and sometimes in manufactured ones. Philosophy, by contrast, thinks about and of animals and animality, humans and humanity. Religious studies investigates not just how traditions conceive animals as such but how animals and animality ought to be. Some skeptics might argue that insisting on a clear distinction between philosophy and religion here is forced if not arbitrary, since philosophy also tends toward the normative and religions invariably reflect and reinforce human meditations. This concern is valid and indeed is acknowledged in the fact that many of the essays here intertwine these perspectives. In part for this reason, this volume organizes the chapters less by discipline than by overall argument.

We first begin to untie the Gordian knot of animal morality by investigating whether and how the very concept and category of morality is permeable, a question explored briefly in this introduction. The first chapter in part 1, "De-humanizing Morality," by Kendy Hess, argues that "moral action" has always been a contested notion. She demonstrates this by tracing the relatively well-known story of the expanding circle of moral concern and the comparatively unfamiliar narrative of the expansion of the circle of moral respect for moral agents. These tracings clearly reveal elastic circles that have bulged to incorporate ever more, indeed, even more than biological humankind. And that is Hess's point: ever since Aristotle, people have argued about what counts as moral agency and who and what are capable of it. Over the centuries we have reached a point where we can seriously consider the possibility that collectives, such as corporations and governments, might qualify as moral agents insofar as they are capable of moral action. To sharpen the conversation, Hess proposes a functionalist definition of moral agency such that any one or any thing able to perform according to that definition would qualify as a moral agent. In this way the discussion avoids making specious claims that nonhuman animals must be "like humans" to qualify as moral agents; rather, it would enable us to say that nonhuman animals are moral agents to the degree that they can function as moral agents.

Some humans, we must admit, do not function as moral agents. It is about this sad truth that Sean Meighoo meditates in chapter 3, "HumAnI(m)Morality." Though he acknowledges the strands of philosophy that labor to extend moral capacity to nonhuman animals, Meighoo would rather unwind the question, turning it around to examine "whether humans possess this capacity in the first place." This search for "any evidence of this humanism among humans" spurs a philosophical critique of humanism that draws on both Nietzsche and the 1930s Surrealist Group in Paris. Both voices lodge strong complaints about humanism, deconstructing it to make the very consideration of human immorality and nonhuman animal morality intelligible in the first place.

In chapter 4, "Not All Dogs Go to Heaven: Judaism's Lessons in Beastly Morality," Mark Goldfeder similarly problematizes the human wont to create binaries, especially in regard to morality and its rewards. Goldfeder pursues the idea of just deserts (good choices produce divine rewards; bad choices, divine punishment) as it is conceived in the Judaic textual tradition. There he finds recurring evidence that animals are also understood to be endowed with rights, protections, privileges, souls, and rewards that perhaps one might have thought reserved for moral humans alone. The dividing line between human and nonhuman animals, he argues, was never as clear-cut as is now broadly assumed. Indeed, Judaic definitions of humanity are notoriously diverse and ambiguous, and there are many features that nonhuman animals undeniably share. Insofar as the definition of humanity transcends biological humanity and the rewards for moral uprightness are not confined to the biologically human, it stands to reason that this tradition recognizes certain nonhuman creatures as morally capable agents.

To build on part 1's argument that the category of the moral is permeable and that entities other than humans can be moral, part 2 brings evidence to support these claims. Frans B. M. de Waal examines non-human expression of the Golden Rule in chapter 5, "Animal Empathy as Moral Building Block." If empathy is other-regarding action, especially in the face of suffering, it probably has expression antecedent to the emergence of *Homo sapiens*. De Waal wonders what nonhuman animal empathy might be, what evidence rightfully demonstrates it, and what empathy might mean, evolutionarily speaking. Insofar as the old is always present in the new, he argues that conspecific mammalian empathy—as observed among the primates he works with—most likely emerged from parental care and the need to cooperate within groups for sustenance and security. Through time and experience, empathy "unblurs" the lines between individuals, reinforcing the importance of appraising others' behaviors and circumstances. Adopting others' perspectives brings about sharper conceptions of self—and others—as morally significant agents, not just morally significant entities.

In chapter 6, "Humans, Other Animals, and the Biology of Morality," Elisabetta Palagi amasses behavioral, physiological, neurocognitive, and endocrinological evidence among various primates, dogs, and even rats to argue that the emotional connectedness presumed in the Golden Rule cannot be reasonably restricted to *Homo sapiens*. Other species, Palagi demonstrates, also engage in mimicry (through, for example, play faces and yawn contagion) to cultivate empathy, a necessary feature for prosociality. Still, it is the spontaneous expression of emotional proximity that truly generates and strengthens affiliations, not those that are offered in response to requests. These and other observations reinforce the argument that the emotional networks in which humans operate are not so different from those of many other species and the morality manifested in these networks is evolutionarily linked.

Perhaps more familiar to the modern human audience than other primates are dogs. In chapter 7, "Moral Mutts: Social Play, Fairness, and Wild Justice," Marc Bekoff argues that play is a morally significant behavior, especially among dogs. Indeed, in and through play, dogs socially demarcate boundaries between acceptable fair play and unreasonable cheating. This distinction is evolutionarily important because cheaters would be not only socially ostracized in a playful setting but also shunned as procreative partners. Cheating, Bekoff concludes, is maladaptive; cooperation is favored and indeed sought out. Individual dogs in a playful setting are free, of course, to choose whether to cheat or cooperate or do a mixture, and they learn through observation of the choices of other dogs. These socialization experiences in a group of dogs at play reinforce the evolutionary claim that cooperation and fairness are necessary components for the very concept of morality. For this reason Bekoff asserts that "there is no reason to assume that social morality is unique to humans."

Dan Demetriou pushes this argument further by weaving observations of play with philosophy of play. In chapter 8, "Fighting Fair: The Ecology of Honor in Humans and Animals," Demetriou distinguishes honor-typical contests from authoritarian ones. The goal in authoritarian contests is to clarify and coordinate hierarchies of control and obedience, whereas honor-typical matches determine the relative prestige of the parties involved. Conspecific challenges or fights among nonhumans are often honor- or rank-seeking behaviors. To be sure, not all creatures that can function with a sense of honor do act honorably, a fact humans sadly demonstrate quite frequently. Demetriou argues that though honor may be a contentious moral value, it nonetheless can reasonably serve as a way to think about nonhuman animal agency in distinctly moral terms.

Part 3, "Reading Animal Morality," explores whether and how religious traditions read animals as moral agents. As Harrison King argues in chapter 9, "Reading, Teaching Insects: Ant Society as Pedagogical Device in Rabbinic Literature," the Judaic textual tradition, for one, demonstrates ways of viewing the nonhuman world, and specifically ants, in light of morality. This is not to say that the textual tradition measures insects vis-à-vis human conceptualizations of morality. Rather, it inscribes ants as creatures distinct from humankind yet nonetheless morally instructive to humankind. Reading animal behavior already inscribed in religious texts bridges the gaps between different ways of knowing, between representing animal agency and historical constructions of the differences between humans and nonhumans and their distinct moral agencies.

The impulse to eat away at the divide between humans and nonhumans is evident also in Buddhist texts, where beasts and humanity share a common destiny in the ongoing cycle of rebirth. In chapter 10, "Jakushin's Dogs and the Goodness of Animals: Preaching the Moral Life of Beasts in Medieval Japanese Tale Literature," Michael Bathgate warns against making universal or univocal claims about Buddhist attitudes toward nonhumans, using medieval Japanese tale literature to demonstrate the complex and conflicting ways that beastly morality (and our moral obligation to beasts) can be imagined. In these texts, the capacity for moral deliberation (and culpability) shared by humans and nonhumans provides the foundations for an ethos of compassion even as it sometimes serves as a trope by which to imagine away the need to act on that ethos.

The final two chapters, constituting part 4, "Reconceiving Animal Morality," dig further into religion, theology, and law for reasons to understand nonhuman animals as moral agents in and of themselves. John Berkman answers the title of chapter 11, "Just Chimpanzees? A Thomistic Perspective on Ethics in a Nonhuman Species," in the affirmative. He arrives at this conclusion by carefully reading Aquinas's thinking about thinking. Insofar as Aquinas links rationality to the ability to think otherwise—to question and reverse a decision—it necessarily becomes linked to some notion of a good beyond the immediate, and this kind of mentation is the sine qua non for morality. Couple this with increasing ethological studies of certain species, and it is possible, necessary even, to conclude that there can—even must—be a Thomistic beastly morality.

In chapter 12, "Brutal Justice? Animal Litigation and the Question of Countertradition," Jonathan K. Crane and Aaron S. Gross make the argument that embedded within the Judaic and Islamic traditions are theologically grounded convictions that nonhuman animals are also rightful religio-legal agents. Three anti-anthropocentric texts from these two traditions lead Crane and Gross to argue, with Derrida, that it would be wrong to claim that any religious tradition completely is devoid of anti-anthropocentric views of rightful nonhuman animal agency. Nor is it sufficient to point to the relative infrequency of such sources as exceptions proving the norm. Rather, it is more honest to appreciate a tradition in all its richness, complete with its embrace of nonhuman animals as rightful litigants—as agents of religious subjectivity and personhood, that is, as rightful moral agents.

KNOTS

The implications of these lines of inquiry are legion, too many to untie, smooth out, and consider in depth here. Still, it could be said that much of animal studies is an attempt to discern human conceptualizations of, attitudes toward, and relations with nonhuman animals. In this way human-kind becomes the central topic of concern instead of nonhuman animals, as is the case in most every other discipline. This reflexive impulse meets with great resistance in this volume, however. Instead of keeping humans as the central object of the scholarly gaze, *Beastly Morality* stays focused on nonhuman animals: this is a book investigating nonhuman animal morality, not human morality.

Nevertheless, the question remains valid. In which ways can and could and should the very question and the very possibility of nonhuman animal morality influence humanity, inclusive of our thinking about, attitudes toward, and relating with nonhuman animals and of organizing ourselves? In the epilogue (chapter 13), three scholars—Ani B. Satz, Lori Marino, and Cynthia Willett—offer preliminary reflections about what animal moral agency might mean. Through their own disciplines—law, psychology, and philosophy, respectively—they propose that these kinds of studies challenge current assumptions about, attitudes toward, and treatment of nonhuman species. Although they do not name them explicitly, these scholars suggest that beastly morality complicates how we think about and treat entertainment animals, pets, primates used in scientific research, and perhaps even food animals, not to mention what it means to be a legally recognizable entity meriting legal protections and troubling some fundamental philosophical assumptions about freedom.

In their distinct ways, these three scholars—indeed the whole book—wonder about the significance of the central question of *Beastly Morality*:

Can we humans think of nonhuman animals as moral agents in and of themselves? If the answer to this question is affirmative, the next question is, How? In which ways can we think so? This volume indicates some possibilities.

No assumption is made here that what follows neatly ties together these or all threads relevant to this line of investigation. This book does not make a neat bow nor complete this project. Rather, it is meant to inspire further inquiry about whether and how the realm of the moral can reasonably and even rightly be uncoiled from humankind and thereby embrace a larger swath of creation. Surely more knots will be encountered along the way.

NOTES

1. Mainstream national media increasingly explore such questions, too. See, for example, Alex Halberstadt, "Zoo Animals and Their Discontents," *New York Times Magazine*, July 3, 2014, about animal depression in zoos, highlighting the work of Dr. Vint Vigra; and Charles Siebert, "Should a Chimp Be Allowed to Sue Its Owner?" *New York Times Magazine*, April 23, 2014, about the NonHuman Rights Project headed by Steven Wise. Both stories were later covered by other media outlets, including CNN, NPR, and CBC.

2. See, for example, Aristotle, *Historia Animalium*, VIII.1.488b4–11.

3. Lex Newman, "Unmasking Descartes's Case for the Bête Machine Doctrine," *Canadian Journal of Philosophy* 31, no. 3 (2001): 389–426, offers a dense clarification and defense of Descartes's *bête machine* doctrine—"the view that brute animals lack not only reason, but any form of consciousness (having no mind or soul)" (389).

4. Immanuel Kant, *Lectures on Ethics*, trans. Peter Heath, ed. Peter Heath and J. B. Schneewind (New York: Cambridge University Press, 2001), 212.

5. See Moses Maimonides, *The Guide of the Perplexed*, trans. Shlomo Pines (Chicago: University of Chicago Press, 1963), part 3, 598–99.

6. The converse also holds true. We also contemplate the human through the lens of the animal, calling ourselves chickens, pigs, sloths, etc. A simple illustration is the vast swath of children's literature bespeaking human values and virtues through nonhuman characters.

7. Another good recent documentary exploring similar issues is *Project Nim* (http://www.project-nim.com).

8. Robert W. Lurz, ed., *The Philosophy of Animal Minds* (Cambridge: Cambridge University Press, 2009), esp. chaps. 6, 11, and 12.

9. Inbal Ben-Ami Bartal, Jean Decety, and Peggy Mason, "Empathy and Pro-Social Behavior in Rats," *Science* 334, no. 6061 (2011): 1427–30.

10. Krom, a deaf chimpanzee, failed to raise infants because she was physically—not mentally—unable to hear their plight. See de Waal's chapter 5 and Berkman's chapter 11 in this volume for more on Krom.

11. See, e.g., Paola Cavalieri, *The Death of the Animal: A Dialogue* (New York: Columbia University Press, 2008); Frans de Waal, Patricia S. Churchland, Telmo Pievani,

and Stefano Parmigiani, eds., *Evolved Morality: The Biology and Philosophy of Human Conscience* (Leiden: Brill, 2014).

12. Job 12:7–10, *Tanakh*, trans. Jewish Publication Society (Philadelphia: Jewish Publication Society, 1985).

13. Matthew Calarco, *Zoographies: The Question of the Animal from Heidegger to Derrida* (New York: Columbia University Press, 2008), 6.

Part One **The Permeability of Morality**

Two De-humanizing Morality

Kendy Hess

FOR CENTURIES, WITHOUT THE SLIGHTEST bit of embarrassment and only the most minimal of caveats, philosophers have assumed that morality was an exclusively human affair. Without bothering to articulate the claim, they have consistently assumed that both moral agents and moral subjects are human—that only human beings could owe or be owed moral consideration.[1] Even today, philosophical discussions of morality constantly assume human wants, needs, capacities, and psychology, and the resulting theories—which are presented as theories of "morality itself" and "moral agency itself"—are thus nothing of the kind. Instead, they present a distinctively *human* morality, one attuned to the wants and needs of humans and blind *in principle* to the wants and needs of the nonhuman world. To this day, the unacknowledged assumptions built into our basic theories of morality ensure that only human beings fit comfortably within those theories (and not even all human beings, at that).

The Utilitarians of the nineteenth century were the first to successfully challenge this practice on at least one front, expanding the circle of moral concern by claiming that nonhuman animals are moral *subjects* (or patients)—that we have moral obligations to them. A minority of contemporary philosophers continue to push the boundaries of this circle outward to encompass living things, ecosystems, and even the planet itself. Until quite recently, though, there has been little sustained attention to the possibility of nonhuman moral *agents*.

Three contemporary debates attempt to fill this void: (1) the well-established debate over whether certain collectives, like corporations and governments, might qualify as moral agents in their own right;[2] (2) the debate over whether artificial agents like robots and computer programs might qualify as moral agents;[3] and (3) the nascent debate over whether certain nonhuman animals might qualify as well, not just as morally considerable subjects but as moral agents.[4] What the three discourses have in common is the need to remove the assumed "humanity"—or perhaps better, the "human-ness"—from the existing accounts of moral agency. It is precisely the paradigm of the human moral agent that is being challenged, so starting from that very paradigm spikes the challenge before it can even be launched.

Yet this *is* the starting point for most philosophical inquiry. The traditional approach to most questions about moral agency is to begin with the paradigm of the human moral agent and apply pressure to it: What does it take, to become this kind of thing or to act in this way? Beginning with a human paradigm, this approach has (of course) yielded distinctively human answers: leisure and education (Aristotle), love of the good (Aquinas), rigorous reasoning (Kant), the ability to perform sophisticated and abstract calculations (Mill), etc. This would not be a failing if philosophers acknowledged that their answers are relevant only to questions about the human practice of moral agency, but of course they do not. The conclusions, drawn from a human paradigm, are treated as if they speak to issues of moral agency per se rather than being limited to human practices of moral agency, and the entire discourse continues according to this unacknowledged constraint. If we begin this inquiry into the possibility of nonhuman moral agents along these traditional anthropocentric lines, we necessarily and covertly convert the question from Can this nonhuman thing be a moral agent? to Can this nonhuman thing—this corporation, this computer, this chimpanzee—be a *human* moral agent? And of course, the answer would be no.

We need a way to explore the possibility of nonhuman moral agents that isn't biased against a positive answer. My goal in this chapter is to provide at least one.

I begin with an extremely brief sketch of the intellectual history involved in this endeavor. As already noted, the circle of moral *concern* (regarding moral subjects) has proven remarkably elastic, and it is worth tracing that progression to see how the expansion was achieved. I then turn to what I call "the circle of moral *respect*" (regarding moral agents).[5] It, too, has expanded, though less explosively, and again the progression is illuminating. I then introduce my proposed approach to the question of moral agency. Rather than starting with human moral agents and looking at how they go about performing moral actions, we should start with the idea of moral action itself and ask which candidates can perform the necessary actions. This is a "functionalist" approach to moral agency, one that defines moral agency in terms of a set of activities or behaviors (in terms of function) rather than in terms of identity; roughly, it treats moral agency as something one *does* rather than something one *is*. The implicit claim is that anything capable of doing what moral agents need to do is, by definition, a moral agent. Now, "moral action" is itself a contested notion, so this approach is unlikely to yield a clear standard acceptable to all. Utilitarians may end up recognizing a different class of moral agents than Kantians, and Aristotelians a different one yet. Nonetheless, this approach gives us a place to start and a path to follow in our efforts to develop an account of moral agency that is not biased toward human capacities in the way so much of the existing work is. I briefly explore the implications that this approach has had for the question of corporate moral agency, then explore the implications for the debate about animal moral agency.[6] I close by raising some concerns.

EXPANDING CIRCLES

I assume that most readers are generally familiar with the myth of the expanding circle of moral concern—the historical expansion of the class of moral subjects.[7] Every step of that expansion was hotly contested in theory and even more hotly (and sometimes violently) contested in practice, and the progression was not nearly as smooth or "unidirectional" as the following sketch suggests. Though I have radically simplified the philosophical theories, almost to the point of caricature, this sketch is accurate as far as it goes, and will suffice to provide a rough outline of the progression that brought us to the current moment, with the circle of moral concern stretched to historic limits.

IN THE BEGINNING, *there was Aristotle.* . . . Western moral philosophy traditionally begins with the ancient Greeks, most particularly with Aristotle and what we now call virtue ethics. In Aristotelian virtue ethics, in a sense, the moral agent himself (and it is a "he") is the only significant moral subject. The moral imperative is that he perfect himself, developing virtues like generosity, honesty, and courage, and other players appear primarily as beneficiaries of his virtues or as victims of his vices. To the extent that this agent might be said to have moral obligations *to* certain others (a rather awkward claim within this framework), those obligations are reciprocal obligations to similar others—the wealthy, educated, powerful, Athenian men who are the focus of Aristotle's moral and political theories. These men, effectively identical to the moral agent, are the only moral subjects within Aristotle's circle of moral concern—the only beings *entitled* to moral consideration in their own right. Aristotle recognized a hierarchy of human beings, and he was quite clear that women, children, slaves, non-Greeks, and even men of the lower classes were not entitled to any particular moral consideration (though it might be wise or virtuous for the moral agent to treat them well). At this point the circle of moral concern included at most the economic, social, political, male elite.[8]

Then came Kant. . . . By the time we reach the Enlightenment, the circle of moral concern has begun to expand. Taking Kant as our familiar exemplar, we have the ringing endorsement of rational autonomy ("humanity") as sufficient grounds for moral concern; Kant even acknowledged that this might include nonhumans, perhaps space aliens.[9] This certainly sounds broadly inclusive, but Kant immediately ruined the effect by explicitly excluding both women and nonwhites,[10] who apparently ranked lower than hypothetical Martians. His focus on rational autonomy at least made wealth, education, and social standing irrelevant to moral standing, and thus expanded the circle of moral concern to include all reasoning and reasonable adult, white males, regardless of class or education. Kant's emphasis on rational autonomy also had an interesting effect: by focusing on an empirically verifiable capacity (like rational autonomy) rather than an identity (like "citizens" or "men"), Kant left himself open to correction on empirical grounds. He committed himself to the claim that certain entities (i.e., those possessing a certain capacity: rational autonomy) are entitled to be treated in certain ways (i.e., respectfully) due to their possession of that capacity. Once this claim had gained acceptance, critics could argue that he was right about the significance of the capacity and wrong—empirically, verifiably wrong—about who or what possessed that capacity. And of course, that is exactly what they did. Over time the circle of moral concern expanded to encompass all competent adult human beings.[11]

Enter the Utilitarians. . . . In the 1800s the Utilitarians blew the circle wide open. Bentham's simple assertion that "the question is not, Can they reason? nor, Can they talk? but, Can they suffer?"[12] immediately expanded the circle to include animals. Mill built on Bentham's insight to demand that we seek to secure "an existence exempt as far as possible from pain, and as rich as possible in enjoyments, both in point of quality and quantity . . . [for] all mankind; and not to them only, but, so far as the nature of things admits, to the whole sentient creation."[13] With this, the circle of moral concern expanded to include all human beings and almost all nonhuman animals.[14]

And then came the environmentalists. The dust hadn't even begun to settle after that philosophical bombshell from the Utilitarians when the environmentalists arrived on the scene in the early 1900s. Albert Schweitzer argued that every living thing embodies a "will to life" and is thus entitled to reverence and a kind of moral concern.[15] This expanded the circle to include plants and, of course, the so-called "lower" animals arguably not captured by the Utilitarian claim. Aldo Leopold noted the historical expansion of moral concern outlined above and then argued that we should extend that moral concern to "the Land" itself—to the dynamic systems that allow energy to flow from the sun to the earth, through various plants and animals, and back to the earth again.[16] Most recently, in the 1970s, James Lovelock and Lynn Margulis suggested that the earth as a whole is effectively a living thing—Gaia—entitled to moral concern.[17] Around the same time, Arne Naess and the other Deep Ecologists took the radical step of suggesting that humanity, while still included in the circle of moral concern, is not even at the center of it.[18] And that brings us to the present.[19] *Thus ends the myth.*

WHILE MUCH OF this is still contested, the general movement is clear. Philosophers have been increasingly willing to look beyond the presence or absence of distinctively human qualities (like rational autonomy) to explore the possibility that more broadly represented qualities like sentience, life, and autopoiesis (the ability of a system to reproduce and maintain itself) are also deserving of moral concern. The circle of moral concern has thus proven to be remarkably elastic—certainly in theory, and even in practice.[20] The circle of moral respect has been less so. While we have radically expanded the class of beings that we (potentially) recognize as moral *subjects*, entitled to moral concern, comparatively little has been done to expand the class of beings that we recognize as moral *agents*, entitled to moral respect.[21] Let me acknowledge that this failure to expand is not necessarily improper. The role of moral agent is far more demanding than the role of moral subject, and it would not be surprising to discover that fewer candidates qualify. Still, it is important to give the possibility of expansion a fair hearing. To that end, it is worth briefly tracing the previous expansions.

Beginning again with Aristotle. . . . Aristotle wasn't particularly interested in the class of moral subjects, or the question of who or what was entitled to moral concern. As noted above, in Aristotelian virtue ethics, the moral agent's primary focus is on himself and the development of his own excellences—most especially the intellectual and moral virtues. Aristotle's moral theory simply doesn't require him to define a class of moral subjects, in the contemporary sense. Aristotle was, however, intensely interested in the question of who was capable of becoming (what we today would call) a full moral agent. He made numerous, detailed claims about who could achieve this status and how to help them do so, and (ironically enough) he justified the existence of a highly stratified and oppressive political structure on the grounds that it was necessary to enable the elite to perfect themselves as moral agents, even at the cost of imposing upon many others. The Aristotelian moral agent is a wealthy and powerful man with "good" friends and family; he is healthy, beautiful, and lucky (yes, lucky), and has shaped himself to be wise, generous, brave, honest, and temperate. This shaping required reason and autonomy, of course, and a strong will.

Aristotle was quite clear that only a very limited few were capable of achieving the kind of excellence he had in mind—the state of full human flourishing, *eudaimonia*. Women, children, slaves, non-Greeks, and members of the lower classes were excluded from this "limited few" because they (allegedly) lacked the capacity to reason properly, lacked the strength of will necessary to conform to reason, or both.[22] It is worth noting that this was not an empirical claim. Aristotle's conclusions about women, slaves, and the rest are grounded primarily in a priori commitments about the essential natures of the feminine, the slave, etc. As a result, their alleged "failures" of reason, fortitude, and the like are not really failures so much as perfectly acceptable limitations of their essential natures. There is nothing wrong with a horse that cannot fly, and nothing wrong with a woman or a slave who does not reason well—it is simply part of their essential nature.[23] If Aristotle encountered a "horse" that could fly, he would be more likely to conclude that it wasn't really a horse than that his ideas about "horse-nature" were wrong. Just so, a woman or slave with superlative powers of reason or will would not be evidence that Aristotle's ideas about women and slaves were wrong; she or he just would not really be a woman or a slave. In this way, Aristotle's claims about who might qualify as a moral agent are not empirical claims, and thus could not be defeated by any amount of empirical evidence.

Leaping forward to Kant. . . . Kant rejects much of Aristotle's framework but retains and sharpens the underlying focus on rational autonomy, which becomes the one essential that is both necessary and sufficient for moral agency. To be a moral agent, one must be an end in oneself, able to create ends for oneself and to identify and adopt universalizable principles (such as the imperative to treat other rational autonomous beings as ends in themselves). This is a purely conceptual claim, as Kant develops it,[24] and unlike Aristotle's claims it does not include any criteria about the kinds of creatures likely to possess the capacity. The question of which creatures do *in fact* possess this capacity is an empirical one, and here Kant had a little trouble applying his own account. Again, Kant himself explicitly excluded women and nonwhites from the circle of moral respect as abruptly as he had excluded them from the circle of moral concern (and on the same grounds). He claimed that women were deficient in their understanding, limited to the beautiful and the "sciences that require wit and a kind of feeling" rather than "a sharp mind, much reflection, and profundity." They were driven by passion and inclination, and their proper role in society was limited to refining and cultivating men.[25] Nonwhite men were similarly deficient.[26] Still, nothing in either the letter of or the justifications for Kant's account of moral agency itself entails this result. In fact, much the opposite.

As with his theory of moral subjects, discussed above, intentionally or not, Kant provided an account of moral agency for which inclusion and exclusion could be challenged on empirical grounds. Despite the flexibility implicit in this account, it has been quite a struggle to expand the circle of moral respect to encompass most adult human beings; there has been little effort to expand it further. The vast majority of the literature on Kantian moral agency assumes that the Kantian agent is human, and thus assumes (without arguing for) the presence of additional capacities not present in the original account—things like consciousness, emotion, and empathy, which then play a role in the exercise of agency.[27] With this, the literature silently excludes candidates (like corporations and computers) that lack these oh-so-human capacities.

Then the Utilitarians. . . . Historically there seems to be a kind of inverse relationship between interest in moral agents and interest in moral subjects. In Aristotle we see intense interest in moral agents and little or no concern with moral subjects; Kant was perhaps more interested in moral agency than moral subjecthood, but since he assumes that the classes are coextensive he doesn't often distinguish between the two. It is thus unsurprising to find that the Utilitarians, so interested in the question of moral subjects, are comparatively uninterested in questions of moral agency. Utilitarianism effectively—albeit silently—relies on a functionalist account of moral agency: The moral agent's obligation is to maximize pleasure and minimize pain, and anything that can do so (in its own right) seems likely to qualify. There is nothing in this account that requires the moral agent to be human, but again, the vast majority of the literature still assumes that the agent is human with additional capacities (consciousness, emotion, empathy) not identified by the original account. Emotion and empathy play an even larger role in discussions of Utilitarian agents than Kantian ones, given the emphasis on relieving suffering.

And the contemporary debate. To my knowledge, environmental philosophers have made few claims about moral agency per se, beyond occasional discussions of the kinds of concerns that should motivate such an agent.[28] The feminist literature includes extensive debate about the exclusionary assumptions implicit in most traditional discussions of moral agency. For example, some have argued that the autonomy so prized by traditional accounts of moral agency must be understood in relational terms, rather than as an independent capacity; others have argued that the very exercise of (apparently unemotional) rationality is in fact dependent on emotion in ways typically obscured by contemporary discourse.[29] Despite these contributions, I am unaware of any discussion in the feminist literature that suggests (or could be used to support) expanding the class of moral agents beyond the human.

AND THAT, AGAIN, brings us to the current day. While the contemporary discourse includes much lively debate about various issues associated with moral agency, the vast majority of it is explicitly or implicitly limited to concerns about the human practice of moral agency. Little of it challenges the human paradigm, or explores the possibility of expanding what I've called the circle of moral respect beyond that limit. As previously noted, there are three contemporary exceptions to this general neglect: (1) the well-established debate over whether certain collectives, like corporations and governments, might qualify as moral agents in their own right; (2) the debate over whether artificial agents, like robots and computer programs, might qualify as moral agents; and (3) the nascent debate over whether certain nonhuman animals might qualify as moral agents. In the next section, I will restrict my discussion to the first, as it is generally the best-developed literature of the three. How have theorists of collectives argued for moral agency in the absence of humanity?

THE MORAL AGENCY OF COLLECTIVES

It is worth noting that many of the philosophers in the collective agency debate have flatly refused to argue for moral agency in the absence of humanity. Some philosophers refuse to recognize the existence of "a collective entity" in the first place, so there's no question of whether "it" might be a moral agent or not: there is no "it" to discuss.[30] Even philosophers willing to recognize (or at least temporarily grant) the existence of a collective entity have refused to recognize it as an agent, much less as a moral agent. Skeptics point to various justifications for this refusal, including the alleged impossibility of basic capacities like intentionality and action, as well as the alleged absence of various higher-order capacities such as rationality, reasons responsiveness, and free will.[31] The philosophers who adopt these positions are generally called "individualists" because they insist that only individuals can possess the necessary capacities. To be more precise, they insist that only *human* individuals can possess the necessary capacities, but the claim about humanity is rarely articulated; it is simply taken to be understood.

Philosophers occupying the contrary position are called "holists," in recognition of their willingness to recognize the existence of the "whole" that is the collective. Holists distinguish among different kinds of collectives, depending on the degree of discipline and coordination among the members. The most highly disciplined and coordinated collectives are called "corporate agents," and holists who argue for the possibility of corporate moral agency generally limit their claims to these kinds of collectives.[32] It is important to remember that the debate is about the moral agency of the collective entity itself—the nonhuman thing that is made of human beings but is not itself human. The question is how to approach the matter: given this nonhuman thing, how do we determine whether it is a moral agent? While holists do not agree among themselves about what approach to take, some general patterns have emerged, and philosophers (and others) interested in the question of animal moral agency may benefit from a review of how the holist debate about corporate moral agency has progressed.[33]

Holist accounts generally begin with the *apparent* or *seeming* moral agency of certain groups of people, like those that form corporations. It is a simple and not particularly contentious fact about the world that corporate agents *seem* to do moral agent-ish kinds of things: they help or harm others while acting in pursuit of chosen ends; they are capable of adapting their behaviors to be more helpful and less harmful; they often modify their behavior in the face of blame or accusation, etc. So we have the initial appearance of moral agency, enough to motivate the inquiry, and the next question is whether this is simply the appearance of moral agency or the real thing. One might expect that the next step would be a debate about the concept or nature of moral agency, in an attempt to establish when "moral agent-ish kinds of things" count as "the real thing." Instead, the debate has ended up revolving around the mechanics.

There have been two basic approaches to the question of whether corporate entities qualify as moral agents. The first focuses on the presence of shared intentions.[34] Here, a group qualifies as an agent when its members possess certain mental states that unite them in certain ways in pursuit of shared goals. Think, for example, of the members of an orchestra concentrating on playing a symphony together, or the workers at a car factory concentrating on working together to make cars. The second approach focuses on internal processes.[35] Here, a group qualifies as an agent when its members consistently conform to certain established procedures: subordinates reporting to their superiors in accordance with established hierarchy, or board members voting on a new policy, for example. In each case, proponents have attempted to answer the question of whether this apparent moral agency was real moral agency by "looking inside" the potential agent to determine *how* it achieved its apparently moral behavior. There has been a great deal of debate between competing accounts both within and across these categories, but the debate has rarely (if ever) revolved around the standards for moral agency per se. Instead, the various paradigms of the (human) moral agent discussed in the previous section are simply assumed, and the participants argue over whether a proposed state, process, or outcome is sufficiently like its human counterpart to qualify. As a result there has been a great deal of discussion about *how* corporate agents perform their allegedly moral actions, and whether they're sufficiently human (though the word is rarely used), but there has been little or no explicit debate about the standard for moral agency itself in the context of this literature.

In an effort to move beyond what seems likely to be a stalemate, I propose a functionalist account of moral agency that can accommodate all of these different approaches. Again, a functionalist account is one that defines the concept in question in terms of a role to be fulfilled or a task to be performed rather than in terms of some kind of essential status or quality. Put crudely, it is about what something does rather than what it is; put more crudely still, if it walks like a duck and quacks like a duck, then it really is a duck. All that remains is to give an account of the role that has to be fulfilled. With regard to moral agency, I propose the following: *a candidate qualifies as a moral agent if and only if it is able to act appropriately on the basis of morally relevant information, because it is morally relevant information*. Thus, the candidate must

1. be able to *act*—be able to shape its behavior on the basis of its own internal states;
2. be able to identify morally relevant information;
3. be able to act upon it appropriately; and
4. be able to do so *because* it is morally relevant information.

This account is intentionally neutral between competing normative theories. What counts as "morally relevant information" will vary depending on which normative theory is adopted: for Utilitarians, morally relevant information will be limited to pleasures and pains; for Kantians, it will focus on rights and duties; for Aristotelians, it will focus on virtues and vices, etc. The "appropriate" action will likewise vary with the normative theory: Utilitarians will require an agent to be able to maximize pleasure and minimize pain; Kantians will require an agent able to identify and conform to universalizable principles; and virtue ethicists will require an agent able to develop the virtues proper to its kind.[36] The question of which normative theory is correct—whether moral obligations revolve around maximizing pleasure and minimizing pain, or conforming to universalizable principles—is also an important one, of course, but it is not the one that concerns us here. The question here is which entities are *bound by* those moral obligations, whatever they are; this account of moral agency makes no commitments regarding which normative theory is correct or best.

It turns out that this account is equally neutral regarding the mechanisms by which these appropriate responses come about. It may be that some corporate agents achieve their actions via shared intentions, while others achieve them via member adherence to established procedures, while others rely on different mechanisms entirely. Fundamentally, it makes no difference so long as there is *some* mechanism (or mechanisms) that make it possible for the corporate agent to act on the basis of morally relevant information. Similarly, the account is neutral regarding the kinds of creature capable of generating such responses. Like the Kantian and Utilitarian standards discussed above (and unlike the Aristotelian standard), it presents a standard for moral agency that makes no necessary reference to human beings or (immediately) to distinctively human capacities; it simply identifies a role to fulfill, a function to perform. With that, it becomes an empirical matter to determine which mechanisms really *are* essential to—and which creatures really *are* capable of—fulfilling that role. Holists have argued at length that corporate agents can do so. Constructing a similar argument would be the task of proponents of animal moral agency.

The only additional requirement established by this account is that the candidate be capable of responding to morally relevant information *because* it is morally relevant information. This final requirement blocks the possibility of identifying as a moral agent one that might (somehow) act in morally appropriate ways (i.e., maximizing pleasure and minimizing pain, conforming to universalizable principles, etc.) through sheer coincidence. Humanized accounts block this possibility by reference to something like explicit intent: the agent must be able to explicitly recognize the situation as morally significant and then explicitly choose to act "morally," either out of some kind of concern for "doing the right thing" or from some motivation that is itself considered "moral" (i.e., empathy). This is certainly one way of meeting the requirement: an agent who explicitly identified a situation as morally significant and intentionally acted appropriately (maximizing pleasure, fulfilling a duty) would be responding appropriately to morally relevant information because it is morally relevant information. However, there is little justification for saying that this is the only acceptable way to meet the requirement, and there are at least two difficulties with presenting it that way. First, this immediately excludes everything but rather sophisticated human beings (it excludes children, and perhaps the cognitively impaired). Again, this exclusiveness does not necessarily mean that the standard is wrong. It is entirely possible that only rather sophisticated human beings are moral agents. But given that only moral agents have moral obligations, this has the result that children and the cognitively impaired have no moral obligations, no reason (at all) to act in ways that generate pleasure for others rather than pain, that express respect rather than contempt, and so forth. That seems both implausible and unfortunate. Second, this standard raises epistemic concerns about how we would *know* that some possible moral agent engaged in this internal process. We could ask, if the candidate were capable of speech, but of course the agent might either lie or be honestly unaware of its own motivations. It seems that the only reliable evidence we could have would be its behavior—that it reliably acted in ways that maximized pleasure and minimized pain, for example. In that case, however, it would be the behavior that fulfills the requirement rather than the internal process that generated it, and we are back to my functionalist account. It may well be that most human moral behavior *is* explicit and intentional in the way that this requirement suggests (though this seems unlikely), but that hardly justifies the much larger claim that *all* moral behavior *must* be like this.[37]

So again, instead of the humanized assumption that the best (or only) way to rule out randomness is to require explicit intent, I suggest it is enough for the agent to act as it does *because of* the morally relevant information. How do we know if the agent is doing so? The same way we know about explicit intent: we ask, if the agent can answer (as can most human beings, and all corporate agents), and we observe the agent's behavior. If the agent reliably[38] responds to choices between pleasure and pain (for others) by maximizing pleasure and minimizing pain, then we have the best possible evidence that it is acting as it is *because of* the fact that pleasure and pain are at stake. If it reliably fulfills some duty of respect or care, then we have the best possible evidence that it is acting as it does *because of* the fact that respect or care is at stake. And so forth. As long as a candidate can act appropriately on the basis of morally relevant information (pleasure and pain, duties and principles, excellences, etc.) and *would not have* acted as it did in the *absence* of said information, it meets this final requirement. Explicit intent is one way of meeting this standard, but a sufficiently strong character trait or felt aversion (to causing pain, being disrespectful, etc.) would work as well, and there are undoubtedly other possibilities. Regardless, phrasing the standard as I have done allows the inquiry to proceed without any explicit or tacit humanizing assumptions.

Approaching the matter from this non-anthropocentric angle puts philosophers of corporate moral agency in much the same situation as philosophers of individual moral agency after Kant and the Utilitarians: we have a description of a capacity that moral agents must possess, of certain actions they must be able to take. All that is left is to examine the world to see which creatures qualify. After Kant, philosophers were able to use his theory to counter his own essentially empirical claims that women and nonwhites did not possess the relevant capacity (rational autonomy) and thus did not qualify as moral agents. Similarly, in the context of the corporate moral agency debate, we can use my approach to counter essentially empirical claims that shared intentions or certain established procedures are necessary for corporate moral agency. Further, we can use this approach to counter claims that phenomenal consciousness, emotion, and empathy are necessary for moral agency. As long as an entity can act morally, in the sense outlined above, it is a moral agent. Once we have identified the qualifying entities as moral agents, we (and they) can begin the process of recognizing them as moral agents and exploring the implications of that status—and holding them morally accountable for their actions.

THE IMPLICATIONS FOR NONHUMAN ANIMAL MORAL AGENCY

This brings us back to the question of whether certain nonhuman animals qualify as moral agents, and we need a way to explore that question that is not unnecessarily biased against a positive answer. Unfortunately, the moral agents envisioned by traditional accounts of moral agency (and the literatures that have grown from them) are so utterly and richly *human* that they are not very helpful in this regard. We do not want to know whether other animals are "like humans"; this misstates the central question, and may lead us astray in our efforts to answer it. We want to know whether they might qualify as moral agents, and I suggest that the functionalist account of moral agency outlined above will help us avoid the many humanizing assumptions otherwise implicit in most traditional accounts of moral agency.

The debate about corporate moral agency begins with ontological issues; fortunately, no one is likely to deny the existence of nonhuman animals, so we can skip that step. Instead, we can begin as the holists do, with the *appearance* of moral agency: do some nonhuman animals do "moral agent-ish kinds of things"? Other essays in this volume, and the vast literature upon which they draw, suggest that they do. The next question, here as with corporate (and artificial) agents, is to ask whether the noted behavior simply looks like moral agency or is the real thing. I would hope that the animal moral agency debate can skip the debate over whether the animals have the "right" processes going on inside and go straight to the question of whether their behavior is moral behavior—whether they are responding appropriately to morally relevant information because it is morally relevant information (as identified by the different normative theories—Utilitarian, Kantian, Aristotelian, or other traditions not mentioned here). When we put the question that way, it seems entirely possible that many nonhuman species do.

Some normative theories seem more likely to support this conclusion than others. For example, it seems more likely that animals would act in ways that increase pleasure and decrease pain *because* those actions increase pleasure and decrease pain, than that they would adopt universalizable principles *because* they are universalizable.[39] Still, that might be enough to make them moral agents on a Utilitarian account, and the Utilitarians (at least) would ask no more. We cannot be more precise about the requirements for moral agency without settling the question of the appropriate normative theory; until that time, we do best to keep our theoretical options open.

I think this is a promising approach, in both its ability to weed out biases and assumptions and its ability to reveal the biases and assumptions already implicit in our moral theorizing. Philosophers have a long, sad history of taking themselves as their exemplars, projecting themselves onto the world and calling those projections "reality." One would hope that we have learned to be skeptical of answers that are too gratifying, affirming our own power and purported uniqueness. I do not have sufficient familiarity with the capacities of nonhuman animals (or computer programs, for that matter) to predict how the inquiry will turn out, but I would be neither surprised nor offended to find that I needed to share the circle of moral respect with some unexpected companions. At the very least, considering the possible moral agency of nonhuman animals forces us to *look* at them, to see the significance they have to themselves and in their own right, and to acknowledge the weight of their gaze.

This prospect raises some interesting questions and concerns, however. First, in recognizing different kinds of moral subjects we acknowledge the possibility that different moral subjects might be entitled to profoundly different kinds of treatment. This, of course, opens the way for a hierarchy—for the idea that some moral subjects are entitled not just to *different* moral concern but to *more* moral concern.[40] In recognizing different kinds of moral agents, then, do we likewise acknowledge the possibility that different moral agents might have profoundly different kinds of obligations?[41] Or that there is some kind of hierarchy of moral agents, such that some moral agents are more important than others? Second, if nonhuman animals *do* qualify as moral agents, what are the implications regarding our moral obligations to them? Are moral agents entitled to different or better moral consideration than mere moral subjects? The epilogue to this volume tries to untangle some of these knots. Third, what are the legal implications? While the law does not recognize categories like "moral subject" or "moral agent," there is a tight theoretical and historical correlation between conceptions of moral agents and conceptions of persons and citizens.[42] If we recognize nonhuman animals as moral agents, must we recognize them as persons, with some or all of the rights that accompany that designation? As citizens?[43] Finally, what would it even *mean* to say that a nonhuman animal "ought" to do something? It is obviously well beyond the scope of this essay to explore such questions, but if the debate about animal moral agency continues, they will have to be addressed.

MORAL AGENCY IS not essentially a human activity. The practice of moral agency may be essential for human beings, but it does not follow that only human beings can practice it. Human beings certainly have their own distinctive ways of engaging in moral agency, just as they have their own distinctive ways of engaging in courtship, building homes, and raising young. But other creatures likewise engage in courtship, build homes, and raise young, and the fact that they go about these things differently than human beings do does not mean that they are (somehow) not really doing them. We do not cling to the idea that we and only we can do such things. We are able to look at the world and recognize other creatures engaging in the same activities, albeit in their own unique ways. There is no reason to treat the practice of moral agency differently.

NOTES

1. The contrast here is between moral agents (entities that bear moral obligations, bound to act in accordance with moral imperatives) and moral subjects (entities that

must be taken into account in a moral calculus, entities entitled to moral consideration). The term "moral agent" is pretty universally accepted for the former, but there is no universally accepted term to designate the latter class. I use "moral subject" here, but others have used "moral patient" and "object of moral concern," among others. I am not trying to take a stand about terminology, so no particular weight should be given to this formulation.

2. See, e.g., Peter A. French, *Collective and Corporate Responsibility* (New York: Columbia University Press, 1984); Christian List and Philip Pettit, *Group Agency: The Possibility, Design, and Status of Corporate Agents* (Oxford: Oxford University Press, 2011). For shorter, more focused treatments, see David Copp, "On the Agency of Certain Collective Entities: An Argument from 'Normative Autonomy,'" *Midwest Studies in Philosophy* 30, no. 1 (2006): 194–221; Copp, "The Collective Moral Autonomy Thesis," *Journal of Social Philosophy* 38, no. 3 (2007): 369–88; Kenneth E. Goodpaster, "The Concept of Corporate Responsibility," *Journal of Business Ethics* 2, no. 1 (1983): 1–22; Kendy M. Hess, "The Free Will of Corporations (and Other Collectives)," *Philosophical Studies* 168, no. 1 (2014): 241–60; Hess, "Because They Can: The Basis for the Moral Obligations of (Certain) Collectives," *Midwest Studies in Philosophy* 38, no. 1 (2014): 203–21; Tracy L. Isaacs, *Moral Responsibility in Collective Contexts* (Oxford: Oxford University Press, 2011); Seumas Miller, "Against the Collective Moral Autonomy Thesis," *Journal of Social Philosophy* 38, no. 3 (2007): 389–409; Pekka Mäkelä, "Collective Agents and Moral Responsibility," *Journal of Social Philosophy* 38, no. 3 (2007): 456–68; Jan Narveson, "Collective Responsibility," *Journal of Ethics* 6, no. 2 (2002): 179–98; Carole Rovane, *The Bounds of Agency: An Essay in Revisionary Metaphysics* (Princeton, NJ: Princeton University Press, 1997).

3. See, e.g., C. Allen, G. Varner, and J. Zinser, "Prolegomena to Any Future Artificial Moral Agent," *Journal of Experimental and Theoretical Artificial Intelligence* 12, no. 3 (2000): 251–61; C. Allen, W. Wallach, and I. Smit, "Why Machine Ethics?," *Intelligent Systems* 21, no. 4 (2006): 12–17; Peter M. Asaro, "What Should We Want from a Robot Ethic?," *International Review of Information Ethics* 6, no. 12 (2006): 9–16; Luciano Floridi and Jeff W. Sanders, "On the Morality of Artificial Agents," *Minds and Machines* 14, no. 3 (2004): 349–79.

4. See, e.g., Grace Clement, "Animals and Moral Agency: The Recent Debate and Its Implications," *Journal of Animal Ethics* 3, no. 1 (2013): 1–14; Urszula Zarosa, "Animals as Moral Agents," *Studies in the Philosophy of Law* 5 (2010): 155–64. There is also some debate about the possibility that young children might qualify as moral agents—see, e.g., Cristina L. Traina, "Children and Moral Agency," *Journal of the Society of Christian Ethics* 29, no. 2 (2009): 19–37. Obviously this final discourse does nothing to question the "humanity" of moral agency, and Traina in fact relies explicitly on the humanness of children, but it does call into question some of the dominant assumptions about the role that sophisticated rationality plays in moral agency.

5. A preliminary note about terminology: There are a number of philosophically significant terms within the discipline of moral philosophy that do not have accepted meanings, and the relationships between the terms and the classes they pick out are even murkier. I am thinking particularly of the terms "person," "moral agent," and "moral subject," both as they function in moral theory and as they function in the different but related context of political theory and law. While I will clearly be making claims about moral agency, I make no claims about the categories of persons, citizens, moral subjects, or the relationships among them (but see Kendy M. Hess, "'If You

Tickle Us': How Corporations Can Be Moral Agents without Being Persons," *Journal of Value Inquiry* 47, no. 3 (2013): 319–35, regarding the relationship between moral agency and personhood).

6. In an effort to keep this reasonably brief and focused, I have not included a section addressing the "artificial agent" literature. Please refer to the sources listed in note 3 for further discussion of that topic.

7. I use the word "myth" here in the sense of "an explaining story," one that generally explains "how things came to be this way. From the beginning to now" (Daniel Quinn, *Ishmael* [New York: Bantam, 1993], 45–59). I do not mean to imply that anything about the progression sketched here is false.

8. I feel compelled to reiterate that this is a radically oversimplified account of Aristotle (and Kant, and Mill, and the rest). It is nonetheless the Aristotle (Kant, Mill) of undergraduate classes everywhere, the philosophers that function as a kind of cultural placeholder for a distinctive set of beliefs and values, and it is in that spirit that I present them here. This is the myth of the expanding circle; a full scholarly presentation of the intellectual history would require thousands of pages but would not, I suggest, differ overly much from the general shape of the myth presented here.

9. Immanuel Kant, *Universal Natural History and Theory of the Heavens* (Arlington, VA: Richer Resources Publications, 2008).

10. For citations to Kant and interesting discussions, see Kurt Mosser, "Kant and Feminism," *Kant-Studien* 90, no. 3 (1999): 322–53; Pauline Kleingeld, "Kant's Second Thoughts on Race," *Philosophical Quarterly* 57, no. 229 (2007): 573–92; Charles W. Mills, "Kant's Untermenschen," in *Race and Racism in Modern Philosophy*, ed. A. Valls (New York: Cornell University Press, 2005), 169–93.

11. While the matter is subject to debate, a straightforward reading of Kant suggests that children and the mentally impaired—i.e., those lacking full rational autonomy—would not be moral subjects entitled to respect, though the moral agent might still have indirect duties with respect to them. See Tom Regan, *The Case for Animal Rights* (New York: Springer, 1987).

12. Jeremy Bentham, *An Introduction to the Principles of Morals and Legislation* (Mineola, NY: Courier Dover Publications, 2007).

13. John S. Mill, *The Basic Writings of John Stuart Mill: On Liberty, the Subjection of Women and Utilitarianism* (New York and Toronto: Random House Digital, Inc., 2010).

14. There is some debate about where to draw the line. For example, it is unclear whether worms and shellfish are included, as it is not entirely clear that they can feel pain or "suffer."

15. Albert Schweitzer, *Civilization and Ethics* (London: A. & C. Black, Limited, 1923).

16. Aldo Leopold and Charles W. Schwartz, *A Sand County Almanac: And Sketches Here and There* (Oxford: Oxford University Press, 1989). See 201–2 for Leopold's brief treatment of the historical developments.

17. James E. Lovelock and Lynn Margulis, "Atmospheric Homeostasis by and for the Biosphere: The Gaia Hypothesis," *Tellus* 26, no. 1 (1974): 2–10.

18. Bill Devall and George Sessions, *Deep Ecology* (Layton, UT: Gibbs Smith, 1985); Arne Naess, "The Shallow and the Deep, Long-Range Ecology Movement: A Summary," *Inquiry* 16, no. 1–4 (1973): 95–100.

19. The feminists have been less active in this literature than in the literature related to moral agency (discussed below), so I have not mentioned them here. To the extent

that the feminists have made a distinctive contribution to this discussion, it probably resides in the literature on the ethics of care. Care ethics challenges the rather myopic focus on "rational autonomy" in the intellectual history sketched above; instead, care ethicists argue that it should be replaced or—more commonly—supplemented by attention to caring (caring for, caring about), with all the attendant implications of emotion and relationships. This might well end up delineating a distinctive circle of moral concern. My thanks to Amandine Catala for pointing this out.

20. In saying this, I do not mean to downplay the extraordinary effort that has been and continues to be expended to ensure that later additions to the circle receive their due.

21. The literature on moral agency is even less developed and less settled than the literature on moral subjects and moral concern (which is saying something). As a result, the significance of being a moral agent is less clear. It is generally accepted that moral subjects are entitled to "moral concern," to be "taken into account" in moral reasoning, but there is no generally accepted parallel term or phrase that captures what moral agents are entitled to. It is generally accepted that being a moral agent entitles one to special consideration, but the content of that "special" is not clear. Most claims for human superiority and entitlement are grounded in our possession of the capacities for moral agency, and being a moral agent clearly entitles you to *something* very important. I simply suggest the phrase "moral respect" to stand for . . . whatever that is. I set aside the question of what, exactly, moral agents are entitled to for another time (though I address some concerns in my concluding remarks).

22. For discussions about Aristotle's attitudes toward women, slaves, and non-Greeks, see Malcolm Heath, "Aristotle on Natural Slavery," *Phronesis: A Journal for Ancient Philosophy* 53, no. 3 (2008): 243–70; Benjamin H. Isaac, *The Invention of Racism in Classical Antiquity* (Princeton, NJ: Princeton University Press, 2006); Nicholas D. Smith, "Plato and Aristotle on the Nature of Women," *Journal of the History of Philosophy* 21, no. 4 (1983): 467–78, and works cited therein. See book 6, chapter 4 of the *Politics* for a sample discussion regarding the exclusion of the working classes (Jonathan Barnes, ed., *Complete Works of Aristotle* [Princeton, NJ: Princeton University Press, 1995]).

23. This is, again, something of a caricature of Aristotle's extremely complex and sophisticated account. In saying that his conclusions are based on commitments about essential natures, I am not suggesting that he recognized women, slaves, and others as different natural kinds from the citizens with whom he was so preoccupied. Nor do I suggest that he saw mechanics and laborers in that way. These "essential natures" need not be biologically based, as they would have to be if they were associated with different natural kinds. Different people have different roles to play in society, and while biology plays a role (especially for women) in shaping people to fulfill those roles, society often plays a greater one. The resulting product is no less essentially shaped to fulfill a specific social role (see Heath, "Aristotle on Natural Slavery," 254–58).

24. Lewis W. Beck, *Kant: Selections* (Upper Saddle River, NJ: Prentice Hall, 1988).

25. For citations to Kant and an interesting discussion, see Mosser, "Kant and Feminism," 322–53.

26. Kant established a four-tiered racial hierarchy with whites (white men) at the top, followed by Asians ("Hindus"), blacks, and Native Americans. According to Kant, Asians can be educated in the arts but not the sciences (as they are incapable of mastering abstract concepts); blacks can be trained to be slaves but cannot be educated and are incapable of working on their own initiative; and Native Americans are completely

inert, impassive, and incapable of being educated at all. See Kleingeld, "Kant's Second Thoughts on Race," and Mills, "Kant's Untermenschen." Kleingeld suggests that Kant radically revised these views in the 1790s, as evidenced by his later works (Kleingeld, "Kant's Second Thoughts on Race," 586–92).

27. See Hess, "Does the Machine Need a Ghost: The Role of Phenomenal Consciousness in Kantian Moral Agency" (ms.), for an argument that Kantian moral agency does not require phenomenal consciousness nor, by extension, empathy or emotion as typically understood.

28. See, e.g., Rosalind Hursthouse, "Environmental Virtue Ethics," in *Working Virtue: Virtue Ethics and Contemporary Moral Problems*, ed. Rebecca L. Walker and Philip J. Ivanhoe (Oxford: Oxford University Press, 2007), 155–72; Allen Thompson, "Radical Hope for Living Well in a Warmer World," *Journal of Agricultural and Environmental Ethics* 23, no. 1–2 (2010): 43–59.

29. For the first, see Catriona Mackenzie and Natalie Stoljar, eds., *Relational Autonomy: Feminist Perspectives on Autonomy, Agency, and the Social Self* (New York: Oxford University Press, 2000); for the second, see, e.g., Alison Jaggar, "Love and Knowledge: Emotion in Feminist Epistemology," *Inquiry* 32, no. 2 (1989): 151–76.

30. The most vehement advocate of this approach is probably Jan Narveson. See, e.g., his "Collective Responsibility."

31. For the broadest approach, *see* Seumas Miller, *Social Action: A Teleological Account* (Cambridge: Cambridge University Press, 2001); Seumas Miller, "Collective Moral Responsibility: An Individualist Account," *Midwest Studies in Philosophy* 30, no. 1 (2006): 176–93; Miller, "Against the Collective Moral Autonomy Thesis." For a sampling of more specific objections, see also Matthew C. Altman, "The Decomposition of the Corporate Body: What Kant Cannot Contribute to Business Ethics," *Journal of Business Ethics* 74, no. 30 (2007): 253–66; Ishtiyaque Haji, "On the Ultimate Responsibility of Collectives," *Midwest Studies in Philosophy* 30 (2006): 292–308; Mitchell. R. Haney, "Corporate Loss of Innocence for the Sake of Accountability," *Journal of Social Philosophy* 35, no. 3 (2004): 391–412; Nani L. Ranken, "Corporations as Persons: Objections to Goodpaster's 'Principle of Moral Projection,'" *Journal of Business Ethics* 6, no. 8 (1987): 633–37; Manuel G. Velasquez, "Why Corporations Are Not Morally Responsible for Anything They Do," *Business and Professional Ethics Journal* 2, no. 3 (1983): 1–18.

32. Examples include highly disciplined, highly structured collectives like corporations, governments, universities, and the rest; the claims are not limited to business entities and do not necessarily extend to less-organized collectives. See Isaacs, *Moral Responsibility in Collective Contexts*, for a preliminary taxonomy, and Christian List, "Three Kinds of Collective Agents," *Erkenntnis* (2014), doi: 10.1007/s10670-014 -9631-z, for further discussion.

33. See, e.g., the works by Copp, French, Goodpaster, List and Pettit, and Rovane cited in note 2.

34. Theorists pursuing this approach include Margaret Gilbert, Seumas Miller, and Raimo Tuomela. See, e.g., M. Gilbert, *On Social Facts* (Princeton, NJ: Princeton University Press, 1992); Margaret Gilbert, "Who's to Blame? Collective Moral Responsibility and Its Implications for Group Members," *Midwest Studies in Philosophy* 30, no. 1 (2006): 94–114; Miller, *Social Action*; Miller, "Collective Moral Responsibility"; Raimo Tuomela and Kaarlo Miller, "We-Intentions," *Philosophical Studies* 53, no. 3 (1988): 367–89.

35. Theorists pursuing this approach include Peter French, Christian List, and Philip Pettit. See, e.g., Peter A. French, "The Corporation as a Moral Person," *American Philosophical Quarterly* 16, no. 3 (1979): 207–15; French, *Collective and Corporate Responsibility*; French, *Responsibility Matters* (Lawrence: University Press of Kansas, 1992); List and Pettit, *Group Agency*; Philip Pettit, "Groups with Minds of Their Own," in *Socializing Metaphysics*, ed. Frederick F. Schmitt (New York: Rowan and Littlefield, 2003), 129–66.

36. Again, see Hess, "Does the Machine Need a Ghost," regarding the possibility that a corporate agent can fulfill the role of Kantian moral agent, and Hess, "A Matter of Corporate Character" (ms.), regarding the possibility that it can fulfill the role of an Aristotelian moral agent. See Hess, "The Free Will of Corporations (and Other Collectives)," more generally about the intentionality and free will of corporate agents.

37. I should perhaps mention that I think corporate agents can meet this "explicit intent" standard, so this is not particularly important for my own project. I just think "explicit intent" is a poor and poorly motivated standard. In addition to the two small difficulties discussed above, there's the further question of why (on earth) this should be necessary, or even desirable. If something *can* act appropriately on the basis of morally relevant information (about pleasure and pain, rights and duties, excellence, etc.), because it is morally relevant information (about pleasure and pain, etc.), then it *should*. If it can do so in the absence of an explicit or articulated intention, then so much the better. And what if it does not? What then? Can we hold it accountable for failing to act as a moral agent should? See the epilogue for further thoughts on such questions.

38. Note that this simply requires regularity, not invariant excellence. It is the rare moral agent who perfectly fulfills her or his (or its) moral obligations. Religions frequently bemoan this fact regarding humans.

39. See de Waal's *Good Natured* for a fascinating discussion along these lines— especially chap. 2, "Sympathy"; Frans B. de Waal, *Good Natured: The Origins of Right and Wrong in Humans and Other Animals* (Cambridge, MA: Harvard University Press, 1996).

40. For egalitarian treatments of disparate classes, see Regan, *The Case for Animal Rights*, and Paul W. Taylor, *Respect for Nature: A Theory of Environmental Ethics* (Princeton, NJ: Princeton University Press, 2011). For inegalitarian treatments, see Robin Attfield, *A Theory of Value and Obligation* (Amsterdam: Rodopi B.V., 1987), and Mary Ann Warren, *Moral Status: Obligations to Persons and Other Living Things* (Oxford: Oxford University Press, 1997).

41. See Hess, "A Matter of Corporate Character," regarding the possibility of distinctive moral obligations for corporations, on an Aristotelian account.

42. See Hess, "'If You Tickle Us,'" for a quick survey; see French, *Collective and Corporate Responsibility*; and List and Pettit, *Group Agency*, for a more extended treatment.

43. This is, of course, a hot topic in the corporate moral agency literature at the time of writing. In 2010 the United States Supreme Court ruled that corporations are entitled to free speech rights under the First Amendment, and in 2014 the Court heard argument on the question of whether corporations are entitled to rights of conscience (see *Citizens United v. Federal Election Commission*, 130 S.Ct. 876, 2010, and *Sebelius v. Hobby Lobby Stores, Inc.*, Docket 13–354).

Three HumAnI(m)Morality

Sean Meighoo

JUST WHEN YOU THOUGHT IT was safe to use punctuation again, I let loose this ill-bred neologism, splicing together the words "morality" and "immorality," "human" and "animal," abusing the privilege of linguistic play granted by even the most indulgent postmodern reader. The meaning of this mongrel term—if there is any meaning to it at all—shifts depending on where you put the accent. If you place the emphasis on the first syllable, this neologism sounds almost exactly like "human immorality," reinscribing the title of this volume, *Beastly Morality*, albeit in a reversed image, like a strange form of mirror writing. The term "beastly" is reflected back to us by the term "human," and the term "morality" reflected back to us by the term "immorality." Certainly, a large part of my essay will be spent reading one highly critical reflection on human immorality, a reflection that appears to have very little to contribute to this volume's stated theme of animal ethics, at least on its surface. If you put the accent on the second syllable of this neologism, however, it seems to sound only like a nonsensical amalgamation of other words, if not other neologisms themselves like "humanimal" and "animorality," the syntagmatic relations composing this term obscured by the associative relations recomposing it in a virtually limitless series of inflections and allusions. Surely enough, in addition to the words "morality" and "immorality," "human" and "animal" from which this neologism was spliced together, it also inscribes within itself the words "orality" and "I," referring us to the practice of spoken language and to the subject who is formed by this practice, respectively, the intimate connection between which, of course, has so long been held to distinguish the human from the animal as such. Moreover, if you repeat the word "humani(m)morality" often enough, you might even be able to sound out "human rights" as well as "animal rights," "human *and* animal rights" as well as "human *or* animal rights"—although this last suggestion of mine, perhaps, finally stretches our literary license too far. In any case, another large part of my essay will be spent reading a more enigmatic meditation on animal morality, a meditation that is justly reputed, I think, to have opened another line of questioning on human ethics itself, a line of questioning that I would like to follow more closely.

Like the capacity for reason or language, the capacity for moral behavior or ethical action has been thought by many philosophers and scientists alike to constitute the key feature that distinguishes humans from other animals. In some recent scholarship, though, this capacity has been extended to nonhuman animals as well. While much of this scholarship itself remains questionable on ethical grounds, it nonetheless stands to make a great contribution to the animal rights movement insofar as it demonstrates that nonhuman animals might also be considered moral agents or ethical subjects.[1] Yet I am interested in following another line of questioning, or rather, I want to turn the question of morality around. Instead of extending the human capacity for morality to nonhuman animals, I want to question whether humans possess this capacity in the first place. Instead of searching for evidence of "humanism" among other animals, I want to question whether there is any evidence of this humanism among humans to begin with. By redirecting the question of morality in this way, I hope to stage an encounter between the discourse of animal rights and the philosophical critique of humanism. More specifically, I want to trace the emergence of what eventually came to be called "antihumanism" within continental philosophy by sharing a close reading of two texts that provide some of its earliest signals. As it turns out, both of these texts are concerned precisely with the question of morality: Friedrich Nietzsche's *Daybreak: Thoughts on the Prejudices of Morality*, and the Surrealist Group's "Murderous Humanitarianism." My claim is that this anti-humanist critique of morality which is undertaken by Nietzsche and the Surrealist Group effectively serves to expose the residual elements of humanism that continue to inform animal rights discourse.

There are thus two different lines of questioning on animal ethics that we might follow here—the Benthamite line of questioning that opens the discourse of animal welfare, animal rights, or animal liberation as such[2] and the Nietzschean line of questioning that augurs the advent of anti-humanism, one line of questioning that promises to redistribute the capacity for morality or ethics from the human to the animal more broadly and another line of questioning that threatens to deconstruct this very capacity. Of course, these two lines of questioning are tightly knotted together, and if we were to pursue either one of these lines far enough, it would inevitably lead us to the other. The Nietzschean line of questioning that I am following in this essay, then, complicates the more popular Benthamite line of questioning on animal ethics without, however, abandoning it entirely, the anti-humanist critique of morality that I want to trace here redirecting the question of moral agency among nonhuman animals even as it rejoins it along the way. It is in this sense that the question of "beastly morality" is also, if not first and foremost, a question of our own humani(m)morality.

ORIGINALLY PUBLISHED IN German in 1881, Nietzsche's *Daybreak* is composed of a long series of aphorisms, divided into five books. Although it greatly resembles his previous work *Human, All Too Human* in terms of its composition, Nietzsche himself seems to have believed that *Daybreak* marked an important shift in his philosophical project, if not a new project altogether, as the title of his text implies. In the preface that he added to the text for its republication in 1886, he declares that it is in *Daybreak* that he "commenced to undermine our *faith in morality*."[3] Indeed, playing on the word "undermine," he opens his preface by introducing himself as "a 'subterranean man' at work, one who tunnels and mines and undermines," even identifying himself as "a solitary mole," what we might call the "undermining" animal par excellence. Of course, Nietzsche goes on to explain that despite his "protracted deprivation of light and air," he is "contented, working there in the dark . . . because he knows what he will thereby also acquire: his own morning, his own redemption, his own *daybreak*," returning to the light and air of day to " 'become a man' again."[4] This subterranean critique of morality which Nietzsche undertakes in *Daybreak* would thus clear the way for his subsequent works that were published over the next few years, including *The Gay Science*, *Thus Spoke Zarathustra*, *Beyond Good and Evil*, and *On the Genealogy of Morals*, before his permanent breakdown in 1889 that was triggered when, as intellectual legend has it, seeing a horse that was being whipped by its coach driver, he threw his arms around the horse's neck and began to cry.

But all legend aside, I am especially interested in reading just one aphorism from *Daybreak*, book 1, section 26, which is itself titled "Animals and morality." In this passage, which occupies no more than the space of a page, Nietzsche makes the argument that morality operates not only within what is often called "civilized society" or what he himself calls "polite society," but in all human societies as well as in animal ones. And the function of all morality, whether it operates in human or animal societies, is to ensure one's own survival, even if this function might seem obvious to us only at the level of the animal: "Social morality [is to be found] in a crude form everywhere, even in the depths of the animal world—and only at this depth do we see the purpose of all these amiable precautions: one wishes to elude one's pursuers and be favoured in the pursuit of one's prey." Nietzsche further argues that even the noblest human enterprise, presumably—the search for truth, philosophy as such—is a modification of the animal's own complex strategy for survival: "Even the sense for truth, which is really the sense for security, man [*sic*] has in common with the animals: one does not want to let oneself be deceived, does not want to mislead oneself, one hearkens mistrustfully to the promptings of one's own passions, one constrains oneself and lies in wait for oneself; the animal understands all this just as man does." Nietzsche comes to the conclusion, then, that far from distinguishing the human from the animal, morality is "animal," as he puts it, placing the human being squarely within the animal world: "The beginnings of justice, as of prudence, moderation, bravery—in short, of all we designate as the *Socratic virtues*, are *animal*: a consequence of that drive which teaches us to seek food and elude enemies. Now if we consider that even the highest human being has only become more elevated and subtle in the nature of his [*sic*] food and in his conception of what is inimical to him, it is not improper to describe the entire phenomenon of morality as animal."[5]

In one sense, Nietzsche's argument on morality in *Daybreak* certainly anticipates much of the recent philosophical and scientific scholarship on the capacity for moral behavior or ethical action among nonhuman animals. Following Nietzsche in this direction, we might say that the human capacity for morality is only one late variation on a prior "animal" capacity.[6] In another sense, however, the force of Nietzsche's argument on morality works in a quite different direction. The effect of his argument, it seems to me, is not to extend the capacity for morality from the human to the animal as much as it is to redefine morality itself, not to expand the range of morality as much as to disperse it. Nietzsche defines morality not by any altruistic concern for others, but rather by what amounts to a narcissistic concern for oneself. He thus calls into question the common presumption that humans are actually capable of altruism themselves, or at least altruism in its purest form—a concern for others to the detriment of oneself, an absolute and unconditional selflessness. While Nietzsche's critique of morality might be read as an argument in favor of existentialist individualism or even Cartesian solipsism—or indeed, as a rigorously philosophical expression of his flagrant male chauvinism[7]—the reading that I am offering here is a more generous one that would call into question the opposition between self and other on which the moral concept of altruism itself continues to depend. In this reading of Nietzsche's text, morality is not structured by any such binary relation, but is instead formed by a complex circuit or relay between oneself and others, rendering altruism practically indistinguishable from narcissism. The moral obligation or duty toward others is not solemnly borne as a sacrifice or burden, then, but joyfully embraced as an affirmation of one's own drive for pleasure.[8] In other words, the concern for others can never be detached from the concern for oneself.

ORIGINALLY PUBLISHED IN English in 1934, "Murderous Humanitarianism" is a short polemical essay against colonialism and racism collectively authored by the Surrealist Group in Paris.[9] Translated from French into English by Samuel Beckett, "Murderous Humanitarianism" provided the Surrealist Group's contribution to the *Negro Anthology*—a massive volume of essays, poems, photographic illustrations, and musical charts on African history and culture in the United States, the Caribbean, South America, Europe, and Africa that was edited and independently published by Nancy Cunard, featuring contributions by Langston Hughes, Zora Neale Hurston, Alain Locke, W. E. B. Du Bois, Nicolás Guillén, George Padmore, and Jomo Kenyatta, among many others, including Ezra Pound and Cunard herself. Although the Surrealist Group does not cite Nietzsche in "Murderous Humanitarianism" at all, I want to suggest nonetheless that this text extends the critique of morality that Nietzsche undertook in *Daybreak*, a critique that remained more or less ignored for some fifty years, much as Nietzsche himself had predicted.[10] Furthermore, it is the Surrealist Group's text in which this critique is directed against humanism as such, thus providing a crucially important though sorely neglected historical link between Nietzsche's critique of morality and the critique of humanism that would so strongly define continental philosophy over the course of the twentieth century.

In marked contrast to Nietzsche's discussion of animals in *Daybreak*, however, the Surrealist Group does not show any interest whatsoever in discussing nonhuman animals themselves in "Murderous Humanitarianism." Rather, it is the exploitation of the proletariat under the conditions of imperial capitalism that concerns them, "whether metropolitan or colonial." In a vitriolic statement spread across two oversized pages of the *Negro Anthology*, they indict the hypocrisy of an avowed humanitarianism that is pressed into service by European colonialists and American racists alike only after the most brutal military power has been used to dispossess, exterminate, and enslave their black and "coloured" subordinates: "For centuries the soldiers, priests and civil agents of imperialism, in a welter of looting, outrage and wholesale murder, have battened with impunity on the coloured races; now it is the turn of the demagogues, with their counterfeit liberalism." Prompted to openly declare its political position by the French Communist Party, the Surrealist Group pledges its support not only for the proletarian revolution at home in France, but also for the struggle against colonialism and racism around the world, and in no uncertain terms: "In a France hideously inflated from having dismembered Europe, made mincemeat of Africa, polluted Oceania and ravaged whole tracts of Asia, we Surréalistes pronounced ourselves in favour of changing the imperialist war, in its chronic and colonial form, into a civil war. Thus we placed our energies at the disposal of the revolution, of the proletariat and its struggles, and defined our attitude towards the colonial problem, and hence towards the colour question." Before concluding their essay by warning the more benevolent imperialists as well as the new "coloured bourgeoisie" that all their "romantic exoticism and modern travel-lust" would not spare them from their impending defeat, the Surrealist Group notes sardonically that "humanists" were full participants in the imperialist project: "In the Antilles, as in America, the fun began with the total extermination of the natives, in spite of their having extended a most cordial reception to the Christopher Columbian invaders. Were they now, in the hour of triumph, and having come so far, to set out empty-handed for home? Never! So they sailed on to Africa and stole men [*sic*]. These were in due course promoted by our humanists to the ranks of slavery."[11]

In the English text of "Murderous Humanitarianism," then—which provides the authoritative text for us since it appears that the original text written in French was never published—the Surrealist Group closely identifies humanism with humanitarianism, using these terms interchangeably. Attacking the professed morality of "our humanists," as they are so derisively called, the Surrealist Group confronts the moral claims of humanitarianism with the long history of human atrocities that have been committed under colonialism and racism in the very name of morality. Of course, the Surrealist Group's argument on humanism remains deeply ambivalent insofar as it is only directed against a hypocritical form of humanitarianism, or as they put it, a "counterfeit liberalism." And yet, the vehement force of their argument seems to suggest that this moral hypocrisy is intrinsic to humanism as such, or at least, humanism as an ideology of rational individualism. In the reading of "Murderous Humanitarianism" that I am offering here, the Surrealist Group thus rejects humanism altogether, rather than simply objecting to its manipulation by European colonialists and American racists on the philosophical grounds of an otherwise morally justified or ethically sound humanism. It is precisely this critique of humanism as such that Jean-Paul Sartre would go on to pursue in his novel *Nausea* as well as in his published address "Existentialism Is a Humanism," to which Martin Heidegger would in turn respond with his "Letter on 'Humanism.'" However, while both Sartre and Heidegger would reject one form of humanism only to propose another form of humanism that each of them would define in his own way, the Surrealist Group does not propose any redefinition of either humanism or humanitarianism in their text at all.

BOTH NIETZSCHE'S CRITIQUE of morality in *Daybreak* and the Surrealist Group's critique of humanism in "Murderous Humanitarianism," then, were pivotal to the emergence of anti-humanism within continental philosophy, even if the term "anti-humanism" itself would not be coined until much later. It is this anti-humanist critique of morality that galvanized the most radical currents of twentieth-century thought, from Marxism and existentialism on one hand to psychoanalysis and structuralism on the other. This anti-humanism, moreover, was established well before the discourse of animal rights was critically taken up within Anglo-American philosophy in the last quarter of the twentieth century. My point here, though, is not to claim any sort of priority for the Nietzschean line of questioning on animal ethics over the Benthamite line of questioning as much as it is to challenge what is still the widespread assumption that anti-humanism has little if anything to contribute to the animal rights movement or to the contemporary field of animal studies.

However, if I have claimed that the anti-humanist critique of morality effectively exposes the residual elements of humanism that continue to inform animal rights discourse, I should also say that the encounter between the discourse of animal rights and the philosophical critique of humanism that I have staged in this essay produces damaging effects on both sides. For animal rights discourse duly calls attention to the strident anthropocentrism that grounds the anti-humanist critique of morality. With only a few exceptions, including Nietzsche himself, anti-humanist thinkers have remained complicit with their humanist peers in their total disregard for nonhuman animals, using them for the sole purpose of demonstrating what it is beyond the capacity for reason that distinguishes the human from the animal as such (more often than not, anti-humanist thinkers have claimed that it is the capacity for language that marks this distinction). Furthermore, this anti-humanist critique of morality has even served to recuperate humanism itself within continental philosophy, albeit in a more subtle form. In this peculiarly anti-humanist form of humanism, the essential immorality of many commonplace human behaviors has been conceded on the very basis that it is only humans who are capable of making moral choices. To put it another way, humans are moral only insofar as they are immoral, or again, the fundamentally human capacity for morality is only confirmed by the fundamentally human capacity for immorality. Curiously enough, this new form of humanism, based on the capacity for morality or ethics rather than reason or language, is quite familiar within the radical discourse of animal liberation as well.[12]

Fully admitting this inherent ambiguity in the anti-humanist critique of morality, then, let me spell out my argument as plainly as I can. It seems to me that any part of the recent scholarship on the capacity for moral behavior or ethical action among nonhuman animals may be seriously contested, regardless of all the sound methods, or indeed, all the good intentions of the scholars in question. This is because the display of moral consideration for others on the part of any nonhuman animal may be shown to provide, or at least to promise, some sort of benefit to the animal itself. Just as the capacity for reason among nonhuman animals is commonly reduced to the operation of "instinct" and the capacity for language reduced to the operation of "code," the capacity for morality or ethics among nonhuman animals may thus be reduced to the operation of "utility" or "instrumentality." The presumption, of course, is that human reason is *not* reducible to instinct, human language is *not* reducible to code, and human morality or ethics is *not* reducible to utility or instrumentality. And it is this presumption which the line of questioning that Nietzsche opened in his work so maddeningly upsets.

There is one more aphorism from *Daybreak* that I would simply like to cite here in its enigmatic entirety, book 4, section 333, which is titled "'Humanity'" (note the scare quotes that Nietzsche places around the word "humanity"): "We do not regard the animals as moral beings. But do you suppose the animals regard us as moral beings?—An animal which could speak said: 'Humanity is a prejudice of which we animals at least are free.'"[13] By following this Nietzschean line of questioning on animal ethics in my essay, I hope to have made some small contribution toward combating what we might call the "humanist prejudice" that informs the concept of morality itself. For without deconstructing the philosophical foundations of humanism that the very concept of morality presupposes, any search for evidence of this much-vaunted morality among nonhuman animals is ultimately bound to fail. What I am calling the deconstruction of the humanist concept of morality, then, would not necessarily demand the expulsion of the terms "morality" and "immorality," "human" and "animal" from our philosophical vocabulary altogether, but it would invite a more careful attention to the ambivalent relations between these terms that give any meaning to the question of animal ethics at all—in a word, to our humani(m)morality.

NOTES

1. Frans de Waal's most recent book, *The Bonobo and the Atheist: In Search of Humanism Among the Primates* (New York: Norton, 2013), provides a very striking illustration of the complicated relationship between this emerging body of scholarship on the capacity for moral behavior or ethical action among nonhuman animals and the political movement for animal rights. While de Waal plainly shows that apes are capable of "humanism"—a term that he does not define anywhere in his text but that he seems to use synonymously with the term "altruism," which he does define (27–28)—he stops short of calling them "moral beings" (17–18, 185, 234–35). This is not to mention the glaring ethical problem of de Waal's laboratory work with nonhuman primates at the Yerkes National Primate Research Center.

2. This line of questioning can be traced back, of course, to Jeremy Bentham's famous question on the capacity for suffering among animals in *An Introduction to the Principles of Morals and Legislation*: "The question is not, Can they *reason?* nor, Can they *talk?* but, Can they *suffer?*" (Jeremy Bentham, *An Introduction to the Principles of Morals and Legislation*, ed. J. H. Burns and H. L. A. Hart, rev. ed. [Oxford: Clarendon Press, 1996], 283, emphasis in original).

3. Friedrich Nietzsche, *Daybreak: Thoughts on the Prejudices of Morality*, ed. Maudemarie Clark and Brian Leiter, trans. R. J. Hollingdale (New York: Cambridge University Press, 1997), 2, emphasis in original.

4. Ibid., 1, emphasis in original.

5. Ibid., 20–21, emphasis in original.

6. De Waal himself begins the first chapter of *The Bonobo and the Atheist* with an epigraph taken from Nietzsche's *Twilight of the Idols* (de Waal, *The Bonobo and the Athe-ist*, 1). He also cites Nietzsche's *On the Genealogy of Morals* in the second chapter of his text to support his own argument on the dissimilarity between the original purpose of an evolutionary trait and its possible uses (ibid., 47–48). Furthermore, playing on what appears to be the unintentional ambiguity in the subtitle of de Waal's book—*In Search of Humanism Among the Primates*—we might even redirect his quasi-Benthamite proj-ect along a more Nietzschean line of questioning by asking whether the "primates" among whom he has so diligently been searching for evidence of humanism include humans themselves as well as apes, monkeys, and other nonhuman primates.

7. While it seems unfair to label Nietzsche a misogynist inasmuch as his frequently disparaging comments on women are matched by his equally flattering remarks about them, it also seems disingenuous to simply absolve him of what I am calling his "male chauvinism" here, as if these flattering remarks on women did not betray his highly prized sense of masculinity as well. In the preface to *Daybreak*, Nietzsche himself calls attention to the significance of this masculine sensibility to his general philosophical project—what he proposes to call the *"self-sublimation of morality"* that has been un-dertaken by those who nonetheless remain *"men of conscience,"* men who, far from hav-ing become sexually indifferent neuters, remain "hostile" to Christianity, romanticism, and patriotism alike, "hostile, in short, to the whole of European *feminism* (or ideal-ism, if you prefer that word), which is for ever [*sic*] 'drawing us upward' and precisely thereby for ever 'bringing us down'" (Nietzsche, *Daybreak*, 4–5, emphasis in original). Furthermore, Nietzsche's decidedly masculinist sense of individualism is contradicted by the details of his own private life—if we may risk the indecency of prying into it here—this "man of conscience" having been placed under the care of his mother, Franziska, after his breakdown in 1889, and then, after Franziska's death in 1897, un-der the care of his sister, the notoriously anti-Semitic Elisabeth Förster-Nietzsche. All this is to say that although we may not be able to reduce the complexity of Nietzsche's critique of morality to his sexist prejudice against women and all things "feminine," we certainly cannot dismiss the critical significance of this prejudice to his work, either. For more on Nietzsche's discourse on woman, cf. Jacques Derrida, *Spurs: Nietzsche's Styles/Éperons: Les Styles de Nietzsche*, trans. Barbara Harlow (Chicago: University of Chicago Press, 1979); Luce Irigaray, *Marine Lover of Friedrich Nietzsche*, trans. Gillian C. Gill (New York: Columbia University Press, 1991); Sarah Kofman, "Baubô: Theological Perversion and Fetishism," trans. Tracy B. Strong, in *Nietzsche's New Seas: Explorations in Philosophy, Aesthetics, and Politics*, ed. Michael Allen Gillespie and Tracy B. Strong (Chicago: University of Chicago Press, 1988), 175–202.

8. My reading of Nietzsche's redefinition or dispersal of morality here draws par-ticularly from the following passage in *Daybreak*, taken from book 4, section 339, "Metamorphosis of duties": "When duty ceases to be a burden but, after long practice, becomes a joyful inclination and a need, the rights of those others to whom our duties, now our inclinations, refer, become something different: namely occasions of pleasant sensations for us. From then onwards, the other becomes, by virtue of his [*sic*] rights, lovable (instead of feared and revered, as heretofore). We are now seeking *pleasure* when we recognise and sustain the sphere of his power" (Nietzsche, *Daybreak*, 163, emphasis in original).

9. The Surrealist Group was a collective of writers and artists that was formally established with the publication of André Breton's *Manifesto of Surrealism* in 1924. The Surrealists, as they are more popularly known, were dedicated to the revolutionary

upheaval of bourgeois society through the liberation of unconscious thought processes in literature and visual art. The text of "Murderous Humanitarianism" itself is signed by Breton, Roger Caillois, René Char, René Crevel, Paul Eluard, J.-M. Monnerot, Benjamin Péret, Yves Tanguy, André Thirion, Pierre Unik, and Pierre Yoyotte.

10. The Surrealist Group does mention Nietzsche among other philosophers and writers in an earlier polemical essay against colonialism, "Revolution Now and Forever!," which was originally published in the group's journal *La Révolution surréaliste* in 1925.

11. Surrealist Group in Paris, "Murderous Humanitarianism," in *Negro: An Anthology*, ed. Nancy Cunard and Hugh Ford, rev. ed. (New York: Continuum, 1970), 352–53.

12. In his classic text *Animal Liberation*, which has widely been credited with sparking the contemporary animal rights movement, Peter Singer himself argues that whereas humans possess the capacity for morality or ethics, other animals do not: "Nonhuman animals are not capable of considering the alternatives, or of reflecting morally on the rights and wrongs of killing for food; they just do it . . . Every reader of this book, on the other hand, is capable of making a moral choice on this matter" (Peter Singer, *Animal Liberation*, rev. ed. [New York: Ecco, 2002], 224).

13. Nietzsche, *Daybreak*, 162.

Four Not All Dogs Go to Heaven

JUDAISM'S LESSONS IN BEASTLY MORALITY

Mark Goldfeder

ON DECEMBER 2, 2013, THE Nonhuman Rights Project (NhRP), a national nonprofit organization working to get actual legal rights for members of nonhuman species, filed a lawsuit in Fulton County, New York, petitioning the judges for a writ of habeas corpus.[1] Habeas corpus allows for a person being held captive to be brought before a court to determine if the imprisonment is lawful. Habeas corpus suits are filed all the time; what made this one historic was that it was not filed for a human being. The writ in question asked the court to formally recognize that a twenty-six-year-old chimpanzee named Tommy was a person, and thereby possessed the legal right not to be bodily detained against his will.[2] One day later, the NhRP filed a similar suit in Niagara Falls, and two days after that a third one on Long Island.

All three lawsuits failed, with all three judges declining to sign the order.[3] One judge held a hearing to explain that while he is indeed an animal lover, he just could not apply NY Code, Article 70: Habeas Corpus to a chimpanzee.[4] Another judge, on a phone hearing, was sympathetic to the cause but did not want to "be the one to make that leap of faith."[5] Still, regardless of the outcome, the reasoning behind the lawsuit is quite simple: the NhRP and its supporters believe that the line between "persons" and "nonpersons" should not be as sharply drawn as it is now. They believe that the current division is artificial and superficial, a line that focuses on microscopic differences in DNA rather than on important and meaningful characteristics, qualities, and emotions that species other than humans might well share.

Although this idea might seem somewhat radical at first glance, from a moral/philosophical perspective these arguments are not that novel. Animal rights and line-drawing have long been a contemplative problem for great thinkers and legal theorists.[6] For many, at least in theory it actually seems almost illogical to deny a complex, autonomous, self-aware creature, capable of communicating its desires, the ability to live as it wishes simply because it looks different. In the words of philosopher Rosalind Hursthouse, for instance:

> Speciesism . . . is just like . . . racism. Racists think that, for instance, the death or enslavement of someone of their own race matters, but that the death or enslavement of someone of a different race does not, despite the fact that a difference in skin colour does not make for a difference in how much one wants to live or be free, or how worthwhile one's life might be, or anything else relevant. Similarly, . . . a speciesist [thinks] that the death or enslavement of a member of their own species matter[s], but that the death or enslavement of a member of a different species . . . d[oes] not, despite the (imagined) fact that the difference in species does not make for a difference in how much the two beings want to live or be free, or how worthwhile their lives might be.[7]

For lawyers, like Steven Wise, the issues are fairly simple and straightforward. What the question boils down to is not whether animals are "human"; they are not, and there is nothing wrong with that. The question is really about whether nonhuman beings can be "legal persons," entitled to some or all human rights. Legal personality makes no claims about sentience, empathy, or even vitality; to have legal personality is simply to be capable of having rights and duties.[8] As Kess demonstrates in chapter 1 of this volume, American courts have long held that the answer to the question of whether nonhuman beings can be legal persons is, at least in some instances, yes.[9] In fact, the Supreme Court in *Burwell v. Hobby Lobby* just affirmed that in some instances nonhuman "persons" (in this case corporations) should be entitled to religious legal rights and protections.[10] For lawyers, then, who only need to look at the bottom line, the question of whether a nonhuman entity can have personhood is simple and decided. For philosophers, however, the question is harder, as we approach the line of *moral* personhood— i.e., actual humanity—instead of just a legal status with a conveniently appropriated name.

But whether we are talking about corporations or animals,[11] and whether we are contemplating granting legal or moral personhood, the idea of moving a well-established line requires a fundamental shift in perspective. In dealing with such a weighty issue, central to our own understanding of the world, it makes sense to at least consider what religion might have to say about the matter, particularly if to see whether the line we take for granted might in fact be only one of many options. This essay will not attempt to answer that question for all religions; it will focus only on Jewish law and lore. It also does not claim to represent the only strain of thought in Judaism or the definitive interpretation of the law; it merely sets out to revisit some of the ancient Judaic texts and understandings, and explore an authentic reading of what this tradition has to say on the subject of nonhuman "persons."

THE CONCEPT OF moral personhood would seem to hinge on the ability to be a moral actor. The idea of divine retribution (i.e., reward and punishment in all its different facets, in both this world and the world to come) is a central tenet of Jewish faith. It is intricately connected to the idea of free will, and the ability to choose rationally between morally acceptable and unacceptable behaviors. Put bluntly: choose well and God will reward you; choose poorly and you will be punished. Those who cannot actually choose their own course of behavior for whatever reason have neither moral responsibility nor culpability; as non-moral actors, they can be neither rewarded nor punished for their actions or inactions.

It has long been assumed that the ability to assess situations and make conscious moral choices is a characteristic unique to mankind. The Bible states that a unique feature of man is his God-like moral intelligence, *lada'at tov vara* (literally, "to know good and evil")—i.e., to differentiate between right and wrong. In the Midrash Genesis Rabbah, the Talmudic sage Rabbi Akiva famously links this concept with free will, and in the Middle Ages the Jewish law codifier Maimonides closed the circle, noting that man is the only creature who resembles God in that he has free will.[12] Yet, is this circle rightfully closed? In light of recent findings, including the work of Frans B. M. de Waal and the research of Steven M. Wise,[13] which shed light on the moral behavior and ethical choices found in the animal kingdom, this essay revisits and explores Judaism's position on animal morality and argues that perhaps that circle is not as unbroken as it might seem.

OUR EXPLORATION STARTS with the idea of animals as divinely ordained creations, formed in God's wisdom and as part of His ineffable plan. Man, for his part, needs both to know and to respect that. The Bible makes specific mention of the moral lessons that man should learn from the other members of the animal kingdom.[14] The Talmud also expands upon these instances. Rabbi Yochanan said: "If the Torah had not been given we could have learnt modesty from the cat, honesty from the ant, chastity from the dove, and good manners from the cock who first coaxes and then mates." There is an entire kabbalistic book dedicated to the subject of how the creatures of creation praise God every day, and as the Midrash Genesis Rabbah notes, oftentimes God performs his wondrous actions through the agency of animals.[15] We can accept the premise then that from a Jewish perspective, animals do perform what we might think of as good—and even noteworthy—deeds.

Jewish law responds by giving animals some rights. A person is not allowed to kill an animal, for instance, unless it is for legitimate human purposes. When an animal kills a person, such as in the case of the murderous ox, the Talmud notes that the Torah took pity on the animal, and made it very hard to prosecute him. In fact, in order to sentence an animal to death, we need the testimony of witnesses and a high court of twenty-three judges. This is the same standard required by the Talmud in any human capital case. By requiring a searching examination before killing an ox, the Torah demonstrates the severity of this matter. More, it suggests that animals are legitimate agents seen by the law to have the right not to be summarily executed without due process.[16]

Humans are not allowed to cause animals pain. Maimonides, in particular, makes it very clear that animals feel not only physical but also emotional pain:

> It is likewise forbidden to slaughter [an animal] and its young on the same day, this being a precautionary measure in order to avoid slaughtering the young animal in front of its mother. For in these cases animals feel very great pain, there being no difference regarding this pain between man and the other animals. For the love and the tenderness of a mother for her child is not consequent upon reason, but upon the activity of the imaginative faculty, which is found in most animals just as it is found in man.[17]

Similarly, Nachmanides, an influential medieval authority, adds that animals sometimes even make behavioral choices based upon their feelings,[18] giving further credence to the idea of animals as being not only capable of feeling emotion but also emotional actors.

Lest one think that the choices animals make are just simple reactions, not based upon intelligent consideration, the Talmud relays several stories about animals making real, conscious decisions. There is, for example, the famous tale of Rabbi Phinehas ben Yair's donkey:

R. Phinehas happened to come to a certain inn. They placed barley before his ass, but it would not eat. It was sifted, but the ass would not eat it. It was carefully picked; still the ass would not eat it. "Perhaps," suggested R. Phinehas, "it is not tithed?" It was at once tithed, and the ass ate it. He, thereupon, exclaimed, "This poor creature is about to do the will of the Creator, and you would feed it with untithed produce!"[19]

It seems that this donkey—and maybe even all donkeys—behaved according to choices between righteous and unrighteous, between good and bad. If divine reward and punishment are based on the making of moral choices and if animals do in fact make good choices, it follows that they are eligible for divine reward and punishment.

Indeed, even the Bible hints that this is the case. On the very last night of their enslavement, when the Jewish people were getting ready for the Exodus from Egypt, the Egyptian houses were full of the cries of families bereft of their firstborns. At midnight, however, at a time when one would expect the animals to join in the howl, they did not; out of respect for the children of Israel, no dog moved its tongue. Later in the Bible, dogs are mentioned again: the nation is told that if an animal is slaughtered improperly and is therefore not kosher, they should not throw the meat away, but rather *lakelev tashlichun oto* (literally, "ye shall cast it to the dogs"). The midrash[20] informs us of the underlying reason:

Scripture says: "Ye shall not eat of anything that dieth of itself; thou mayest give it unto the stranger that is within thy gates. . . ." Hence, what must Scripture mean by saying: "Ye shall cast it to the dogs"? To the dogs and to such as are like dogs. . . . This is to teach you that the Holy One, blessed be He, does not withhold the reward of any creature.[21]

That verse and rabbinic explanation are an excellent starting point for the question of beastly morality and just reward, but are not entirely satisfying in and of themselves. Here is why. In general Jewish philosophy, the discussions revolving around reward and punishment usually focus on life after death, i.e., reward and punishment in the world to come. And so the next question that we have to ask is, Do animals have souls that endure beyond physical death?

Rabbi Moshe Chaim Luzzato (commonly referred to as "Ramchal"), an influential kabbalist and philosopher of the eighteenth century,[22] wrote that animals do in fact have souls. Ramchal asserted that "one type of soul [*nefesh*] that man has is the same that exists in all living creatures. It is this [animal] soul that is responsible for man's natural feelings and intelligence."[23]

If animals do have souls, then one would expect them to receive reward in the next world for the things they have done in this world. The canonic responsa literature, during the period of Jewish masters known as the Gaonim (scholars of a period roughly from the sixth to the eleventh centuries),[24] provides such an opinion. With regard to animals that die for good (i.e., legitimate) reasons, Rabbi Sherira Gaon, writing in the tenth century, explicitly states, "We are of the opinion that all living creatures, the slaughtering and killing of which God has permitted, have a reward, which they may expect."[25] This implies that animals have notions of futurity akin to humans insofar as they too conceive of futures beyond physical demise.

Bringing us back full circle, a set of midrashim attributed to Rabbi Akiva—the same Talmudic Rabbi Akiva of the first century who linked reward and punishment to free will—goes one step further than the Geonim.[26] The midrash tells us that animals will even have the ultimate reward: they will participate and be included in the eventual resurrection of the dead.

> When God renews His world, He himself takes charge of the work of renewal. He arranges all the regulations of the last ones, those of the future world . . . the order of each and every generation, of every being, of every animal, and of every bird. . . . I have caused all human beings and all creatures to die in this world, and I shall restore their spirit and soul to them and revive them in the World to Come.[27]

Considering the amount of literature in the Jewish textual tradition on the concept of human morality and divine reward and punishment, it seems rather odd that if animals make the same kinds of choices as humans, though perhaps of a different sort or degree, we would have to rely on an obscure reference to make the case that they too share in reaping rewards in the hereafter. More information on the process of rewarding animals is necessary to understand the concept of beastly morality under Jewish law. The remainder of this essay focuses on that mystery and attempts to answer the question of the great textual lacuna on beastly morality.

WE START BY noting that the line between humans and animals was not as clear-cut in ancient (rabbinic) times as it is now. Throughout the discussions in rabbinic literature, we encounter part-human and part-animal beings, such as mermaids and other monsters.[28] The rabbis, as legal theorists, not scientists, were more interested in how to classify such creatures than in whether these creatures actually existed. From their statements and rulings across the Babylonian Talmud, the Jerusalem Talmud, and the midrashic lore, one can get a sense of the criteria that they used in determining what exactly it was that gave a creature that elusive title we tend to call—for lack of a better word—humanity, with the accompanying rights and benefits.

Jewish law recognizes some of the classic tests of humanity such as biology, moral intelligence and communicative ability, free will, and so on. However, I will argue here that it is the shifting contextual/functionality test of humanity, as developed in the Jerusalem Talmud, that is the origin of our obligations to certain animals above and beyond our general obligation not to harm nonhuman life for no reason—and indeed our fundamental understanding of animals in general. If animals display human characteristics—if they look human, or act human in some meaningful cognitive way—they deserve not only human rights but also mutual respect. From a Jewish law perspective, they are, in fact, at some level, "human."[29] That might explain the dearth of specifically animal-focused discussions of morality and compensation; if animals are displaying what we might at first call beastly morality, then perhaps according to Jewish law they have by definition already crossed or started crossing the line into humanity.

There are several places throughout the Bible and the Talmud where humans are referred to as *yelud isha* (literally, "those born of woman"). In describing Eve, the Targum Onkelos, an early and influential commentary, notes that the verse refers to her as "the mother of all humanity," because she, Eve, is the progenitor of mankind; anyone born from Eve or her descendants is considered part of mankind. This seems to argue for a traditional speciesist definition, and some Jewish law authorities have taken that definition to be authoritative fact.[30]

One story from the Talmud, which tells us how a rabbi created a "golem," a humanoid automaton, seems to support such a reading:

Rab[bah] said: If the righteous desired it, they could be creators, for it is written. But your iniquities have distinguished between [you and your God]. Rabbah created a man, and sent him to R. Zera. R. Zera spoke to him, but received no answer. Thereupon he said unto him: "Thou art a creature of the magicians. Return to thy dust."[31]

The fact that Rabbi Zera destroyed the golem tells us at least one fundamental thing: "killing" this golem was not considered murder. Why? Because—according to traditional argument—humanity is defined as having been born from a woman, no matter how similar to humanity something looks. While several rabbinic decisors do agree that this is the working definition, they also add some important points. The first is that because humanity is species driven, no human, no matter how many abnormalities or deficiencies, mental or physical, loses the status of personhood. Similarly, miscarried fetuses are human for the purpose of mourning and burial. This leads us to a startling conclusion: if humanity is species driven, as descendants of Eve, then even according to traditional Judeo-Christian sources, humans are descended from nonhuman animals, as Adam and Eve were in no sense of the words "born of woman."[32]

And yet this "born of woman" technicality cannot be the definition of humanity under Jewish law, or halacha. Halacha is meant to address reality on the ground, and so what happens when we are introduced to a creature that for all intents and purposes looks and acts human, but according to our definition is not? Would anyone feel comfortable telling children who were formed in vitro, or who finished their development in an artificial incubator, that they are not fully human and are therefore not entitled to their basic human rights?

The simple answer is to retain the speciesist argument and redefine "born of woman" to mean just having human DNA; the biblical usage of that phraseology may have been a simple way of referring to the usual method of possessing precise human biological specifications, but not necessarily the only one. I suggest that this is not the case, and that indeed halacha has developed an alternative proposition for humanity, one that has important relevance for any discussion of animals. This is based upon a fascinating discussion of tractate Niddah of the Jerusalem Talmud.

Rabbi Yasa states in the name of Rabbi Yochanan: "If [a creature] has a human body but its face is of an animal, it is not human; if [a creature] has an animal body, but its [face is] human, it is human." This would indicate that when the simple definition does not apply, one examines the creature for "human" features, specifically, a human visage. However, the Talmud continues:

> Yet suppose it is entirely human, but its face is animal like, and it is learning Torah? Can one say to it "come and be slaughtered?" [Rather one cannot]. Or consider if it is entirely animal like, but its face human, and it is plowing the field [acting like an animal] do we come and say to it, "come and perform levirate marriage [*yibum*] and divorce [*chalitza*]?" [Rather, one cannot.]
>
> The [T]almudic conclusion seems to be simple. Sometimes, when dealing with a "creature" that does not conform to the simple definition of humanness—borne from a human mother—one examines context to determine if it is human. Does it study Torah (differential equations would do fine for this purpose, too) or is it at the pulling end of a plow?[33]

According to the Talmud, when we cannot apply the biological definition of a human—which may in fact still be the general default definition for the status of personhood—then we apply the contextual definition of a human if it fits. This lends additional support to the idea that a genetically engineered person, even one fully incubated artificially, would be human, as it would have both human attributes and abilities and would behave as humans do. But it also means that great apes, bonobos, and all other primates who sign, communicate, and interact like people meet the contextual definition insofar as they do as humans do, and thus in theory might in some cases be considered people, not animals, by halacha.

While this is the central tenet here, it is also important to point out that there are other possible definitions of halachic humanity, although it is unclear if these are definitions or more aptly descriptive features of humanity. One is the moral intelligence test, based on the verse in Genesis *lada'at tov vara* (literally, "to know [differentiate] between good and evil"). As noted above, Rabbi Akiva famously links this notion with free will, and Maimonides claims that what makes man special is that he is the only creature who resembles God in that he has free will.[34] If Maimonides is right, and if animals have the will to make moral choices, then animals are people too, according to halacha.

Others have wanted to classify speech as a possible halachic criterion for humanity, but that raises some age-old considerations; a human who cannot speak is still human, and there are in fact animals, ranging from gorillas to parrots, that can both communicate and speak. This is not just a modern phenomenon that began with Alex, the African Grey parrot;

the Babylonian Talmud notes that a certain Rabbi Illish met a man who understood the language of birds, and King Solomon was famously able to converse with some animals.[35]

Since we are not willing to give or take away a status of personhood solely on the basis of sounds or motions, the idea of speech, or more generally communication, must be linked to a concept. When we talk about speech as a characteristic of humanity, it means the ability not just to know but to express the differentiation between good and evil. This may not be a separate definition at all, but rather just a description or a test for knowledge of moral intelligence. Or it might be a description or test for our contextual/functional lens—i.e., does this animal behave, contextually, like a human being, exhibiting what we would think of as clearly human intelligence? For instance, does the animal speak? Does the animal communicate, and have knowledge? In all of these ways, at least some animals are "human."[36]

This idea is not far-fetched. The truth is that the early rabbis, although they did not have bonobos who could sign, did deal with what they felt were border cases of humanity. The classic example is a Mishnah in tractate Kilayim, which discusses the creature called *adnei hasadeh*, also known as a *yadua*. While the rabbinic descriptions are terse, the creature seems much like Bigfoot; the influential medieval scholar Rabbi Shlomo Yitzchaki, in his commentary on Job, describes the creature as having the form of a man while really being an animal of the field. Maimonides, however, in describing this creature, notes that its speech is similar to a human's, but is unintelligible. Most importantly, he refers to it in his commentary on the Mishnah as *al nasnas*, which is in fact an Arabic word for "monkey." The Tiferet Yisrael explicitly provides that these sources refer to what we call an orangutan.[37]

The Talmud quotes two opinions as to whether or not, from a Jewish law standpoint, we are dealing with humans here. It is, however, unclear if the two positions are in conflict, with one saying yes and one saying no, or if the status is simply that these beings are somewhere in between—i.e., everyone agrees that for some things they are considered human and for other things they are not. According to at least some important commentators, however, this creature is a full human being. The Jerusalem Talmud in fact refers to it as a *bar nosh d'tor* (literally, a "mountain man"). Presumably, this fits our earlier definition, also from the Jerusalem Talmud: contextually this creature exhibits characteristics that make it seem human, and therefore it is human. What we see clearly from the discussion of the *adnei hasadeh* is that just as we established before, humanness need not be defined solely with reference to a human parent; it may also be defined by a clear, independent functionality test. Either is sufficient to make one human according to Jewish law.[38]

While acknowledging that the Jewish tradition is quite expansive and subject to various interpretations, given the evidence presented in this essay, we find that Judaism's teachings are in fact quite compatible with a broader and deeper understanding of beastly morality. From the biblical comment that we have much to learn from the ways of the animal kingdom to the ancient text of Perek Shira (describing, in part, the ways in which animals serve and praise God in nature), the notion that animals have the potential for morality has long been part of the Judaic tradition, and the idea has found resonance in a variety of specific areas within Jewish thought. Philosophically speaking, Nachmanides's assertion that animals do have some form of free will coincides nicely with the numerous statements throughout the Talmud and the Midrash that involve animals receiving their punishments and just rewards. Theologically, the Gaonic responsa asserting that animals receive recompense in the afterlife for their worldly afflictions and efforts makes sense given the stories in the Talmud of righteous animals separating tithes, and sheds light on the basis for the Midrash that has them taking part in the Great Resurrection. Practically speaking, the biblical ox that is put on trial by a panel of twenty-three judges demonstrates the weight that the concept of animal morality is given in the legal arena.[39]

In conclusion, if there does seem to be a disproportionately small amount of literature on the subject of beastly morality, perhaps it is because Judaism already had a broader and deeper understanding of what it means to be practically human.

On the basis of the Jerusalem Talmud's contextual definition of humanity, it is quite possible that some of the morally responsible subjects of Professor de Waal's and Professor Wise's research were already—from a Jewish perspective—more human than not, with many of the associated rights, duties, privileges, and expectations.

NOTES

1. Parts of this article have appeared in the *Global Journal of Animal Law* (http://www.gjal.abo.fi/?page=get_issue&id=2013-02), and much of the material comes from a piece first published in *Animal Law* 20, no. 1 [2013]).

2. See Brandon Keim, "A Chimp's Day in Court: Inside the Historic Demand for Nonhuman Rights," *Wired*, December 6, 2013, http://www.wired.com/2013/12/chimpanzee-personhood-nonhuman-right/.

3. The NhRP quickly announced that it was expecting this and that it would appeal. See http://www.nonhumanrightsproject.org/2013/12/10/press-release-on-ny-judges-decisions/ for the NhRP press release on the matter.

4. Statements of Judge Joseph Sise, Fulton County Court. See Brandon Keim, "Judge Rules Chimps Can't Be Legal Persons but Activists Vow to Fight On," *Wired*, December 9, 2013, http://www.wired.com/wiredscience/2013/12/chimpanzee-personhood-claims-denied/.

5. Ibid.

6. Scott Wilson, "Animals and Ethics," *Internet Encyclopedia of Philosophy* (2010), http://www.iep.utm.edu/anim-eth/; see Tom Regan, *The Case for Animal Rights* (Netherlands: Springer, 1987).

7. Rosalind Hursthouse, *Beginning Lives* (Oxford: Blackwell's, 1987), 102–3.

8. See Bryant Smith, "Legal Personality," *Yale Law Journal* 37, no. 3 (1928): 283–99.

9. Peter A. French, "The Corporation as a Moral Person," *American Philosophical Quarterly* 16, no. 3 (1979): 207–15.

10. *Burwell v. Hobby Lobby*, 573 U.S. ___ (2014); see Katie McDonough, "Can a Corporation Have a Religion?: Hobby Lobby Challenge to Contraception Mandate Heads to Supreme Court," *Salon*, November 25, 2013, http://www.salon.com/2013/11/25/can_a_corporation_have_a_religion_hobby_lobby_challenge_to_contraception_mandate_heads_to_supreme_court/.

11. See, generally, Michael D. Riard, "Toward a General Theory of Constitutional Personhood: A Theory of Constitutional Personhood for Transgenic Humanoid Species," *UCLA L. Rev.* 39 (1991): 1425.

12. *Genesis Rabbah: The Judaic Commentary to the Book of Genesis, A New American Translation*, vol. 1, 21:5, 233, trans. Jacob Neusner (Atlanta: Scholars Press, 1985) [hereinafter *Genesis Rabbah*]; Maimonides, *Mishneh Torah* 5:1, 41, trans. Philip Birnbaum (New York: Hebrew Publishing Company, 1967).

13. Frans de Waal, *The Bonobo and the Atheist: In Search of Humanism among the Primates* (New York: Norton, 2013); Steven M. Wise, *Rattling the Cage: Toward Legal Rights for Animals* (Cambridge, MA: Perseus Books Group, 2000).

14. Psalms 104:24 (King James Version of the Bible, hereafter King James); see Rabbi Moshe Cordovero, *Tomer Devorah* [The Palm Tree of Deborah], trans. Moshe Miller (Southfield, MI: Targum Press, 1993), 50 (stating that just as God "sustains all creatures . . . so, too, should man do good to all, not despising any creature"). E.g., Proverbs 6:6 (KJV) ("Go to the ant, thou sluggard; consider her ways and be wise").

15. Rabbi Dr. I. Epstein, ed. and trans., *The Babylonian Talmud*, vol. 2, Erubin 100b, 698, (London: Soncino Press, 1948). See Malachi Beit-Arié, *Perek Shira: Songs of Praise for the Creator* (Jerusalem: Jewish National and University Library, 1990) (ascribing songs to land animals, winged creatures, insects, and residents of the waters, all of which praise their Creator). See *Genesis Rabbah*, 10:7 ("Even things that you regard as completely superfluous to the creation of the world, for instance, fleas, gnats, and flies, also fall into the classification of things that were part of the creation of the world. . . . And the Holy One, blessed be he, carries out his purposes even with a snake, scorpion, gnat, or frog").

16. See Commentary of Rema to Shulchan Aruch Even Haezer 5:14 (discussing legitimate purposes, e.g., medical purposes); see also Nachmanides, *Commentary on the Torah: Leviticus 17:11*, trans. Charles B. Chavel (New York: Shilo Publishing House, 1974) (discussing the same). See Exodus 21:28 (King James) ("If an ox gore a man or a woman, that they die: then the ox shall be surely stoned, and his flesh shall not be eaten; but the owner of the ox shall be quit"); Jacob Schachter and H. Freedman, trans., *The Babylonian Talmud*, vol. 1, Sanhedrin 55a, 375 (New York: Rebecca Bennet Publications, 1959); *Commentary of Rashi to Babylonian Talmud Sanhedrin*, 55a; Sefer HaChinuch (the unwarranted killing of an animal, i.e., killing an animal for illegitimate human purposes, is rated as bloodshed that is only a little less severe than killing a person); see also Schachter and Freedman, *The Babylonian Talmud*, vol. 1, Sanhedrin 2a, 2 ("The ox to be stoned is tried by twenty-three. . . . The death sentence on the wolf or the lion or the bear or the leopard or the hyena or the serpent is to be passed by twenty-three," and "Capital cases are adjudicated by twenty-three"). For more on religions and animals in courts, see Bathgate (chapter 10) and Crane and Gross (chapter 12) in this volume.

17. Maimonides, *The Guide of the Perplexed*, pt. 3, ch. 48, trans. Shlomo Pines (Chicago: University of Chicago Press, 1963), 599 (emphasis omitted).

18. Nachmanides, *Commentary on the Torah: Bereishis/Genesis* 1:29.

19. Rabbi Epstein, *The Babylonian Talmud*, vol. 2, Chullin 7a–b.

20. Exodus 11:5–6; 11:7; 22:31 (King James). A midrash is "an ancient Jewish exposition of a passage of the scriptures." Philip Babcock Gove, ed., *Webster's Third New International Dictionary* (Springfield, MA: Merriam-Webster, 1993), 1431.

21. Jacob Z. Lauterbach, trans., *Mekhilta de-Rabbi Ishmael*, 2d ed., vol. 2, Kaspa, ch. 2, 466 (Philadelphia: Jewish Publication Society, 2004).

22. See Dan Cohn-Sherbok, *The Dictionary of Jewish Biography* (London: Continuum, 2005), 187 (describing Ramchal as an Italian kabbalist and philosopher); see also Samuel J. Levine, "Further Reflections on the Role of Religion in Lawyering and in Life," *Regent University Law Review* 11, no. 31 (1998–1999): 34 (describing Ramchal as a great eighteenth-century ethicist).

23. Moshe Chaim Luzzatto, *The Way of God*, pt. 3, 1:1, trans. Aryeh Kaplan, 6th rev. ed. (Jerusalem: Feldheim Publishers, 1996).

24. George Horowitz, *The Spirit of Jewish Law: A Brief Account of Biblical and Rabbinical Jurisprudence with a Special Note on Jewish Law and the State of Israel* (New York: Central Book Company, 1953), 40–42.

25. Rabbi Natan Slifkin, *Man and Beast: Our Relationships with Animals in Jewish Law and Thought* (Israel: Zoo Torah, 2006), 114 (quoting Rabbi Sherira Gaon, Teshuvos HaGeonim no. 375).

26. Cohn-Sherbok, *The Dictionary of Jewish Biography*, 8; see *Genesis Rabbah*, 21:6 (discussing Rabbi Akiva's linkage of reward and punishment to free will).

27. Slifkin, *Man and Beast*, 71 n. 1 (quoting Osiyos D'Rabbi Akiva, Os aleph).

28. See Rabbi Natan Slifkin, *Sacred Monsters: Mysterious and Mythical Creatures of Scripture, Talmud and Midrash* (Israel: Zoo Torah, 2007), 19 (discussing references to mystical creatures present throughout Jewish literature); see also *The Book of Jasher* 61:15 (J. H. Parry, 1887), accessed November 16, 2013, http://www.ccel.org/a /anonymous/jasher [http://perma.cc/BXA6-LL2U] ("Zepho . . . came into the cave and he looked and behold, a large animal was devouring the ox; from the middle upward it resembled a man, and from the middle downward it resembled an animal").

29. See below, Jerusalem Talmud, Niddah 3:2. See *Babylonian Talmud*, Baba Mezi'a 31a, for a discussion of man's duty toward animals generally; see also Rabbi Dr. Asher Meir, "Animal Suffering: The Jewish View," *Virtual Jerusalem*, August 25, 2013, accessed November 16, 2013, http://www.virtualjerusalem.com/judaism .php?Itemid=10453 [http://perma.cc/ouwkvjpTeZ1] (discussing that, according to the Babylonian Talmud, Baba Mezi'a 31a, the reference to "unloading" pack animals in Exodus 23:5 is one source for the prohibition of animal suffering). See Rabbi Michael J. Broyde, "Cloning People and Jewish Law: A Preliminary Analysis," pt. III(D), *Jewish Law*, accessed November 16, 2013, http://www.jlaw.com/Articles/cloning .html [[http://perma.cc/ooQEWj29WjC], (asserting that "humanness" is not dependent on intelligence, and noting the ambiguity in categorizing something as "animal" or "human").

30. See, e.g., Job 14:1 (King James) ("Man that is born of a woman . . . " [emphasis omitted]). See also Rabbi Epstein, *The Babylonian Talmud* , vol. 3, Yoma 75b, 698 (London: Soncino Press, 1948) ("[F]or is there one born of woman"). Israel Drazin, *Targum Onkelos to Deuteronomy 1* (New York: KTAV Publishing House, 1982); Rabbi A. M. Silbermann and Rev. M. Rosenbaum, trans., *Targum Onkelos Commentary to Genesis* 3:20 (Jerusalem: Silbermann Fam., 1934); Responsa Chacham Tzvi 93; see Rabbi Michael J. Broyde, "Genetically Engineering People: A Jewish Law Analysis of Personhood," *St. Thomas L. Rev.* 13, no. 2 (2001): 890 (noting that, while there are different interpretations as to what makes one human, some groups adopt the "from a human mother" formulation as the exclusive definition of humanness).

31. Schachter and Freedman, *The Babylonian Talmud*, vol. 1, Sanhedrin 65b, 446.

32. See, e.g., Moshe Cordovero, *Pardes Rimonim* [Orchard of Pomegranates], ch. 24, § 10 (discussing killing a "golem"); Rabbi Avraham Azulai, Chessed LeAvraham, Maayan Revi'i nahar 30 (discussing the same). See also Shut Teshuva Me'ahava 1:53; Chazon Ish YD. 118:4, Chida, Birkei Yosef Even HaEzer 4:8; Sidrei Taharot, Oholot 5a.

33. Broyde, "Cloning People and Jewish Law," pt. 3 (D) (quoting the Jerusalem Talmud, Niddah 3:2).

34. Genesis 3:22 (King James); "Commentary of Rashi to Genesis 3:22," Chabad.org, accessed November 16, 2013, http:// www.chabad.org/library/bible_cdo/aid/8167 showrashi=true [http:// perma.cc/oprzpHMGcxc]; *Genesis Rabbah*, 21:7; Maimonides, *Mishneh* Torah, 5:1, 41–42.

35. See Steven M. Wise, *Drawing the Line: Science and the Case for Animal Rights* (Cambridge, MA: Perseus Books Group, 2002), 87–91 (describing the author's interaction with Alex and Alex's ability to speak and identify colors and sounds); Maurice Simon, trans., *The Babylonian Talmud*, vol. 1, Gittin 45a, 198 (New York: Rebecca Bennet Publications, 1959); Midrash Tanhuma B, Mavo; Ruth Rabbah 1:17; Eccl. Rabbah 2:25.

36. In our modern world of widespread corporate personhood, the idea of extending what we think of as "humanity" for some purposes and not for others is not shocking. See, e.g., *Citizens United v. Fed. Election Commn.*, 558 U.S. 310, 342 (2010) (recognizing that First Amendment protection extends to corporations).

37. Rabbi Epstein, *The Babylonian Talmud*, Kilayim 8:5, 132 (London: Soncino Press, 1961); Schachter and Freedman, *The Babylonian Talmud*, vol. 1, Sanhedrin 65b, 445; Shlomo Yitzchaki, *Commentary of Rashi* on Job 6:23; Maimonides, *Commentary to the Mishnah Kilayim* 8:5; see also Shlomo E. Glicksberg, "Judaism and Evolution

in Four Dimensions: Biological, Spiritual, Cultural, and Intellectual," in *Origin(s) of Design in Nature: A Fresh, Interdisciplinary Look at How Design Emerges in Complex Systems, Especially Life,* ed. Liz Swan et al. (Netherlands: Springer, 2012), 212; Maimonides, *Commentary to the Mishnah Kilayim* 8:5.The idea of monkeys as intermediates between man and animal is well founded in Jewish thought. Discussing the four basic levels of Creation (minerals, plants, animals, and man), Rabbi Yosef Albo writes that just as coral life and sea sponges represent the intermediate existence between the plant and animal kingdoms, so too does the monkey represent the intermediate stage between animals and man. Yosef Albo, *Sefer Halkarim* [The Book of Principles] 3:1; Israel Lipschitz, Tiferet Yisrael, Yachin to the Mishnah Kilayim 8.

38. Jerusalem Talmud, Kilayim 8:5. See, e.g., Rash Mishantz, *Commentary on Mishnah Kilayim 8:5* (arguing that the creature is a human); Rav Ovadia Bartenura, *Commentary on Mishnah Kilayim 8:5*; Jerusalem Talmud, Kilayim 8:5. See R. Akiva Eiger, *Commentary to Yoreh Deah* 2 (stating that monkeys cannot perform ritual slaughter not because they are not human but because they are not observant Jews); see also Maharasha, Chidushei Aggadot to Tractate Sanhedrin (implying that if something is alive, like an animal, and exhibits human characteristics, we would in fact consider it human).

39. Proverbs 6:6 (King James). Malachi Beit-Arié, *Perek Shira*. Nachmanides, *Commentary on the Torah: Bereishis/*Genesis 1:29. See note 25 and accompanying text (discussing the possibility of reward for animals that die for good reasons). Rabbi Epstein, *The Babylonian Talmud*, Chullin 7a–b, 29. Slifkin, *Man and Beast*, 71n.1 (quoting Osiyos D'Rabbi Akiva, Os Aleph). See note 16 and accompanying text (discussing the standards for putting an animal to death).

Part Two **Observing Animal Morality**

Five Animal Empathy as Moral Building Block

Frans B. M. de Waal

ONCE UPON A TIME, THE United States had a president known for a peculiar facial display. In an act of controlled emotion, he would bite his lower lip and tell his audience, "I feel your pain."

Whether the display was sincere is not the issue here; how we are affected by another's predicament is. Empathy is second nature to us, so much so that anyone devoid of it strikes us as dangerous, mentally ill, or both. At the movies, we can't help but get inside the skin of the characters on the screen. We despair when their gigantic ship sinks; we exult when they finally stare into the eyes of a long-lost lover.

We are so used to empathy that we take it for granted, yet it is essential to human society as we know it. Our morality depends on it. How could anyone be expected to follow the Golden Rule without the capacity to mentally trade places with a fellow human being? It is logical to assume that this capacity came first, giving rise to the Golden Rule itself. The act of perspective-taking is summed up by one of the most enduring definitions of empathy that we have, formulated by Adam Smith as "changing places in fancy with the sufferer."[1] Even Smith, the father of economics, best known for emphasizing self-interest as the lifeblood of human economy, understood that the concepts of self-interest and empathy don't conflict.[2] Empathy makes us reach out to others, first just emotionally, but later in life also by understanding their situation.

This capacity likely evolved because it served our ancestors' survival in two ways. First, like every mammal, we need to be sensitive to the needs of our offspring. Second, our species depends on cooperation, which means that we individually do better if we are surrounded by healthy, capable group mates. Taking care of them is just a matter of enlightened

FIGURE 5.1 An example of consolation among chimpanzees: A juvenile puts an arm around a screaming adult male, who has just been defeated in a fight with his rival. Consolation probably reflects empathy, as the objective of the consoler seems to be to alleviate the distress of the other. *Source*: Photograph by Frans de Waal.

self-interest. This argument—empathy in our own interest as the glue of society—is in fact quite old in biology, and goes back to Peter Kropotkin,[3] who himself was inspired in this by Adam Smith.[4]

ANIMAL EMPATHY

It is hard to imagine that empathy—a characteristic so basic to the human species that it emerges early in life and is accompanied by strong physiological reactions—came into existence only when our lineage split off from that of the apes. It must be far older than that. Examples of empathy in other animals would suggest that it arose long before our species made its appearance.

Evolution rarely throws anything out. Instead, structures are transformed, modified, co-opted for other functions, or tweaked in another direction. The frontal fins of fish became the front limbs of land animals, which over time turned into hoofs, paws, wings, and hands. Just as there is morphological continuity, there is also behavioral continuity in the animal kingdom. Specifically, over the last several decades, we've seen increasing evidence of empathy in species other than our own. One piece of evidence came unintentionally out of a developmental study by Carolyn Zahn-Waxler, a research psychologist at the National Institute of Mental Health. She visited people's homes to find out how young children respond to family members' emotions. She instructed people to pretend to sob, cry, or choke, and found that some household pets seemed as worried

FIGURE 5.2 Empathy combined with perspective-taking enables helping behavior tailored to the other's specific needs, known as targeted helping. In this case, a mother chimpanzee reaches to help her son out of a tree after he screamed and begged for her attention. *Source*: Photograph by Frans de Waal.

as the children were by the feigned distress of the family members. The pets hovered nearby and put their heads in their owners' laps.[5] Recently, this experiment has been repeated but with a focus on the pets rather than the children in the family, concluding that they showed first-stage empathy, which is emotional contagion. Some dogs whined or whimpered when they heard their owners cry.[6]

But perhaps the most compelling evidence for the strength of animal empathy came from a group of psychiatrists led by Jules Masserman at Northwestern University. The researchers reported in 1964 that rhesus monkeys refused to pull a chain that delivered food to themselves if doing so gave a shock to a companion. One monkey stopped pulling the chain for twelve days after witnessing another monkey receive a shock. Those primates were literally starving themselves to avoid shocking another animal.[7]

The anthropoid apes, our closest relatives, are even more remarkable. Yerkes reported how his bonobo, Prince Chim, was so extraordinarily concerned and protective toward his sickly chimpanzee companion, Panzee, that the scientific establishment might not accept his claims: "If I were to tell of his altruistic and obviously sympathetic behavior towards Panzee, I should be suspected of idealizing an ape."[8] What Yerkes was hinting at here is that Western science, especially in his day but still today, is always more comfortable with negative portrayals of animals (as competitive or aggressive) than with positive ones, in which animals are depicted as nice to each other. Statements to the latter effect are regarded with skepticism, as romantic or idealistic.[9]

Nadia Ladygina-Kohts, a primatological pioneer, noticed similar empathic tendencies in her young chimpanzee, Joni, whom she raised at the beginning of the last century, in Moscow. Kohts, who analyzed Joni's behavior in the minutest detail, discovered that the only way to get him off the roof of her house after an escape—much more effective than any reward or threat of punishment—was by arousing sympathy:

> If I pretend to be crying, close my eyes and weep, Joni immediately stops his plays or any other activities, quickly runs over to me, all excited and shagged, from the most remote places in the house, such as the roof or the ceiling of his cage, from where I could not drive him down despite my persistent calls and entreaties. He hastily runs around me, as if looking for the offender; looking at my face, he tenderly takes my chin in his palm, lightly touches my face

with his finger, as though trying to understand what is happening, and turns around, clenching his toes into firm fists.[10]

These observations suggest that apart from emotional connectedness, apes have an appreciation of the other's situation and show a degree of perspective-taking. One striking report in this regard concerns a bonobo female named Kuni, who found a wounded bird in her enclosure at Twycross Zoo, in England. Kuni picked up the bird, and when her keeper urged her to let it go, she climbed to the highest point of the highest tree, carefully unfolded the bird's wings and spread them wide open, one wing in each hand, before throwing it as hard as she could toward the barrier of the enclosure. When the bird fell short, Kuni climbed down and guarded it until the end of the day, when it flew to safety. Obviously, what Kuni did would have been inappropriate toward a member of her own species. Having seen birds in flight many times, she seemed to have a notion of what would be good for a bird, thus giving us an anthropoid illustration of Smith's "changing places in fancy."

This is not to say that all we have are anecdotes. Systematic studies have been conducted on so-called consolation behavior. Consolation is defined as friendly or reassuring behavior by a bystander toward a victim of aggression. For example, chimpanzee A attacks chimpanzee B, after which bystander C comes over and embraces or grooms B. After thousands such observations, we know that consolation occurs regularly and exceeds baseline levels of contact. In other words, it is a demonstrable tendency that probably reflects empathy, since the objective of the consoler seems to be to alleviate the distress of the victim. Indeed, the usual effect of this kind of behavior is that the victim stops screaming, yelping, and showing other signs of distress,[11] and there are clear behavioral signs of a stress-reducing effect. Using self-scratching as an external sign of anxiety, Fraser, Stahl, and Aureli demonstrated that chimpanzees show this behavior less after having received consolation than without it.[12]

A BOTTOM-UP VIEW OF EMPATHY

The above examples help to explain why, to the biologist, a Russian doll is such a satisfying plaything, especially if it has a historical dimension. I own a doll of Russian president Vladimir Putin, within whom we discover Yeltsin, Gorbachev, Brezhnev, Khrushchev, Stalin, and Lenin, in that order.

Finding a little Lenin and Stalin within Putin will hardly surprise most political analysts. The same is true for biological traits: the old always remains present in the new.

This is relevant to the debate about the origins of empathy, especially because of the tendency in some disciplines, such as psychology, to put human capacities on a pedestal. Some even argue that empathy is uniquely human.[13] Instead of placing empathy in the upper regions of human cognition, it is probably best to start out examining the simplest possible processes, some perhaps even at the cellular level. In fact, recent neuroscience research suggests that very basic neural processes may underlie empathy. Researchers at the University of Parma, in Italy, were the first to report that monkeys have special brain cells that become active not only if the monkey grasps an object with its hand but also if it merely watches another do the same. Since these cells are activated as much by doing as by seeing someone else do, they are known as mirror neurons, or "monkey see, monkey do" neurons.[14]

It seems that developmentally and evolutionarily, advanced forms of empathy are preceded by and grow out of more elementary ones. Empathy probably evolved in the context of the parental care that characterizes all mammals. Signaling their state through smiling and crying, human infants urge their caregiver to take action, and caregivers are sensitive to these signals. This also applies to other primates. The survival value of these interactions is evident from the case of a deaf female chimpanzee I have known named Krom, who gave birth to a succession of infants and had intense positive interest in them. But because she was deaf, she wouldn't notice her babies' calls of distress, even if she sat down on them. Krom's case illustrates that without the proper mechanism for understanding and responding to a child's needs, a species will not survive. During the 180 million years of mammalian evolution, females who responded to their offspring's needs out-reproduced those who were cold and distant. Having descended from a long line of mothers who nursed, fed, cleaned, carried, comforted, and defended their young, we should not be surprised, therefore, by gender differences in human empathy, which appear well before socialization. Such sex differences are found in the second year of life, with girls showing more concern for others than boys. The literature on adult gender differences is more equivocal and contested, to be sure, yet women have been found to be better readers of subtle affective cues than men, and women report stronger empathic reactions.[15] Similar sex differences also exist among chimpanzees.[16]

Empathy also plays a role in cooperation. One needs to pay close atten-tion to the activities and goals of others to cooperate effectively. A lion-ess needs to notice quickly when other lionesses go into hunting mode, so that she can join them and contribute to the pride's success. A male chimpanzee needs to pay attention to his buddy's rivalries and skirmishes with others so that he can help out whenever needed, thus ensuring the political success of their partnership. Effective cooperation requires being exquisitely in tune with the emotional states and goals of others.[17]

Within a bottom-up framework, the focus is not so much on the high-est levels of empathy, but rather on its simplest forms, and how these combine with increased cognition to produce more-complex forms of empathy. How did this transformation take place? The evolution of em-pathy runs from shared emotions and intentions between individuals to a greater self/other distinction—that is, an "unblurring" of the lines be-tween individuals. As a result, one's own experience is distinguished from that of another person, even though at the same time we are vicariously affected by the other's. This process culminates in a cognitive appraisal of the other's behavior and situation: we adopt the other's perspective.

As in a Russian doll, however, the outer layers always contain an inner core. Instead of evolution having replaced simpler forms of empathy with forms that are more advanced, the latter are sophisticated elaborations on the former and remain dependent on them. This also means that empa-thy comes naturally to us. It is not something we learn only later in life, or something that is culturally constructed. At heart, it is an automated response that we fine-tune and elaborate upon in the course of our lives, until it reaches a level at which it becomes such a complex response that it is hard to recognize its origin in simpler responses, such as body mimicry and emotional contagion.

MORAL SENTIMENTS

Ever since Aristotle, moral philosophers, including David Hume, Adam Smith, and Edward Westermarck, have argued that there are two distinct layers to human morality: (1) moral emotions or sentiments and (2) the capacity for moral judgment and reasoning. We tend to focus on the first layer when we compare humans with other animals because it is closer to direct behavioral expression and hence is easier to measure. Investigating the extent to which primates are capable of moral judgment and reasoning is a much more challenging task, and the lack of data in this area constrains what conclusions can be drawn. Regardless of this limitation, moral sentiments are a necessary starting point for investigations of the origins of morality. These sentiments are the very building blocks of morality in that they reflect the tendencies and capacities (e.g., the capacities for empathy and perspective-taking) without which human morality as we know it would be unthinkable. The moral sentiments, and their underlying capacities, however, are not necessarily *objects* of morality. For example, we would with Westermarck classify the tendency for retribution as a prerequisite for a rule-based, just society—hence as a critical building block of morality—whereas we might at the same time morally disapprove of many of its expressions.[18] Furthermore, as Railton points out, many important building blocks of morality, such as deliberation and the capacity to adjust one's own behavior to compensate for another's limitations, are essential to morality without necessarily being "dedicated" to moral tasks.[19]

Distinguishing between the behaviors that we judge and the capacities that make these behaviors and judgments possible seems to be a major source of confusion. This confusion is not new; it goes all the way back to Seton, who tried to determine analogues in animals to the Ten Commandments.[20] Even if such analogues exist, they tell us very little about the origins of morality. Consequently, we need to sharply distinguish the moral evaluation of animal behavior—which is a naive and rather useless enterprise—from the search for moral abilities and tendencies in animals other than ourselves. Empathy is one of those critical capacities. It is not sufficient for morality, but surely human morality would be unthinkable without our tendency to be interested in others and making their situation to some extent our own.[21]

NOTES

1. A. Smith, *A Theory of Moral Sentiments* (New York: Modern Library, 1937 [1759]), 10.

2. See Meighoo's treatment of Nietzsche's view of self-interest and altruism, in chapter 3 of this volume.

3. P. Kropotkin, *Mutual Aid: A Factor of Evolution* (New York: New York University Press, 1972 [1902]).

4. L. A. Dugatkin, "Strange Bedfellows: A Russian Prince, a Scottish Economist, and the Role of Empathy in Early Theories for the Evolution of Cooperation," *Journal of Experimental Zoology, Part B: Molecular and Developmental Evolution* 320B (2013): 407–11.

5. C. Zahn-Waxler, B. Hollenbeck, and M. Radke-Yarrow, "The Origins of Empathy and Altruism," in *Advances in Animal Welfare Science*, ed. M. W. Fox and L. D. Mickley (Washington, DC: Humane Society of the United States, 1984), 21–39.

6. D. Custance and J. Mayer, "Empathic-Like Responding by Domestic Dogs (Canis familiaris) to Distress in Humans: An Exploratory Study," *Animal Cognition* 15 (2012): 851–59.

7. J. Masserman, M. S. Wechkin, and W. Terris, "Altruistic Behavior in Rhesus Monkeys," *American Journal of Psychiatry* 121(1964): 584–85.

8. R. M. Yerkes, *Almost Human* (New York: Century, 1925).

9. Frans de Waal, *Good Natured: The Origins of Right and Wrong in Humans and Other Animals* (Cambridge, MA: Harvard University Press, 1996).

10. N. N. Ladygina-Kohts, *Infant Chimpanzee and Human Child: A Classic 1935 Comparative Study of Ape Emotions and Intelligence*, ed. F. B. M. de Waal (New York: Oxford University Press, 2001 [1935]), 121.

11. M. T. Romero, M. A. Castellanos, and F. B. M. de Waal, "Consolation as Possible Expression of Sympathetic Concern Among Chimpanzees," *Proceedings of the National Academy of Sciences, USA* 107 (2010): 12110–15; Z. Clay and F. B. M. de Waal, "Development of Socio-emotional Competence in Bonobos," *Proceedings of the National Academy of Sciences, USA* (2013), doi:10.1073/pnas.1316449110.

12. O. N. Fraser, D. Stahl, and F. Aureli, "Stress Reduction through Consolation in Chimpanzees," *Proceedings of the National Academy of Sciences USA* 105 (2008): 8557–62.

13. D. J. Povinelli, "Can Animals Empathize?," *Scientific American Presents: Exploring Intelligence* 9 (1998): 67, 72–75.

14. G. di Pellegrino, L. Fadiga, L. Fogassi, V. Gallese, and G. Rizzolatti, "Understanding Motor Events: A Neurophysiological Study," *Experimental Brain Research* 91 (1992): 176–80.

15. S. D. Preston, "The Origins of Altruism in Offspring Care," *Psychological Bulletin* 139 (2013): 1305–41; M. L. Hoffman, "Sex Differences in Empathy and Related Behaviors," *Psychological Bulletin* 84 (1977): 712–22; C. Zahn-Waxler, M. Radke-Yarrow, E. Wagner, and M. Chapman, "Development of Concern for Others," *Developmental Psychology* 28 (1992): 126–36; J. A. Hall, "Gender Effects in Decoding Nonverbal Cues," *Psychological Bulletin* 85 (1978): 845–57; N. Eisenberg and R. A. Fabes, "Prosocial Development," in *Social, Emotional, and Personality Development*, vol. 3 of *Handbook of Child Psychology*, ed. W. Damon and N. Eisenberg, 701–78 (New York: Wiley, 1998).

16. Romero, Castellanos, and de Waal, "Consolation as Possible Expression of Sympathetic Concern Among Chimpanzees."

17. This holds true with regard to play. See Bekoff, chapter 7 of this volume.

18. E. Westermarck, *The Origin and Development of the Moral Ideas*, 2nd ed. (London: Macmillan, 1912 [1908]), 1.

19. P. Railton, "Darwinian Building Blocks," *Journal of Consciousness Studies* 7 (2000): 55–59.

20. E. T. Seton, *The Natural History of the Ten Commandments* (New York: Scribner's, 1907).

21. F. B. M. de Waal, *The Bonobo and the Atheist: In Search of Humanism Among the Primates* (New York: Norton, 2013).

Six Humans, Other Animals, and the Biology of Morality

Elisabetta Palagi

FOR LUCA

THE GOLDEN RULE, ACCORDING TO which we are to "do unto others as you would have them do unto you," has been put forth, mainly by philosophers and theologians, as an important basis of morality.[1] The Oxford English Dictionary defines "morality" as the "principles concerning the distinction between right and wrong or good and bad behavior." This definition includes the term "principle," which, according to the same dictionary, means "a fundamental truth or proposition that serves as the foundation for a system of belief or behavior or for a chain of reasoning." From these authoritative definitions it appears clear that the concept of morality is commonly considered to be an outcome of a complex rationality and theoretical reasoning and, consequently, a phenomenon completely cleaved to our nature as *human* beings. It is not surprising, then, that in the most popular interpretation, the term "morality" can be attributed only to humans. But can we actually argue that moral behaviors are exclusively linked to our most rational nature?

For example, are the strong sensations we experience when witnessing a violent event (such as child abuse) or an extremely selfless behavior (sacrificing one's own life to save another) the outcome of a pure reasoning process or, instead, are they the reaction of other, deeper and visceral parts of our organism? The perception of wrong and right—the process at the basis of moral reactions—lies within our entire being: the mind and the body. The negative and positive emotions of others naturally and organically resonate within us and provoke a similar emotional response. That individuals are able to transpose the pain or happiness of others into similar feelings of their own is fundamental to our very being. This suggests that the original Golden Rule requiring that an individual somehow relate to another ("non-self") can be understood in light of the older biological mechanism of "emotional resonance," which leads two individuals to feel the same, and thereby to fulfill the "being alike" principle, itself a necessary prerequisite to applying the Golden Rule as such.[2]

The skill to unconsciously apply the "like me" correspondence between self and others, through bodily communication, also represents an essential prerequisite to forming and establishing social bonds between individuals. The proximate factor explaining bodily resonance was identified in the perception-action mechanism, which consists of the involuntary reenactment of an observed behavior or facial expression. Neurophysiological evidence of this coupling derived from the discovery of mirror neurons that stimulated (and is still stimulating) much debate in the neuroscience world. This set of neurons, first described in the prefrontal cortex of the rhesus macaque, fires when the subject either performs a motor action or observes the action performed by another. A mirror system for understanding action and imitation, homologous to that of macaques, was later discovered in humans. The observation of a facial expression activates subcortical brain areas in the subject. These include limbic structures, which are activated both when the subject feels a given emotion and when the subject observes the same emotion in the facial expression of others (emotional resonance). This matching mechanism does not require any kind of conscious awareness and functions as an emotional bridge between different subjects. Thanks to this mechanism, two individuals can synchronize their affective states and perhaps engage in cooperative, prosocial, and (why not?) altruistic behaviors. Indeed, it has been observed that individuals who cooperate successfully with others and maintain peaceful relationships are more likely to be well integrated in their group and are able to accomplish survival activities in a more effective way.[3] In this perspective a "moral brain" is adaptive and, therefore, favored by natural selection.

Until a few years ago, self-other affective matching was attributed to humans only. Yet many researchers soon became aware that the only possibility we had to understand even the most complex forms of human empathy was to look at other branches on the evolutionary tree. As a result of this new interest, some convincing data emerged on similar phenomena in other species. Apes, monkeys, and even dogs and rats have become good models to study for the origin and evolutionary history of human empathic and prosocial potential. These nonhuman animals can serve as a precious Noah's ark that can help us to shed light on the origin of the contested phenomenon of human nature: morality.

SAME FACE . . . SAME EMOTION

In humans, emotions expressed through facial displays can strongly affect rational decisions, opinions, and beliefs. Numerous experiments demonstrate the strict linkage between the capacity to promptly react to facial expressions of others and empathy. For example, Dimberg and Thunberg found that participants with high empathy scores responded more rapidly and with larger zygomatic muscle activity to happy faces compared to angry ones.[4] The same participants reacted more rapidly and with larger corrugator muscle activity to angry faces than to happy faces. That is, people mirror the facial expressions that they observe: they smile when seeing grins and scowl when seeing frowns. Moreover, they reported feeling the emotions linked to those specific facial expressions: happiness and anger. On the other hand, the participants who scored low on empathy values did not react to either happy or angry faces with facial muscle activity and reported no emotional response or feelings. These authors suggested that rapid and unconscious facial mimicry may be an important mechanism for emotional and empathic contagion.

The *same face–same emotion* mechanism is an extremely adaptive phenomenon. It regulates dyadic relations and favors the formation of strong, enduring social bonds, which in turn enhance reproductive success.[5]

On this point, Minagawa-Kawai and coworkers discovered that human mothers mimicked the smiles of their own infants more promptly than they did the smiles of unfamiliar infants.[6] The authors found that the promptness of response in mother-infant pairs had a neurobiological correspondence. The faster response was associated with an increased activation in the regions around the orbitofrontal cortex in mothers who were viewing their own infant's smile than in those viewing an unfamiliar infant's smile. In these mothers, specific neuronal regions involved in positive emotional regulation were activated by viewing both familiar and unfamiliar infants, but the magnitude of activation was greater when affective attachment was involved.

Considering the importance that facial mimicry might play in regulating social interactions, it was proposed that this phenomenon was more widespread than previously thought and not confined to humans. In nonhuman primates, this phenomenon was investigated for the first time in the orang-utan, *Pongo pygmaeus*.[7] In this study, orang-utans viewed a playful facial expression (play face) made by a playmate and then produced a congruent expression within one second. Such responses appear to be homologous with that found in *Homo sapiens*. Recently, Mancini, Ferrari and Palagi found this response in a monkey species, the gelada (*Theropithecus gelada*).[8] The presence of homologous facial mimicry in humans, apes, and monkeys shows that this response has deep evolutionary roots.

Geladas in particular are a good model species for testing hypotheses on mimicry and emotional contagion because they show high levels of social affiliation, spend much time grooming, and frequently embrace one another.[9] They also engage in high levels of social play even as adults and frequently use playful facial displays to fine-tune their playful interactions.[10] The typical facial expression accompanying play is the so-called "play face" (PF), which is performed keeping the mouth opened with only the lower teeth exposed. The "full play face" (FPF) is a more intense variant in which the lower and upper teeth and gums are exposed while the lips are kept actively retracted.[11] Gelada facial mimicry is extremely accurate, and the motor resonance is precise. As in a mirror, animals are able to finely discriminate and exactly reproduce the two variants: play face in response to play face (PF/PF) and full play face in response to full play face (FPF/FPF). This shared emotional/sensorimotor representation has an impact in promoting a sense of familiarity between two individuals. It facilitates emotional connection and improves social affiliation.[12] A further important hint highlighting the linkage between mimicry and emotional connection in geladas involves mother-infant interactions. Mother-infant dyads, compared to unrelated pairs, were characterized by higher levels of mimicry and by the fastest responses. Mother-infant mimicry thus differed both quantitatively and qualitatively from the mimicry between unrelated subjects. The fine facial coordination occurring between mothers and their infants has been extensively documented in humans as well.[13] These exchanges of affective matching are crucial for neuropsychological maturation and for the infant attachment to the mother.[14] In nonhuman primates, facial mimicry could reflect one of the core elements of the mother-infant relationships and might represent an important indicator of the quality of the first and most basic bond that individuals—human and primate alike—establish during life.

Another phenomenon that has attracted the attention of psychologists and anthropologists over the last decade is yawn contagion. Well known in humans since the end of 1980s thanks to the pioneering work of Robert Provine, yawn contagion has recently been linked to the empathic skills of the infected subjects. Contagion starts when children develop the ability to properly identify the emotions of others. Importantly, emotional contagion is impaired in subjects who suffer from empathy disorders, such as autism, even though recent studies suggest that the lack of yawn contagion in autistic subjects could be due to attention biases more than actual impairment of the empathic sphere. Moreover, psychological studies have clearly demonstrated that yawn response susceptibility strongly correlates with self-reported scores of empathy (based on self-face recognition and faux-pas theory of mind tasks). Different neuroimaging and EEG studies converge in supporting the empathic basis of yawn contagion, which involves part of the brain areas involved in empathy processing. Norscia and Palagi found in humans that the rate of contagion was greatest in response to kin, then friends, then acquaintances, and lastly strangers, just as it is for measures of empathy. Related individuals showed the highest level of contagion, in terms of frequency of yawn responses. Strangers and acquaintances showed longer delays in the yawn response (latency) compared to friends and kin. This outcome suggests that yawn neuronal activation magnitude in contagion differs as a function of subject familiarity, according to the empathic gradient.[15] Thanks to a mixed model analysis, the authors found that yawn contagion was driven by inter-individual emotional closeness and not by other variables such as gender and nationality. Belonging to the different genders or different nationalities is not important, but it is the strength of our bonding and the synchronization of our affective state that really matters.

The empathic nature of yawn contagion was found not only in humans but also in other animals. Apparently, yawn contagion is a good candidate for deep exploration through a cross-species approach, insofar as it is a building block of empathy. A recent experimental study demonstrated that although chimpanzees paid more attention to videos of unfamiliar subjects yawning, they yawned more when viewing videos of familiar individuals yawning. This result suggests an ingroup-versus-outgroup bias in contagion.[16] By collecting data on a group of semi-free-ranging bonobos (*Pan paniscus*), Demuru and Palagi demonstrated that in this species yawn contagion followed the same empathic gradient found in humans.[17]

Contagion was higher in kin and individuals sharing a good relationship, measured via affinitive contacts, than in subjects sharing weak bonds. Empathy thus plays a role in the modulation of contagion phenomenon in the great apes, not just in humans.

Monkeys are also infected by yawns. Again, geladas have given us a good opportunity to explore the role of face-to-face emotional communication in nonhuman animals. Palagi and colleagues found that geladas preferentially responded to yawn stimulus from subjects with whom they exchanged high levels of grooming.[18] This relation persisted after controlling for the effect of spatial association and led the authors to hypothesize that emotional proximity rather than spatial proximity best predicts yawn contagion. The power of mimicry as social glue became even clearer when Paukner and colleagues demonstrated that being imitated increases the propensity to engage in social affiliation with the imitator.[19] In an elegant experiment, the researchers put some capuchin monkeys in front of two human experimenters. The first experimenter (imitator) replicated the exact gestures done by the monkey, and the other experimenter performed some actions that differed slightly. The reaction of the monkeys was quite clear: they spent more time in proximity to—and exchanged a higher number of tokens with—the better imitator than with the poorer imitator. The experiment underlines the importance of body-to-body communication (e.g., mimicry and contagion) in shaping emotional and social connection between subjects, even across species.

Data supporting the hypothesis of the empathic nature of yawn contagion come also from our "best friend," the dog. Romero and colleagues found that dogs yawned more frequently after a familiar human (the owner) yawned than an unfamiliar person.[20] The susceptibility of dogs strongly correlates with the emotional proximity between the trigger and the responder. To exclude that the yawn response could result from the anxiety experienced by dogs during the trials, Romero and colleagues measured each subject's heart rate both during yawning and in controls. The heart rate did not differ, suggesting that yawn contagion in dogs is not linked to the potential stress caused by the experimental condition. Dogs and humans share a long common history, and the process of domestication has selected a set of social-cognitive abilities that enable dogs to emotionally communicate with humans in unique ways.[21] Interspecific contagion shown by domesticated dogs is modulated by affective components of the behavior and may indicate that rudimentary forms of empathy are present *in* this species and perhaps even *from* this nonhuman species.[22]

In human children, emotional expression and anger are important predictors of empathy and, in turn, empathy strongly predicts prosocial behaviors.[23] A further hint supporting the possible link between yawn contagion and empathy comes from numerous studies. Both naturalistic and experimental approaches have correlated yawn contagion with prosocial behaviors. Prosocial behaviors are hypothesized to be tied to empathy, consolation, and targeted helping.[24] Consolation may be dependent on emotional contagion. The perception of another's distress leads to a matching state in the observer, followed by sympathetic concern. The observers then perform prosocial acts toward the other. This is how consolation is born.

FROM EMOTIONAL CONTAGION TO SYMPATHETIC CONCERN: WHEN ANIMALS ACT AS MORAL AGENTS

Empathy is a multilayered phenomenon whose building blocks represent a preexisting framework for nesting more complex emotional and cognitive processes.[25] From this perspective, cross-species research gives us the possibility to explore empathy capacities as a bottom-up emotional and developmental process of the brain.[26] New strategies are needed to resolve the degree to which empathy is fundamentally an affective-emotional or cognitive process of the brain and, if so, how empathy connects to a variety of higher complex cognitive capacities. Some driving questions include how and when an animal transposes an emotional response to the emotions of others into an act that can help others, and in what ways the ontogenetic trajectories and life experiences are important to acquire social competence and, ultimately, act prosocially toward others.

One of the most elucidating examples of prosocial behavior comes from the rat, a highly playful and cognitive species, which has provided much information about the basal building blocks of even the most complex forms of empathy.[27] Play behavior in rats has great importance in the maturation of the medial prefrontal cortex (mPFC). This brain area receives input from all other cortical regions and functions to plan and direct motor, cognitive, affective, and social behavior across time.[28] Panksepp and Panksepp highlighted the importance of social interaction such as rough-and-tumble play in "*providing fundamental learning experience for higher forms of empathy.*"[29] They indicated that mPCF is one of the most important "empathic" parts of the brain, which is also sensitive to social play during ontogeny. The empathic side of rats has been recently explored and tested in an experiment carried out by Ben-Ami Bartal and colleagues.[30] A rat was placed in an arena with a cage-mate trapped in a transparent tube. The free rat quickly learned to open the tube and set the cage-mate free. The rat continued to open the tube containing the trapped companion even when another tube containing chocolate was available in the cage. In this case, the free rat opened both tubes and shared the chocolate. Obviously, it is possible that the responses of the free rat may have been caused in part by its own high stress at hearing cage-mate alarm calls. However, given neurological evidence that witnessing distress in others activates many of the same brain areas as experiencing distress oneself, this distinction becomes difficult to disambiguate. This experiment suggests that reflexive empathy and imitation in both humans and other animals have evolved because they promote affiliation and social bonding.[31]

The human act of providing comfort to a distressed subject is widely accepted as a crucial behavior revealing the empathic potential of individuals.[32] In nonhuman primates, consolation has been behaviorally described as the first affinitive contact occurring between the victim of an aggression and a bystander not involved in the aggression.[33] The comforting gesture generally leads to an improvement of the psychological and affective state of the victims by reducing their anxiety.[34] In order to provide comfort, as a first step, the potential consoler has to perceive the emotional state of the victim (emotional contagion). As a second step, he/she has to spontaneously react in an appropriate way by making a friendly gesture toward the victim and alleviating the victim's distress. The victim may also ask for a friendly contact, but in this case, the affiliative contact provided by the bystander cannot be defined as consolation. Why? What is the difference in the two types of affiliation and how are the two kinds of affiliation perceived by the victim?

Palagi and Norscia tried to answer these questions by studying the consolation mechanism in bonobos, since bonobos frequently engage in reciprocal helping and cooperation, show high levels of tolerance with both in-group and out-group members, and are characterized by a hierarchy that is not tightly structured.[35] The egalitarianism of the bonobo society is probably *a* reason if not *the* reason why consolation is widespread in this species. In bonobos, both spontaneous and requested affiliation protects victims against further attack. Probably the mere proximity of other group members is sufficient to deter the recruitment of the aggressive contact. Yet Palagi and Norscia found that only spontaneous affiliation, and not the gestures coming from a direct request, improved the emotional state of a victim by reducing its anxiety, measured as self-scratching, a valid behavioral indicator of anxiety in both human and nonhuman primates.[36] This result indicates that the improvement of the emotional state of the victim depends not on the gesture itself but on its spontaneity. Hence, what makes the difference is the victim's perception of the motivational autonomy of the consoler, who does not require any kind of invitation to provide comfort: *You care about me; this is helpful to me.* Sambo and colleagues found that distressed patients scored lower on pain ratings when they were observed by high-empathic bystanders compared to low-empathic bystanders.[37] Hence, perceived spontaneous empathy makes a difference in humans as well, not just in other primates.

Bonobos preferentially directed the spontaneous comforting gestures toward kin, then to "friends" (individuals most frequently engaging in affinitive interactions with the consoler), and finally to "acquaintances" (individuals weakly bonded to the consoler). As with yawn contagion, bonobo consolation follows an empathic gradient similar to that operating among humans.[38] The indirect linkage between consolation and yawn contagion found in the bonobo could be ascertained by experimental and naturalistic studies directly correlating consolation with phenomena of empathic sensorimotor resonance, not only in apes but also in other primate and nonprimate species.

Empathic and prosocial behaviors have foundations not only at neurological levels (e.g., mirror neurons), but also at endocrinological levels. To illustrate, interesting data are emerging from studies on the oxytocinergic system. In humans and other social mammals, oxytocin facilitates attachment between mother and offspring and potentiates bonding between mating partners. Moreover, it was shown in humans that empathy raises oxytocin levels and affects subsequent generosity toward strangers. In chimpanzees (*Pan troglodytes*), Wittig and colleagues found that food sharing, a cooperative and prosocial event, may play a key role in social bonding under the influence of oxytocin. Oxytocin levels were higher after food sharing than after grooming and other forms of social feeding. Wittig et al. concluded that via the oxytocinergic system, food sharing can co-opt neurobiological mechanisms evolved to support mother-infant bonding during lactation sessions and may act as a facilitator of bonding and cooperation between unrelated subjects. This finding is consistent with data coming from humans. As in chimpanzees, oxytocin levels in humans rise after episodes of empathy and affect subsequent generosity toward strangers.[39]

Similarly intriguing results are accumulating from naturalistic (non-invasive and non-manufactured) observations on monkeys, which represent a new challenge in the studies of animal morality insofar as they are finding evidence of morality's building blocks in species beyond the great apes. Geladas, for example, tend to provide support more to victims of aggression than to aggressors, even though aggressors often have high-ranking status (e.g., the alpha male). The support offered during the aggressive interactions is generally exchanged with long grooming sessions that the victim directs toward the supporter (Palagi, personal observations). Would it be too much to say that such behaviors bespeak what we often mean by "gratitude"?

There are also observations providing evidence of consolation in monkeys. In geladas, bystanders affiliate with victims of aggression, especially after attacks of high intensity (Palagi et al., unpublished data). Moreover, as it occurs for consolation in human and nonhuman apes, "monkey consolation" actually provides comfort to the victim and is positively affected by the quality of the relationship and familiarity between subjects.[40] In *Macaca tonkeana*, consolation reduced anxiety in victims especially when reconciliation did not occur and protected them against renewed attacks by the former aggressor. On the whole, our results support the view that a combination of emotional contagion and sympathetic concern (so far described for humans and apes only) is at work also in monkeys, thus opening new scenarios on the evolutionary pathways of animal empathy.[41]

IN CONCLUSION, WE humans, much as many other social animals, live completely nestled in an emotional network that makes us socially interdependent beings. The use that humans and other social animals make of the emotions triggered by the perception of others' pain, happiness, sadness, and joy clearly depends on a huge array of factors, both internal and external, that can either inhibit or facilitate the empathic response. That said, such shared mechanisms cannot be easily dismissed.

Indeed, our brains have a long evolutionary history, one shared with that of other mammal species, especially apes and monkeys. Our most sophisticated emotional and cognitive capacities are sustained by brain structures that anatomically integrate preexisting ones. This evolutionary continuity with other animals explains why we cannot understand the origins of our own moral potential without keeping in mind that we are, in fact, at base and at most, animals.

NOTES

1. N. Duxbury, "Golden Rule Reasoning, Moral Judgment, and Law," *Notre Dame Law Review* 84, no. 4 (2009): 1529–606. I am grateful to Jonathan K. Crane for his kind invitation to contribute to this book. I wish to thank Marc Bekoff, Gordon Burghardt, Matthew Campbell, Giada Cordoni, Elisa Demuru, Frans de Waal, Pier Francesco Ferrari, Stefano Parmigiani, Sergio Pellis, Barbara Smuts, Marek Špinka, Roscoe Stanyon, and Peter Verbeek for sharing with me some basic ideas on the concepts of cooperation, fairness, empathy, and morality in animals. I thank Ivan Norscia and Roscoe Stanyon for the accurate revision of the manuscript and for support and encouragement they regularly give me. Finally, I am grateful to all the colleagues of the NIMBioS Working Group (http://www.nimbios.org/workinggroups/WG_play) for the stimulating input on one of the most controversial behaviors an ethologist can come across.

2. F. B. M. de Waal, *The Bonobo and the Atheist: In Search of Humanism among the Primates* (New York: Norton, 2013).

3. J. H. Pfeifer, M. Iacoboni, J. C. Mazziotta, and M. Dapretto, "Mirroring Others' Emotions Relates to Empathy and Interpersonal Competence in Children," *Neuro-Image* 39 (2008): 2076–85; R. van Baaren, L. Janssen, T. L. Chartrand, and A. Dijksterhuis, "Where Is the Love? The Social Aspects of Mimicry," *Philosophical Transactions of the Royal Society B: Biological Sciences* 364 (2009): 2381–89; S. D. Preston, and F. B. M. de Waal, "Empathy: Its Ultimate and Proximate Bases," *Behavioral and Brain Sciences* 25, no. 1 (2002): 1–20; V. Gallese, C. Keysers, and G. Rizzolatti, "A Unifying View of the Basis of Social Cognition," *Trends in Cognitive Sciences* 8 (2004): 396–403; I. Dinstein, C. Thomas, M. Behrmann, and D. J. Heeger, "Mirror up to Nature," *Current Biology* 18, no. 1 (2008): R13–R18; V. Gallese, L. Fadiga, L. Fogassi, and G. Rizzolatti, "Action Recognition in the Premotor Cortex," *Brain* 119 (1996): 593–609; P. F. Ferrari, V. Gallese, G. Rizzolatti, and L. Fogassi, "Mirror Neurons Responding to the Observation of Ingestive and Communicative Mouth Actions in the Monkey Ventral Premotor Cortex," *European Journal of Neuroscience* 17 (2003): 1703–14; G. Rizzolatti and L. Craighero, "The Mirror Neuron System," *Annual Review of Neuroscience* 27 (2004): 169–92; T. Singer, "The Neuronal Basis and Ontogeny of Empathy and Mind Reading: Review of Literature and Implications for Future Research," *Neuroscience Biobehavioral Reviews* 30 (2006): 855–63; F. B. M. de Waal, *Peacemaking among Primates* (Cambridge, MA: Harvard University Press, 1989).

4. U. Dimberg and M. Thunberg, "Empathy, Emotional Contagion, and Rapid Facial Reactions to Angry and Happy Facial Expressions," *Psychology Chinese Journal* 1 (2012): 118–27, doi: 10.1002/pchj.4.

5. J. H. Capella, "The Facial Feedback Hypothesis in Human Interaction: Review and Speculation," *Journal of Language and Social Psychology* 12 (1993): 13–29; R. B. van Baaren, R. W. Holland, K. Kawakami, and A. van Knippenberg, "Mimicry and Prosocial Behavior," *Psychological Science* 15 (2004): 71–74; J. B. Silk, J. C. Beehner, T. J.

Bergman, C. Crockford, A. L. Engh, L. R. Moscovice, R. M. Wittig, R. M. Seyfarth, and D. L. Cheney, "The Benefits of Social Capital: Close Social Bonds among Female Baboons Enhance Offspring Survival," *Proceedings of the Royal Society B: Biological Sciences* 276 (2009): 3099–3104.

6. Y. Minagawa-Kawai, S. I. Matsuoka, N. Dan, and K. Naoi, "Prefrontal Activation Associated with Social Attachment: Facial-Emotion Recognition in Mothers and Infants," *Cerebral Cortex* 19 (2009): 284–92.

7. M. Davila-Ross, S. Menzler, and E. Zimmermann, "Rapid Facial Mimicry in Orangutan Play," *Biology Letters* 4 (2008): 27–30.

8. G. Mancini, P. F. Ferrari, and E. Palagi, "Rapid Facial Mimicry in Geladas," *Scientific Reports* 3 (2013): 1527, doi:10.1038/srep01527.

9. V. Pallante, P. F. Ferrari, and E. Palagi, "Not Only a Human Affair: Embracing Behaviour in *Theropithecus gelada*," *Folia Primatol* 84 (2013): 309.

10. E. Palagi and G. Mancini, "Playing with the Face: Playful Facial 'Chattering' and Signal Modulation in a Monkey Species (*Theropithecus gelada*)," *Journal of Comparative Psychology* 125 (2011): 11–21.

11. Ibid.

12. G. Mancini, P. F. Ferrari, and E. Palagi, "In Play We Trust: Rapid Facial Mimicry Predicts the Duration of Playful Interactions in Geladas," *PLoS ONE* 8, no. 6 (2013): e66481, doi:10.1371/journal.pone.0066481.

13. R. Feldman, "Parent-Infant Synchrony and the Construction of Shared Timing; Physiological Precursors, Developmental Outcomes, and Risk Conditions," *Journal of Child Psychology and Psychiatry* 49 (2007): 329–54.

14. R. Feldman, "The Relational Basis of Adolescent Adjustment: Trajectories of Mother-Child Interactive Behaviors from Infancy to Adolescence Shape Adolescents' Adaptation," *Attachment and Human Development* 12 (2010): 173–92.

15. R. R. Provine, "Faces as Releasers of Contagious Yawning: An Approach to Face Perception Using Normal Human Subjects," *Bulletin of the Psychonomic Society* 27 (1989): 211–14; Singer, "The Neuronal Basis and Ontogeny of Empathy and Mind Reading"; A. Millen and J. R. Anderson, "Neither Infants nor Toddlers Catch Yawns from Their Mothers," *Biology Letters* 7 (2011): 440–42; M. S. Helt, I. M. Eigsti, P. J. Snyder, and D. A. Fein, "Contagious Yawning in Autistic and Typical Development," *Child Development* 81 (2010): 1620–31; S. A. Usui, A. Senju, Y. Kikuchi, et al., "Presence of Contagious Yawning in Children with Autism Spectrum Disorder," *Autism Research and Treatment*, Article ID 971686 (2013), doi:10.1155/2013/971686; S. M. Platek, S. R. Critton, T. E. Myers, and G. G. Gallup, Jr., "Contagious Yawning: The Role of Self-Awareness and Mental State Attribution," *Cognitive Brain Research* 17 (2003): 223–27; N. R. Cooper, I. Puzzo, A. D. Pawley, R. A. Bowes-Mulligan, E. V. Kirkpatrick, P. A. Antoniou, and S. Kennett, "Bridging a Yawning Chasm: EEG Investigations into the Debate concerning the Role of the Human Mirror Neuron System in Contagious Yawning," *Cognitive, Affective, and Behavioral Neuroscience* 12 (2012): 393–405; H. Haker, W. Kawohl, U. Herwig, and W. Rössler, "Mirror Neuron Activity during Contagious Yawning—An fMRI Study," *Brain Imaging and Behavior* 7, no. 1 (2013): 28–34; I. Norscia and E. Palagi, "Yawn Contagion and Empathy in *Homo sapiens*," *PLoS ONE* 6 (2011): e28472, doi:10.1371/journal.pone.0028472; Preston and de Waal, "Empathy," 1–20.

16. M. W. Campbell, and F. B. M. de Waal, "Ingroup-Outgroup Bias in Contagious Yawning by Chimpanzees Supports Link to Empathy," *PLoS ONE* 6, no. 4 (2011): e18283, doi:10.1371/journal.pone.0018283.

17. E. Demuru and E. Palagi, "In Bonobos Yawn Contagion Is Higher among Kin and Friends," *PLoS ONE* 7, no. 11 (2012): e49613, doi:10.1371/journal.pone.0049613.

18. E. Palagi, A. Leon, G. Mancini, and P. F. Ferrari, "Contagious Yawning in Gelada Baboons as a Possible Expression of Empathy," *Proceedings of the National Academy of Sciences, USA* 106 (2009): 19262–67.

19. A. Paukner, S. J. Suomi, E. Visalberghi, and P. F. Ferrari, "Capuchin Monkeys Display Affiliation toward Humans Who Imitate Them," *Science* 325 (2009): 880–83.

20. T. Romero, A. Konno, and T. Hasegawa, "Familiarity Bias and Physiological Responses in Contagious Yawning by Dogs Support Link to Empathy," *PLoS ONE* 8, no. 8 (2013): e71365, doi:10.1371/journal.pone.0071365.

21. B. Hare, M. Brown, C. Williamson, and M. Tomasello, "The Domestication of Social Cognition in Dogs," *Science* 298 (2002): 1634–36.

22. M. Bekoff and J. Pierce, *Wild Justice: The Moral Lives of Animals* (Chicago: University of Chicago Press, 2009). Also see Bekoff, chapter 7 in this volume.

23. J. Strayer and W. Roberts, "Empathy and Observed Anger and Aggression in Five-Year-Olds," *Social Development* 13 (2004): 1–13.

24. E. Palagi, T. Paoli, and S. Borgognini, "Reconciliation and Consolation in Captive Bonobos (*Pan paniscus*)," *American Journal of Primatology* 62 (2004): 15–30; O. N. Fraser, D. Stahl, and F. Aureli, "Stress Reduction through Consolation in Chimpanzees," *Proceedings of the National Academy of Sciences of the United States of America* 105 (2008): 8557–62; T. Romero, M. A. Castellanos, and F. B. M. de Waal, "Consolation as Possible Expression of Sympathetic Concern among Chimpanzees," *Proceedings of the National Academy of Sciences of the United States of America* 107 (2010): 12110–15; B. Hare and J. Tan, "How Much of Our Cooperative Behavior Is Human?," in *The Primate Mind: Built to Connect with Other Minds,* ed. F. B. M. de Waal and P. F. Ferrari (Cambridge, MA: Harvard University Press, 2012), 175–93; F. B. M. de Waal, "Putting the Altruism Back into Altruism: The Evolution of Empathy," *Annual Review of Psychology* 59 (2008): 279–300.

25. E. E. Hecht, D. A. Gutman, T. M. Preuss, M. M. Sanchez, L. A. Parr, et al., "Process versus Product in Social Learning: Comparative Diffusion Tensor Imaging of Neural Systems for Action Execution-Observation Matching in Macaques, Chimpanzees, and Humans," *Cerebral Cortex* 23, no. 5 (2012): 1014–24; J. Panksepp and J. B. Panksepp, "Toward a Cross-Species Understanding of Empathy," *Trends in Neurosciences* 36, no. 8 (2013): 489–96.

26. F. B. M. de Waal, "A Bottom-Up View of Empathy," in *The Primate Mind,* ed. F. B. M. de Waal and P. F. Ferrari (Cambridge, MA: Harvard University Press, 2012), 121–38.

27. Panksepp and Panksepp, "Toward a Cross-Species Understanding of Empathy."

28. H. C. Bell, S. M. Pellis, and B. Kolb, "Juvenile Play Experience and the Development of the Orbitofrontal and Medial Prefrontal Cortices," *Behavioural Brain Research* 207 (2010): 7–13.

29. Panksepp and Panksepp, "Toward a Cross-Species Understanding of Empathy," 492.

30. Ben-Ami Bartal, J. Decety, and P. Mason, "Empathy and Prosocial Behavior in Rats," *Science* 334 (2011): 1427–30.

31. R. M. Seyfarth and D. L. Cheney, "Affiliation, Empathy, and the Origins of Theory of Mind," *Proceedings of the National Academy of Sciences of the United States of America* 110 (2013): 10349–56.

32. K. K. Fujisawa, N. Kutsukake, and T. Hasegawa, "Peacemaking and Consolation in Japanese Preschoolers Witnessing Peer Aggression," *Journal of Comparative Psychology* 120 (2006): 48–57; N. Eisenberg, *The Caring Child* (Cambridge, MA: Harvard University Press, 1992).

33. F. B. M. de Waal and A. van Roosmalen, "Reconciliation and Consolation among Chimpanzees," *Behavioral Ecology Sociobiology* 5 (1979): 55–66.

34. Fraser, Stahl, and Aureli, "Stress Reduction through Consolation in Chimpanzees"; Romero, Castellanos, and de Waal, "Consolation as Possible Expression of Sympathetic Concern among Chimpanzees," 12110–15.

35. E. Palagi and I. Norscia, "Bonobos Protect and Console Friends and Kin," *PLoS ONE* 8, no. 11 (2013): e79290, doi:10.1371/journal.pone.0079290; T. Paoli and E. Palagi, "What Does Agonistic Dominance Imply in Bonobos?," in *Bonobos: Behaviour, Ecology, and Conservation*, ed. T. Furuichi and J. Thompson (New York: Springer-Verlag, 2008), 35–54; Hare and Tan, "How Much of Our Cooperative Behavior Is Human?"

36. Palagi and Norscia, "Bonobos Protect and Console Friends and Kin."

37. C. F. Sambo, M. Howard, M. Kopelman, S. Williams, and A. Fotopoulou, "Knowing You Care: Effects of Perceived Empathy and Attachment Style on Pain Perception," *PAIN* 151 (2010): 687–93.

38. Preston and de Waal, "Empathy."

39. T. R. Insel, "The Challenge of Translation in Social Neuroscience: A Review of Oxytocin, Vasopressin, and Affiliative Behavior," *Neuron* 25 (2010): 768–79; M. C. Soares, R. Bshary, L. Fusani, W. Goymann, M. Hau, K. Hirschenhauser, and R. F. Oliveira, "Hormonal Mechanisms of Cooperative Behavior," *Philosophical Transactions of the Royal Society B: Biological Sciences* 365 (2010): 2737–50; J. A. Barraza and P. J. Zak, "Empathy toward Strangers Triggers Oxytocin Release and Subsequent Generosity," *Annals of the New York Academy of Sciences* 1167 (2009): 182–89; R. M. Wittig, C. Crockford, T. Deschner, K. E. Langergraber, T. E. Ziegler, and K. Zuberbühler, "Food Sharing Is Linked to Urinary Oxytocin Levels and Bonding in Related and Unrelated Wild Chimpanzees," *Proceedings of the Royal Society B: Biological Sciences* 281, no. 20133096 (2014).

40. E. Palagi, S. Dall'Olio, E. Demuru, and R. Stanyon, "Exploring the Evolutionary Foundations of Empathy: Consolation in Monkeys," *Evolution and Human Behavior* (in press) (2014), http://dx.doi.org/10.1016/j.evolhumbehav.2014.04.002.

41. Preston and de Waal, "Empathy: Its Ultimate and Proximate Bases," 1–20; Palagi, Dall'Olio, Demuru, and Stanyon, "Exploring the Evolutionary Foundations of Empathy: Consolation in Monkeys."

Seven Moral Mutts

SOCIAL PLAY, FAIRNESS, AND WILD JUSTICE

Marc Bekoff

DOMESTICATED DOGS ARE FASCINATING MAMMALS.[1] We created them in our own image, often favoring traits that compromise their health and longevity, and they also vary greatly in size, shape, mass, color, coat, personality, and behavior. And because they are easy to observe and to identify reliably in various environments, dogs are wonderful candidates for the study of a wide variety of behaviors, including social play.[2] Not only have we learned much about the nitty-gritty details of what dogs do when they play (for example, how they ask another dog to play, how they announce their intentions, how cheaters are treated, and how they apologize and forgive transgressions against the rules of fair play), but we have also generated some theories about the evolution of social behavior and moral sentiments—wild justice. Moreover, fair play is tightly linked to the evolution of social tolerance, social reciprocity, individual fitness, and peaceful relationships among group-living animals. That is, kernels of what we humans know as and call morality are evident in canine play. For this reason, this essay assumes we will never learn about animal morality if we close the door on the possibility that it even exists.

The popular literature abounds with books about dogs, and myths prevail that are based on casual observations here and there rather than on detailed, systematic studies. Because of our close relationship with dogs, there is a tendency to embellish them, especially in popular literature, but there really is no need to do so. We do not have to exaggerate their cognitive, emotional, and moral capacities to make them more interesting or alluring.[3] Nor do we have to study dogs only to learn more about how they compare to other animals, such as nonhuman primates. In fact, because the wide diversity of extant dogs shares a common heritage, they lend themselves nicely to studies in which they are compared to wild relatives such as wolves and coyotes. To be sure, dogs, like other animals, do what they need to do to be dogs and should not be pushed aside as not worth studying because they are "mere artifacts."[4] We need to represent dogs as who they are and not as who or what we want them to be. If we pay careful attention to available data, we see that they have evolved highly developed cognitive and emotional skills. The study of dogs at play is as good a place as any to start to see who they really are.

WHY STUDY PLAY?

Early in my career I was told (especially by fieldworkers) that it was a waste of time to study dogs and play behavior. Some people told me that "real ethologists" do not study dogs because they are artifacts—merely "creations of man"—and we cannot really learn much about the behavior of wild animals by studying them. In the 1970s, those who studied dogs were mostly veterinarians and people interested in practical applications of behavioral data. Concerning play, some people thought of it as a wastebasket into which behavior patterns that were difficult to understand should be tossed, and some people thought that understanding play was not important for researchers interested in behavioral development. Others, however—among them my Ph.D. mentor, Michael W. Fox—realized that play was essential to normal social, cognitive, and physical development and that people just had not taken the time to study it in detail.[5] One reason it has been so difficult to study play is that it is a hodgepodge or kaleidoscope of many different activities from various social contexts, and it takes a lot of time to learn about the details of this fascinating behavior. It can take hours and hours to conduct frame-by-frame analyses of as few as ten minutes of playtime captured on video, but that kind of analysis is essential to gaining an understanding of this behavioral phenotype.

In order to generate interest in detailed comparative systematic studies of play, I organized a symposium that centered on this fascinating behavior.[6] I also began detailed studies, which have now lasted more than four decades, focusing on what animals do when they play. I developed a lengthy ethogram (a list of the actions the animals perform in a variety of contexts; and data were collected that had no obvious connection to the then scanty extant theory).[7] However, over time, the zeitgeist changed and some of the data found homes as new hypotheses and theories materialized. The study of dogs at play came to involve interdisciplinary collaboration, with non-invasive research that can readily be conducted in dog parks and in various non-captive settings. Such study generates results that can enrich the lives of individuals and provides information that can be used to more fully understand and integrate dogs and other canids into society.[8]

The payoff from studying play has been significant. I am thrilled that I and others did not give in to the skepticism, because now it is clear that detailed studies of play can inform the development of "big theories" concerning the evolution of social behavior, fairness, cooperation, cognitive and moral capacities, and moral behavior, including the question of whether animals have a "theory of mind." Analyses of play can also provide insights into individual survival and reproductive fitness, and build a bridge between ontogenetic and phylogenetic inquiries.[9] There is honor in playing and play-fighting fairly (see chapter 8 in this volume).

One example of how studies of play can have far-reaching applications is the fact that play is a voluntary and cooperative behavior and is linked to the development of social skills and animals coming to know "right" from "wrong"—the development of fairness and moral sentiments, including social justice.[10] To illustrate, dogs and other animals choose when to play and when not to play, and in most instances they can quit whenever they choose to do so. However, when dogs and other animals play with one another they learn, for example, how hard they can bite or slam into their partner without the other animal terminating the encounter as if they are asking, "Wasn't this supposed to be play?" or running away. Later I will write about what we have learned about coyotes who do not play fair and how they are shunned by group members because of it. To be clear, this essay is not meant to be a review of the field, but it does show that detailed observations of social play—a behavior previously tossed aside because it was considered a waste of time to study—can inform the development of "big theories" in a number of different areas, including and perhaps especially that of animal morality.

There are no substitutes for careful observation and description; this stage of study is critical for the generation of experiments, models, and theory. In my studies I take a strongly evolutionary and ecological approach, using Niko Tinbergen's integrative ideas about the questions with which ethological studies should be concerned: namely, evolution, adaptation, causation, and ontogeny (development and the emergence of individual differences).[11] Gordon Burghardt later suggested adding "subjective experience" to Tinbergen's scheme.[12]

So, concerning play, we can ask: Why did play evolve? How does it promote survival value and reproductive fitness and allow individuals to come to terms with social situation in which they find themselves? What causes play? How does play develop? What is the experience of animals in play—the emotional side of play? Over time, studies of play have become much more detailed and theoretically driven.[13]

WHAT IS THIS ACTIVITY CALLED PLAY?

What is play? The deceptively simple question has troubled researchers for many years. A well-received definition of social play that I developed with John Byers is "social play is an activity directed toward another individual in which actions from other contexts are used in modified forms and in altered sequences."[14] Our definition centers on what animals do when they play, or the structure of play, rather than on possible functions of play. Nonetheless, the definition is not without problems, for it would seem to apply, for example, to stereotypical behaviors such as the repetitive pacing or excessive self-grooming sometimes evinced by caged animals. It is difficult to see how to state a non-arbitrary restriction on the range of behaviors that may constitute play. Gordon Burghardt's characterization of play as having five criteria attempts to do this. He notes: "Playful activities can be characterized as being (1) incompletely functional in the context expressed; (2) voluntary, pleasurable, or self-rewarding; (3) different structurally or temporally from related serious behavior systems; (4) expressed repeatedly during at least some part of an animal's life span; and (5) initiated in benign situations."[15]

Our definition also highlights the fact that when animals play they use actions that are also used in activities such as predation (hunting), reproduction (mating), and aggression. Full-blown threatening and submitting only rarely, if ever, occur during play. Behavior patterns that are used in anti-predatory behavior also are observed in play. This is especially so in prey animals such as ungulates (deer, elk, moose, gazelles), who run about in unpredictable zigzag patterns during play. During play, actions may be changed in their form and intensity and combined in a wide variety of unpredictable sequences. In juvenile chimpanzees the unpredictability of play increases compared to the same activity among infants;

indeed, the play sessions are more complex and variable in pattern use.[16] In polecats, coyotes, and American black bears, biting in play-fighting is inhibited when compared to biting in real fighting.[17] Clawing in bears is also inhibited and less intense, an example of self-handicapping that is observed in many diverse species.[18] Play in bears also is non-vocal, and biting and clawing are directed to more parts of the body of another individual during play than during aggression.

Play sequences may also be more variable and less predictable than those performed in "true" predation or aggression because individuals are, in part, mixing actions from a number of different contexts. As there are more actions for individuals to choose from, it is not surprising that play sequences are significantly more variable than agonistic sequences of behavior.[19] "Significantly more variable" simply means that it is more difficult to predict which actions will follow one another during play than, say, during real predation or aggression, when sequences of motor patterns are more highly structured. During play among dogs, coyotes, or wolves one might see the following sequence: biting, chasing, wrestling, body slamming, wrestling, mouthing, chasing, lunging, biting, and wrestling, whereas during aggression the sequence would more likely be threatening, chasing, lunging, attacking, biting, wrestling, and then one individual submitting to the other. Curiously, young canids do not show gender differences in play.[20]

In the wild, animals do not spend a lot of time engaging in social play, but this does not mean that play is unimportant. Much wild animal play is spontaneous; it is common to see two animals sniffing the ground or walking about and then beginning to play when they cross each other's path or bump into each other. The amount of time and energy that young mammals devote to various types of play is usually less than 10 percent of the total time and energy they devote to various activities other than rest or sleep.[21] This holds true for captive animals as well. Captive adult wolves typically play about 9 percent of the total time they are active.[22] Whether in the wild or in captivity, play in most species occurs mainly during infant and juvenile life. Adults do engage in social play, but usually less often than the young of their species.[23]

THE FAIR WAY TO PLAY

Although play is fun, it is also serious business. When animals play, they are constantly working to understand and follow the rules and to communicate their intentions to play fairly. They fine-tune their behavior on the run, carefully monitoring the behavior of their play partners and paying close attention to infractions of the agreed-upon rules. Fair play in animals involves four basic components: ask first, be honest, follow the rules, and admit when you're wrong. When the rules of play are violated and when fairness breaks down, so does play.[24]

To learn about the dynamics of play it is essential to pay attention to subtle details that are lost in superficial analyses. Dogs and other animals keep track of what is happening when they play, so we need to do this also. My studies of play are based on careful observation and analyses of videotape. I watch tapes of play one frame at a time to see what the animals are doing and how they exchange information about their motivations, intentions, and desires to play. This is tedious work, and some of my students who were excited about studying dog play had second thoughts after watching the same video frames over and over again. But when they then were able to go out and watch dogs play and understand what was happening, they came to appreciate that while studying play can be hard work it is well worth the effort.

By studying play we may be able to learn about what may be going on in individuals' minds, what they feel, what they are thinking about, what they want, and what they are likely to do during a social encounter. Because of the intermingling of actions from different contexts, it is important to ask several questions: "What are animals feeling when they play?" "How do animals know that they are playing?" How do they communicate their desires or intentions to play or to continue to play?" and "How is the play mood maintained?"

Because there is a chance that various behavior patterns that are performed during ongoing social play can be misinterpreted, individuals need to tell others "I want to play with you," "This is still play no matter what I am going to do to you," or "This is still play regardless of what I just did to you." An agreement to play rather than to fight, mate, or engage in predatory activities can be negotiated in various ways. Individuals may use behavior patterns called "play signals" or "play markers" to initiate play or to maintain and prevent termination of a play mood by "punctuating" play sequences with these actions when it is likely that a particular behavior may have been, or may be, misinterpreted. There are also auditory (play sounds such as play panting), olfactory (play odors), and tactile signals.

To illustrate how animals communicate their intentions and desires to play, let's consider domesticated dogs and their wild relatives. One action that is very common in play among canids is the "bow." A dog asks another to play by bowing: crouching on her forelimbs, raising her hind end in the air, and often barking and wagging her tail as she bows. Bows occur almost exclusively in the context of social play. The bow is a highly ritualized and stereotyped movement. Bows are modal action patterns (MAPs) in that they are strongly stereotyped and distinctive and recognizable, but they are not always performed precisely the same as fixed action patterns.[25] Bows stimulate recipients to engage or to continue to engage in social play. Evolutionarily speaking, when cashed out as "intentional icons," players (senders and receivers of bows) can be seen as "cooperating devices," in that the disposition of senders to produce play-soliciting signals and the disposition of receivers of play signals to respond appropriately to play invitations, have evolved together.[26]

Bows occur throughout play sequences, but most commonly are performed at the beginning or toward the middle of playful encounters. And, of course, bows have to be seen by other dogs. In her research on play in dogs, Horowitz discovered that play signals were "sent nearly exclusively to forward-facing conspecifics while attention-getting behaviors were used most often when a playmate was facing away, and before signaling an interest to play."[27]

To solve the problems that might be caused by confusing play with mating or fighting, many different species, including canids, have evolved signals, such as the bow, that function to establish and to maintain a play "mood." My students and I discovered that play signals in infant domestic dogs, wolves, and coyotes were used non-randomly in a bout, especially when biting accompanied by rapid side-to-side shaking of the head, was performed. Youngsters also were using bows with a purpose in mind. Bows are used right at the beginning of play to tell another dog, "I want to play with you," and they're also used right before biting accompanied by rapid side-to-side head shaking, as if to say, "I'm going to bite you hard, but it's still in play," and right after vigorous biting, as if to say, "I'm sorry I just bit you so hard, but it was play." We also learned that play bows performed at the beginning of play sequences are always less variable (that is, more stereotyped or "fixed") than those performed in the middle of play sessions.[28] This difference could reflect the fact that after play has been officially initiated there is less of a need to communicate that it is still play.

Bows essentially serve as punctuation, an exclamation point (!), to call attention to what the dog wants to tell his friend.[29] For example, biting accompanied by rapid side-to-side shaking of the head is performed during serious aggressive and predatory encounters and can easily be misinterpreted if its meaning is not modified by a play signal like the bow. Bows thus reduce the likelihood of aggression and help to establish a "play mood." Just as this is true for domestic dogs, bows also reduce the likelihood of aggression in African wild dogs. Dogs and their wild relatives rapidly learn how to play fairly, and the appropriate response to play bows seems to be innate or learned during the course of only a very few interactions with littermates.

PLAY SIGNALS, HONESTY, AND CHEATING

Play bows are honest signals, signs of trust. There is little evidence that social play is a manipulative activity. Play signals are rarely used to deceive others in canids or other species. My own long-term studies indicate that deceptive signaling is so rare that I cannot recall more than a few occurrences in thousands of play sequences. Cheaters are unlikely to be chosen as play partners because others can simply refuse to play with them. Infant coyotes who mislead others into playing so that they can dominate them have difficulty getting other young coyotes to play with them. Research shows that animals who violate that trust are often ostracized, suggesting that violation of the rules of play is maladaptive and can disrupt the efficient functioning of the group.[30]

My students and I have discovered that among dogs, coyotes, and wolves, individuals who do not play fairly find that their invitations to play are ignored or that they're simply avoided by other group members. My long-term field research on coyotes living in the Grand Teton National Park in Wyoming[31] shows that coyotes who don't play fairly often leave their pack because they don't form strong social bonds. Such loners suffer higher mortality than those who remain with others.

A major message from such research on captive and wild canids is clear: *Don't bow if you don't want to play. Play means play.* Cheating is maladaptive. These field data also show how studies of the development of play in captive animals that are virtually impossible to conduct in the wild can inform what is happening in the wild. (This is not an endorsement of keeping animals in captivity.) The data also strongly suggest that these animals have a "theory of mind" and that the victim of a deceiver sees through the deceiver's intent and decides not to play; they are problem solvers, not automatons, and they decide not to play when the interaction is not cooperative, symmetrical, and fair. I realize that some people might claim that studies designed to find out whether other animals have a theory of mind do not support the claim that they do. Nonetheless, it may be that direct observations are as useful, or even more useful, for learning about what is happening in the heads of other animals.

In domestic dogs there is little tolerance for non-cooperative cheaters. Cheaters may be avoided or chased out of play groups. There seems to a sense of what is right, wrong, and fair in that dogs, like coyotes and (I assume) other social animals, actively make the decision that it is not "right" or "okay" to ask another to play and then try to dominate or mate with that other. Even in rats, fairness and trust are important in the dynamics of playful interactions. Sergio Pellis discovered that sequences of rat play consist of individuals assessing and monitoring one another and then fine-tuning and changing their own behavior to maintain the play mood.[32] When the rules of play are violated, when fairness breaks down, so does play.

Playing by the rules is not about winning or losing. In my own research I did not look at play bouts as having been "won" or "lost," mainly because they were not in any obvious way related to an individual's position in the social/dominance hierarchy, in the leadership of their group, or of their social status with the individual with whom they were playing. Burghardt also noted that there were not individual winners and losers in play.[33] Comparative research has shown that play may be important in the development of motor and physical training, cognitive/motor training, or other social skills. However, it is difficult to generalize about possible functions of play across species. While play-fighting (also called rough-and-tumble play) does not appear to be important in the development of motor training for fighting skills in laboratory rats, it may be important for juvenile chimpanzees.[34]

Play thus may serve a number of functions simultaneously, such as socialization, exercise, practice, cognitive development, or training for the unexpected[35]—the last theory being based on the kaleidoscopic (unpredictable) nature of play sequences. Play may also have an "anxiolytic effect" by reducing anxiety during tense situations (for example, pre-feeding time) and preventing escalation to an aggressive encounter. Chimpanzees, bonobos, and juvenile gorillas, for example, show an increase in social play during pre-feeding periods compared to other times.[36] No matter what the functions of play may be, many researchers believe that play provides important nourishment for brain growth and helps to rewire the brain, increasing the connections between neurons in the cerebral cortex.[37]

There also are trade-offs in play that serve to maintain fair play. Animals engage in two activities that help create an equal and fair playing field: self-handicapping and role-reversing. Self-handicapping (or "play inhibition") occurs when individuals perform behavior patterns that might compromise them outside of play. Coyotes, for example, will inhibit the intensity of their bites, thus abiding by the rules and helping to maintain the play mood.[38] The fur of young coyotes is very thin, and intense bites are painful and cause high-pitched squeals. In adult wolves, a bite can generate as much as 1,500 pounds of pressure per square inch, so there is a good reason to inhibit its force. Role-reversing happens when a dominant animal performs an action during play that would not normally occur during real aggression. For example, a dominant wolf would not roll over on his back during fighting, making himself more vulnerable to attack, but would do so while playing. Bauer and Smuts discovered that role reversals are not always necessary but they probably do facilitate play.[39]

FINE-TUNING, FAIR PLAY, AND EVOLUTION

Individuals of different species fine-tune ongoing play sequences to maintain a play mood and to prevent play from escalating into real aggression. Detailed analyses of film show that in canids there are subtle and fleeting movements and rapid exchanges of eye contact that suggest that players are exchanging information on the run, from moment to moment, to make certain everything is all right, that this is still play. Dogs and their wild relatives communicate with one another (and with us) using their faces, eyes, ears, tails, bodies, and various gaits and vocalizations. They combine facial expressions and tail positions with different types of barks to communicate what they want, what they intend to do, or how they feel. Dogs and wolves have more than a dozen facial expressions, a wide variety of tail positions, and numerous vocalizations, postures, and gaits; the number of possible combinations of all of these modes of communication is staggering. Individuals who do not want to play do not play. By using play and other special contexts (such as greetings, courtship, or ritualized fighting) to communicate about relationships, animals can convey intentions and emotions "on the run" and negotiate and renegotiate the terms of a relationship while minimizing the risk of injury or misunderstanding.[40] These cognitive and emotional capacities are necessary for animals, including humans, to make decisions about whether an ongoing interaction is, or feels, right or wrong and to change behavior accordingly. All of this evidence of contextual and consequential thinking clearly demonstrates that nonhuman animals are not non-thinking automatons.[41] These capacities can and should figure into how we treat these sophisticated and sensitive animals.

Playtime generally is safe time, and individuals can quit whenever they want to. Transgressions and mistakes are forgiven and others accept apologies, especially when one player is a youngster who is not yet a competitor for social status, food, or mates, or when the "cheater" has not been viewed as such yet because he or she has not violated the rules of play too frequently. Individuals must cooperate with one another when they play, and they must negotiate agreements to play. "Uncooperative play" is in fact impossible, an oxymoron, and so it is likely that natural selection weeds out those who do not play by the accepted and negotiated rules.

Still, why might animals continually keep track of what they and others are doing and modify and fine-tune play on the run while they are playing? Why might they try hard to share another individual's intentions? Why do animals carefully use play signals to tell others that they really want to play, not to try to dominate them? Why do they engage in self-handicapping and role-reversing? Why do animals behave fairly? By "behave fairly," I mean that animals often have social expectations when they engage in various sorts of social encounters that, if they are violated, amount to being treated unfairly because of a lapse in social etiquette.

During early development there is a small time window when young mammals can play without being responsible for their own well-being. Parents and other adults feed them and protect them from intruders. This time period is generally referred to as the "socialization period," for this is when species-typical social skills are learned most rapidly. It is important for individuals to engage in some play, and there is a premium for playing fairly if one is to be able to play at all. If individuals do not play fairly, they may not be able to find willing play partners in the future. In coyotes, for example, youngsters are hesitant to play with an individual who does not play fairly or with an individual whom they fear. In many species individuals also show play-partner preferences, and it is possible that these preferences are based on the trust that specific individuals place in one another, or that it is more fruitful for an animal to test its cognitive and physical skills with a particular partner, or that play with a certain partner is useful for strengthening the social relationship with that partner.[42] Because social play cannot occur in the absence of cooperation or fairness, it might be a "foundation of fairness."

Such foundations of fairness include learning how hard to bite, how roughly to treat others, and how to resolve conflicts. There are codes of social conduct that regulate actions that are and are not permissible, and the existence of these codes is related to the evolution of social morality. What could be a better atmosphere in which to learn social skills than during social play, where there are few penalties for transgressions? Individuals might also generalize codes of conduct learned in playing with each other to other group members and to other situations such as food sharing, defending resources, grooming, and giving care. We need much more research focusing on these questions.

Social morality, in this case behaving fairly, is an adaptation shared by many mammals. Behaving fairly evolved because it helped young animals to acquire social skills and other skills needed to mature into adults. Without social play individuals would lose out, and group cohesion would suffer as well.[43] Morality evolved because it is adaptive, because it helps animals, including humans, survive and thrive in particular environments and groups. There is no reason to assume that social morality is unique to humans.[44]

For all these reasons, mammalian social play is a good choice for a behavior to study in order to learn more about the evolution of fairness and social morality, even in humans. If one is a "good" Darwinian, it is premature to claim that only humans can be empathic and moral beings. Indeed, Niko Tinbergen and renowned fieldworkers including Hans Kruuk and George Schaller have suggested looking to other social carnivores to gain insights into the evolution of social behavior in humans.[45]

THE IMPLICATIONS OF PLAY

Despite some lingering (and rapidly declining) skepticism about whether or not other animals are conscious or experience deep and enduring emotions, it is now time to stop ignoring who these animals really are and to stop pretending that we do not know that they are indeed conscious and feeling beings who experience a wide range of emotions.[46] It is not rocket science. The minds of other animals are not "that private" so as to make it impossible to know what they want, need, and feel. And there is no doubt that dogs and other animals love to play and enjoy it deeply. They voluntarily seek it out relentlessly, take certain risks, play to exhaustion, and return to seeking playmates after very little rest.

We must also make every effort to use this information on behalf of individual animals. Indeed, in July 2012 a group of renowned scientists met at Cambridge University and finally declared that animals are truly conscious, then produced a long-overdue document that they called the Cambridge Declaration on Consciousness.[47] They wrote, "Current evidence indicates that non-human animals have the neuroanatomical, neurochemical, and neurophysiological substrates of conscious states along with the capacity to exhibit intentional behaviors. Consequently, the weight of evidence indicates that humans are not unique in possessing the neurological substrates that generate consciousness. Non-human animals, including all mammals and birds, and many other creatures, including octopuses, also possess these neurological substrates." They could also have included fish, for whom the evidence supporting sentience and consciousness is also compelling.[48] Jessica Pierce and I and others have argued that animals use these neurological substrates to engage in moral reflection readily evident in their play.[49]

Although we really have known for a much longer period of time that other animals are conscious and sophisticated thinkers interacting with each other and their environs, perhaps this highly publicized declaration will be helpful for radically improving animal well-being. We can only hope that this declaration is not merely gratuitous hand waving. I have proposed a Universal Declaration on Animal Sentience that expands the Cambridge Declaration and also notes that we must factor sentience into the decisions we make about how we treat other animals.[50]

While Steven Wise's Nonhuman Rights Project labors to achieve legal recognition of nonhuman animals, Oxford University's animal welfarist Marian Dawkins has claimed that we really still do not know if other animals are conscious and that we should " remain skeptical and agnostic [about consciousness] . . . Militantly agnostic if necessary."[51] However, there is now a wealth of scientific data that make such skepticism about animal consciousness, and surely militant agnosticism, anti-scientific and even harmful to animals. The Cambridge Declaration on Consciousness, based on the same information available to Dawkins, shows this to be so.

Perhaps what I call "Dawkins' dangerous idea" will now finally be shelved, given the conclusions of the Cambridge Declaration.[52]

A PROSPECTIVE VIEW OF PLAY

So, where are we? Play is a voluntary activity and individuals can quit when they have had enough or want to do something else.[53] Cheating and deception are extremely rare, and there are good reasons for individuals to play fairly. Social play may be a unique category of behavior because inequalities between players are more tolerated than in other social situations. Play cannot occur if individuals choose not to engage in the activity, and the equality (or symmetry) needed for play to continue makes it different from other forms of seemingly cooperative behavior such as hunting and caregiving. This sort of symmetry, or egalitarianism, is thought to be a precondition for the evolution of social morality in humans.[54]

It is clear that morality and virtue did not suddenly appear in the evolutionary epic beginning with humans. While fair play in animals may be a rudimentary form of social morality, it still could be a forerunner of more-complex and more-sophisticated moral systems, such as those found among humans. It is self-serving anthropocentrism to claim that we are the only moral beings in the animal kingdom. The origins of virtue, egalitarianism, and morality are more ancient that our own species, and all have biological bases. But we will never learn about animal morality if we close the door on the possibility that it exists. Our moral capacities have to have older roots from which they have evolved, and existing data (especially from play) support this claim. However, in the spirit of learning about the fascinating lives of other animals, learning more about us is clearly not the only reason or the main reason to learn more about them.

Animals can have fun, be nice to one another, be fair, and honor the trust that each has for the other. In order to play, they have to do just this, because most (if not all) individuals in a group will benefit from adopting this behavioral strategy, and group stability may also be fostered. Numerous mechanisms (play invitation signals, variations in the sequencing of actions performed during play when compared to other contexts, self-handicapping, role-reversing) have evolved to facilitate the initiation and maintenance of social play in numerous mammals—to keep others engaged—so that agreeing to play fairly and the resulting benefits of doing so can be readily achieved. To be sure, there are marked species differences in the development of play in dogs, coyotes, and wolves that can be related to variations in species-typical social organization, and play among these canids follows strict rules of social interaction that center on fairness and trust. Nevertheless, the study of social play is related to questions about animal emotions and moral behavior.

Social play clearly is fun for the players. Thus, future research can also consider whether it is possible for animals to have "too much fun" or to behave "too fairly," following up on research on humans in the field called "diagonal psychology," which shows that there can be negative consequences associated with being too full of oneself or being "too happy."[55] Thus one can ask whether there is stabilizing selection for fun and fairness that reins in the possible costs of behavior that can be too risky or too costly, including social play.[56] While there are bits of data that inform this area of inquiry, it really is wide open for further detailed study.

While we know quite a bit about animal social play, there still is much to learn about the details of playful interactions. Much of what we already know about the development, evolution, and social dynamics of play has come from detailed comparative research on domestic dogs and their wild relatives, and this information and the methods of study can be used to learn more about play in other nonhuman animals and the need for "wild play" in human animals.[57] Studying play is challenging and exciting, and I hope that additional detailed studies from a wide variety of species will be forthcoming. These data are essential for enriching our understanding of the evolution of play across diverse species, how ecological variables influence the development of play in individuals of the same species, and how an individual's playful experiences (or the lack thereof) influence his or her future behavior.

NOTES

1. I thank Jonathan K. Crane for inviting me to write this essay and for his insightful and challenging comments. Parts of this paper have appeared in some of my earlier essays as noted and also in an essay titled "The Significance of Ethological Studies: Playing and Peeing," in *Dog Behavior and Cognition*, ed. Alexandra Horowitz (New York: Springer, 2014), 59–75, from which much of the introduction and some text is taken.

2. Ibid.

3. Marc Bekoff, *The Emotional Lives of Animals* (Novato, CA: New World Library, 2007); Alexandra Horowitz, *Inside of a Dog: What Dogs See, Smell, and Know* (New York: Scribner's, 2009); Adam Miklosi, *Dog Behavior, Evolution, and Cognition* (New York: Oxford University Press, 2009); Brian Hare and Vanessa Woods, *The Genius of Dogs: How Dogs Are Smarter Than You Think* (New York: Plume, 2013).

4. Michael W. Fox and Marc Bekoff, "The Behaviour of Dogs," in *The Behaviour of Domestic Animals*, ed. E. S. E. Hafez, 3rd ed. (London: Bailliere, Tindall, 1975), 370–409.

5. For discussions about possible functions of play, see J. Wayne Lazar and Gordon D. Beckhorn, "Social Play or the Development of Social Behavior in Ferrets (*Mustela putorius*)?," *American Zoologist* 14 (1974): 405–14; Marc Bekoff and John A. Byers, "A Critical Reanalysis of the Ontogeny and Phylogeny of Mammalian Social and Locomotor Play: An Ethological Hornet's Nest," in *Behavioral Development: The Bielefeld Interdisciplinary Project*, ed. K. Immelmann, G. Barlow, M. Main, and L. Petrinovich (Cambridge and New York: Cambridge University Press, 1981), 296–337; Marek Spinka, Ruth. C. Newberry, and Marc Bekoff, "Mammalian Play: Training for the Unexpected," *Quarterly Review of Biology* 76 (2001): 141–68; Elisabetta Palagi, Giada Cordoni, and Silvana Borgognini Tarli, "Immediate and Delayed Benefits of Play Behaviour: New Evidence from Chimpanzees," *Ethology* 110 (2004): 949–62; Gordon M. Burghardt, *The Genesis of Animal Play: Testing the Limits* (Cambridge, MA: MIT Press, 2005); Sergio Pellis and Vivien Pellis, *The Playful Brain: Venturing to the Limits of Neuroscience* (London: Oneworld Publications, 2010); Elisabetta Palagi, "Playing at Every Age: Modalities and Potential Functions in Non-human Primates," in *The Oxford Handbook of the Development of Play*, ed. A. D. Pellegrini (New York: Oxford University Press, 2011), 70–82.

6. Marc Bekoff, ed., "Social Play in Mammals," *American Zoologist* 14 (1974): 265–436.

7. Marc Bekoff, "The Development of Social Interaction, Play, and Metacommunication in Mammals: An Ethological Perspective," *Quarterly Review of Biology* 47 (1972): 412–34; Marc Bekoff, "Social Play and Play-Soliciting by Infant Canids," *American Zoologist* 14 (1974): 323–40; Marc Bekoff, "Social Communication in Canids: Evidence for the Evolution of a Stereotyped Mammalian Display," *Science* 197 (1977): 1097–99.

8. Marc Bekoff and Jessica Pierce, *Wild Justice: The Moral Lives of Animals* (Chicago: University of Chicago Press, 2009); Jessica Pierce and Marc Bekoff, "Wild Justice Redux: What We Know about Social Justice in Animals and Why It Matters," *Social Justice Research* (special issue, ed. Sarah Brosnan) 25 (2012): 122–39.

9. Marc Bekoff, "Mammalian Dispersal and the Ontogeny of Individual Behavioral Phenotypes," *American Naturalist* 111 (1977b): 715–32.

10. Marc Bekoff, "Wild Justice and Fair Play: Cooperation, Forgiveness, and Morality in Animals," *Biology and Philosophy* 19 (2004): 489–520; Lee A. Dugatkin and Marc Bekoff, "Play and the Evolution of Fairness: A Game Theory Model," *Behavioural Processes* 60 (2003): 209–14; Bekoff and Pierce, *Wild Justice*; Giada Cordoni and Elisabetta Palagi, "Ontogenetic Trajectories of Chimpanzee Social Play: Similarities with Humans," *PlosOne* 6 (2011): e27344, doi: 10.1371/journal.pone.0027344; Pierce and Bekoff, "Wild Justice Redux"; Sarah Brosnan, ed., "Justice in Animals," *Social Justice Research* 25: 109–231 (2012).

11. Niko Tinbergen, *The Study of Instinct* (New York: Oxford University Press, 1951); Niko Tinbergen, "On Aims and Methods of Ethology," *Zeitschrift für Tierpsychologie* 20 (1963): 410–33.

12. Gordon Burghardt, "Amending Tinbergen: A Fifth Aim for Ethology," in *Anthropomorphism, Anecdote, and Animals: The Emperor's New Clothes?*, ed. R. W. Mitchell, N. Thompson, and L. Miles (Albany, NY: SUNY Press, 1997), 254–76. For further discussion about how Tinbergen's ideas can be applied to behavioral studies

in general, see Peter M. Kappeler, Louise Barrett, Daniel T. Blumstein, and Tim H. Clutton-Brock, "Constraints and Flexibility in Mammalian Social Behaviour: Introduction and Synthesis," *Philosophical Transactions of the Royal Society B* 368 (2013), http://rstb.royalsocietypublishing.org/content/368/1618/20120337; and Louise Barrett, Daniel T. Blumstein, Tim H. Clutton-Brock, and Peter M. Kappeler, "Taking Note of Tinbergen, or: The Promise of a Biology of Behavior." *Philosophical Transactions of the Royal Society B* 368 (2013). http://rstb.royalsocietypublishing.org /content/368/1618/20120352; for cognitive ethological inquiries in particular (the study of animal minds), see Dale Jamieson and Marc Bekoff, "On Aims and Methods of Cognitive Ethology," *Philosophy of Science Association* 2 (1993): 110–24.

13. A chronology of this progress can be found in Bekoff, "Social Play in Mammals"; Donald Symons, *Play and Aggression: A Study of Rhesus Monkeys* (New York: Columbia University Press, 1978); Robert M. Fagen, *Animal Play Behavior* (New York: Oxford University Press, 1981); Marc Bekoff and John A. Byers, "A Critical Reanalysis of the Ontogeny and Phylogeny of Mammalian Social and Locomotor Play: An Ethological Hornet's Nest," in *Behavioral Development: The Bielefeld Interdisciplinary Project*, ed. K. Immelmann, G. Barlow, M. Main, and L. Petrinovich (Cambridge: Cambridge University Press, 1981), 296–337; Marc Bekoff and John A. Byers, eds., *Animal Play: Evolutionary, Comparative, and Ecological Perspectives* (New York: Cambridge University Press, 1998); Burghardt, *The Genesis of Animal Play*; Pellis and Pellis, *The Playful Brain*.

14. For further discussion, see Bekoff and Byers, "A Critical Reanalysis of the Ontogeny and Phylogeny of Mammalian Social and Locomotor Play"; Burghardt, *The Genesis of Animal Play*.

15. Burghardt, *The Genesis of Animal Play*, 382.

16. See Cordoni and Palagi, "Ontogenetic Trajectories of Chimpanzee Social Play."

17. Marc Bekoff, "Social Play Behavior and Social Morality," in *Encyclopedia of Animal Behavior*, ed. Marc Bekoff (Westport, CT: Greenwood Press, 2004), 833–45.

18. J. D. Henry and S. M. Herrero, "Social Play in the American Black Bear: Its Similarities to Canid Social Play and an Examination of Its Identifying Characteristics," *American Zoologist* 14 (1974): 371–89.

19. Harriet L. Hill and Marc Bekoff, "The Variability of Some Motor Components of Social Play and Agonistic Behaviour in Infant Eastern Coyotes," *Canis latrans* var, *Animal Behaviour* 25 (1977): 907–9; Bekoff and Byers, "A Critical Reanalysis of the Ontogeny and Phylogeny of Mammalian Social and Locomotor Play."

20. Bekoff, "Social Play and Play-Soliciting by Infant Canids"; Maxeen Biben, "Comparative Ontogeny of Social Behavior in Three South American Canids, the Maned Wolf, Crab-Eating Fox and Bush Dog: Implications for Sociality," *Animal Behaviour* 31 (1983): 814–26.

21. Essays in Bekoff and Byers, eds., *Animal Play*.

22. Giada Cordoni, "Social Play in Captive Wolves (*Canis lupus*): Not Only an Immature Affair," *Behaviour* 146 (2009): 1363–85.

23. For a notable exception, see Elisabetta Palagi, "Social Play in Bonobos (*Pan paniscus*) and Chimpanzees (*Pan troglodytes*): Implications for Natural Social Systems and Interindividual Relationships," *American Journal of Physical Anthropology* 129 (2006): 418–26.

24. Bekoff and Pierce, *Wild Justice*; Pierce and Bekoff, "Wild Justice Redux."

25. George Barlow, "Modal Action Patterns," in *How Animals Communicate*, ed. Thomas Sebeok (Bloomington: Indiana University Press, 1977), 98–134; Bekoff, "Social Communication in Canids."

26. Marc Bekoff and Colin Allen, "Intentional Icons: Towards an Evolutionary Cognitive Ethology," *Ethology* 91(1992): 1–16.

27. Alexandra Horowitz, "Attention to Attention in Domestic Dog (*Canis familiaris*) Dyadic Play," *Animal Cognition* 12 (2008): 107–18. http://link.springer.com /article/10.1007%2Fs10071-008-0175-y?LI=true#page-2.

28. Bekoff, "Social Communication in Canids."

29. Marc Bekoff, "Play Signals as Punctuation: The Structure of Social Play in Canids," *Behaviour* 132 (1995), 419–29.

30. Bekoff and Pierce, *Wild Justice*.

31. Summarized in Marc Bekoff and Michael C. Wells, "Social Ecology and Behavior of Coyotes," *Advances in the Study of Behavior* 16 (1986): 251–38.

32. Sergio Pellis, "Keeping in Touch: Play Fighting and Social Knowledge," in *The Cognitive Animal*, ed. M. Bekoff, C. Allen, and G. M. Burghardt (Cambridge, MA: MIT Press, 2002).

33. Gordon M. Burghardt, "Play," in *Encyclopedia of Animal Behavior*, ed. M. D. Breed and J. Moore (Oxford: Academic Press, 2010), 2:740–44.

34. Pellis and Pellis, *The Playful Brain*; Giada Cordoni, personal communication.

35. Spinka, Newberry, and Bekoff, "Mammalian Play."

36. Palagi, "Social Play in Bonobos (*Pan paniscus*) and Chimpanzees (*Pan troglodytes*)." Elisabetta Palagi, Daniela Antonacci, and Giada Cordoni, "Fine-tuning of Social Play in Juvenile Lowland Gorillas (*Gorilla gorilla gorilla*)," *Developmental Psychobiology* 49 (2007): 433–45.

37. For more information on comparative studies about brains and play, see Kerrie P. Lewis and Robert A. Barton, "Amygdala Size and Hypothalamus Size Predict Social Play Frequency in Nonhuman Primates: A Comparative Analysis Using Independent Contrasts," *Journal of Comparative Psychology* 120 (2006): 31–37; Kerrie L. Graham, "Coevolutionary Relationship between Striatum Size and Social Play in Nonhuman Primates," *American Journal of Primatology* 73, no. 4 (2010): 314–22; Kerrie L. Graham and Gordon M. Burghardt, "Current Perspectives on the Biological Study of Play: Signs of Progress," *Quarterly Review of Biology* 85 (2010): 393–418.

38. Bekoff, "Social Play and Play-Soliciting by Infant Canids."

39. Erika B. Bauer and Barbara B. Smuts, "Cooperation and Competition during Dyadic Play in Domestic Dogs, *Canis familiaris*," *Animal Behaviour* 73 (2007): 489–99.

40. Camille Ward and Barbara B. Smuts, "Why Does Carnivore Play Matter?," *Journal of Developmental Processes* 2 (2007): 31–38.

41. Bekoff, *The Emotional Lives of Animals*; Marc Bekoff, *The Animal Manifesto: Six Reasons for Expanding Our Compassion Footprint* (Novato, CA: New World Library, 2010); Marc Bekoff, *Why Dogs Hump and Bees Get Depressed: The Fascinating Science of Animal Intelligence, Emotions, Friendship, and Conservation* (Novato, CA: New World Library, 2013).

42. Cordoni and Palagi, "Ontogenetic Trajectories of Chimpanzee Social Play"; Elisabetta Palagi and Giada Cordoni, "The Right Time to Happen: Play Developmental Divergence in the Two *Pan* Species," *PLoS ONE* 7, no. 12 (2012): e52767, doi:10.1371/journal.pone.0052767.

43. E.g., Daniela Antonacci, Ivan Norscia, and Elisabetta Palagi, "Stranger to Familiar: Wild Strepsirhines Manage Xenophobia by Playing," *PLoS ONE* 5, no. 10 (2010): e13218, doi:10.1371/journal.pone.0013218; Cordoni and Palagi, "Ontogenetic Trajectories of Chimpanzee Social Play."

44. Bekoff and Pierce, *Wild Justice*; Robert W. Sussman and C. Robert Cloninger, eds., *Origins of Altruism and Cooperation* (New York: Springer, 2011); Sarah Brosnan, ed., "Justice in Animals"; Frans de Waal, *The Bonobo and the Atheist: In Search of Humanism among the Primates* (New York: Norton, 2014).

45. E.g., George B. Schaller and Gordon R. Lowther, "The Relevance of Carnivore Behavior to the Study of Early Hominids," *Southwestern Journal of Anthropology* 25 (1969): 307–41.

46. Marc Bekoff, "A Universal Declaration of Animal Sentience: No Pretending," *Psychology Today*, June 20, 2013, http://www.psychologytoday.com/blog/animal-emotions/201306/universal-declaration-animal-sentience-no-pretending; Bekoff, *Why Dogs Hump and Bees Get Depressed*; Marc Bekoff, ed., *Ignoring Nature No More: The Case for Compassionate Conservation* (Chicago: University of Chicago Press, 2013); Marc Bekoff, *Rewilding Our Hearts: Building Pathways of Compassion and Coexistence* (Novato, CA: New World Library, 2014).

47. Cambridge Declaration on Consciousness (2012), http://fcmconference.org and www.psychologytoday.com/blog/animal-emotions/201208/scientists-finally-conclude-nonhuman-animals-areconscious-beings.

48. Victoria Braithwaite, *Do Fish Feel Pain?* (New York: Oxford University Press, 2010).

49. Bekoff and Pierce, *Wild Justice*; Pierce and Bekoff, "Wild Justice Redux"; Brosnan, "Justice in Animals."

50. Bekoff, "A Universal Declaration of Animal Sentience."

51. Marian Dawkins, *Why Animals Matter* (New York: Oxford University Press, 2012), 177.

52. Bekoff, "A Universal Declaration of Animal Sentience"; Bekoff, *Why Dogs Hump and Bees Get Depressed*

53. See also Peter Gray, "The Play Theory of Hunter-Gatherer Egalitarianism," in *Ancestral Landscapes in Human Evolution*, ed. D. Narvaez, K. Valentino, A. Fuentes, J. McKenna, and P. Gray (New York: Oxford University Press, 2014).

54. Bekoff and Pierce, *Wild Justice*; Francesca Ciani, Stefania Dall'Olio, Roscoe Stanyon, and Elisabetta Palagi, "Social Tolerance and Adult Play in Macaque Societies: A Comparison with Different Human Cultures," *Animal Behaviour* 84 (2012): 1313–22.

55. Randolph M. Nesse, "Natural Selection and the Elusiveness of Happiness," *Philosophical Transactions of the Royal Society B* 359 (2004): 1333–47; see June Gruber, H. C. Devlin, and J. Moskowitz, "Seeing Both Sides: An Introduction to the Light and Dark Sides of Positive Emotion," in *Positive Emotion: The Light Sides and Dark Sides*, ed. J. Gruber and J. Moskowitz (New York: Oxford University Press, 2014).

56. Marc Bekoff, "Can Animals Be Too Happy or Have Too Much Fun?," *Psychology Today*, March 16, 2014, http://www.psychologytoday.com/blog/animal-emotions/201403/can-animals-be-too-happy-or-have-too-much-fun.

57. Marc Bekoff, "The Need for 'Wild Play': Let Children Be the Animals They Need to Be," *Psychology Today*, February 25, 2012, http://www.psychologytoday.com/blog/animal-emotions/201202/the-need-wild-play-let-children-be-the-animals-they-need-be.

Eight Fighting Fair

THE ECOLOGY OF HONOR IN HUMANS AND ANIMALS

Dan Demetriou

IN JUNE OF 1813, CAPTAIN Philip Broke of the HMS *Shannon* challenged his counterpart, Captain James Lawrence of the USS *Chesapeake*, to a ship-to-ship duel. Broke hoped to restore British national honor, which was badly bruised at this point in the War of 1812. The problem for Broke was that half a dozen Royal Navy ships had recently been sunk or captured by American frigates of roughly equal size. These defeats in no way challenged British naval supremacy, but they traumatized British pride and self-image. As the great war anthem "Rule, Britannia" tells us, the British had come to see their rule of the waves not only as essential to their freedom, but as a divine command. And for the Royal Navy in particular, mere dominance by overwhelming force wasn't enough: after decades of victorious actions against often larger European forces, British sailors understandably came to see themselves—sailor to sailor, officer to officer—as without rival. Their recent losses to the U.S. Navy cast that opinion into doubt.

Charged with blockading the Americans in Boston as part of a larger British effort to strangle American trade, Broke had previously tried to engage the American *President* and *Constitution* with his *Shannon* and *Tenendos*, but the prudent American commodore of that squadron, John Rogers, exploited a thick fog and sneaked out of Boston harbor without a scratch. Frustrated by this, Broke pressed the point with Lawrence. He ordered away all the other ships of his squadron, desperate to draw the more powerful, fresher, and more heavily manned *Chesapeake* into single action. And lest there be any doubt about his purpose, he fired off this challenge to Lawrence.

H.B.M. ship *Shannon*, off Boston,
June, 1813

Sir,

As the *Chesapeake* appears now ready for sea, I request that you will do
me the favour to meet the *Shannon* with her, ship to ship, to try the fortune of our respective flags. To an officer of your character, it requires
some apology for proceeding to further particulars. Be assured, sir, that
it is not from any doubt I can entertain of your wishing to close with
my proposal, but merely to provide an answer to any objection that
might be made, and very reasonably, upon the chance of our receiving unfair support. After [the] diligent attention which we had paid to
Commodore Rogers, the pains I took to detach all force but the *Shannon* and *Tenedos* to such a distance that they could not possibly join in
any action fought in sight of the capes, and the various verbal messages
which had been sent into Boston to that effect, we were much disap-
pointed to find the commodore had eluded us by sailing on the first
chance, after the prevailing easterly winds had obliged us to keep an off-
ing from the coast. He, perhaps, wished for some stronger assurance of
a fair meeting. I am therefore, induced to address you more particularly,
and to assure you that what I write, I pledge my honour to perform to
the utmost of my power.

The *Shannon* mounts twenty-four guns upon her broadside, and one
light boat-gun—eighteen-pounders upon her maindeck, and thirty-two
pound carronades on her quarterdeck and forecastle, and is manned
with a complement of 300 men and boys (a large proportion of the
latter), besides thirty seamen, boys and passengers, who were taken out
of recaptured vessels lately. I am thus minute, because a report has pre-
vailed in some of the Boston papers that we had 150 men additional
lent to us from *La Hogue*, which really never was the case. *La Hogue*
is now gone to Halifax for provisions, and I will send all other ships
beyond the power of interfering with us, and meet you wherever it
is most agreeable to you, within the limits of the under mentioned
rendezvous. . . .

If you will favour me with any plan of signals or telegraph, I will warn
you (if sailing under this promise) should any of my friends be too nigh,
or anywhere in sight, until I can detach them out of my way; or I would

sail with you, under a flag of truce, to any place you think safest from our cruisers, hauling it down when fair to begin hostilities.

You must, sir, be aware that my proposals are highly advantageous to you, as you cannot proceed to sea singly in the *Chesapeake* without imminent risk of being crushed by the superior force of the numerous British squadrons which are now abroad, where all your efforts, in case of rencontre, would, however gallant, be perfectly hopeless. I entreat you, sir, not to imagine that I am urged by mere personal vanity to the wish of meeting the *Chesapeake*, or that I depend only upon your personal ambition for your acceding to this invitation: we have both nobler motives. You will feel it as a compliment if I say that the result of our meeting may be the most grateful service I can render to my country; and I doubt not, that you, equally confident of success, will feel convinced that it is only by repeated triumphs, in even combats, that your little navy can now hope to console your country for the loss of that trade it can no longer protect. Favour me with a speedy reply. We are short of provisions and water, and cannot stay long here.

I have the honour to be, sir,
Your obedient, humble servant,
P.B.V. BROKE,
Captain of H.B.M. ship Shannon.

N.B. For the general service of watching your coast it is requisite for me to keep another ship in company to support me with her guns and boats, when employed near the land, and particularly to aid each other if either ship, in chase, should get on shore. You must be aware that I cannot, consistently with my duty, waive so great an advantage for this general service by detaching my consort without an assurance on your part of meeting me directly, and that you will neither seek nor admit aid from any other of your armed vessels if I dispatch mine expressly for the sake of meeting you. Should any special order restrain from thus answering a formal challenge, you may yet oblige me by keeping my proposal a secret, and appointing any place you like to meet us (within 300 miles of Boston) in a given number of days after you sail; as, unless you agree to an interview, I may be busied on other service and, perhaps, be at a distance from Boston when you go to sea. Choose your terms, *but let us meet.* (n.a. 1893)

This remarkable letter helps us see, from the inside, what makes an honor-minded person tick. The word "fair" appears twice and "unfair" once, but in fact the entire letter is devoted to assuring Lawrence that Broke will take every possible measure to ensure a fair fight. Indeed, without quoting the letter in full we would miss the "minute" details and contingencies Broke considers to ensure that his proposed "interview" with Lawrence is fair to the American.

Philosophers and behavioral economists discuss fairness a great deal, but usually in the context of distributing material goods. Broke, however, is interested in a fair distribution of a good of a different sort: a zero-sum good that we will refer to as *competitive prestige*, and one much more often discussed by sports commentators than philosophers. What Broke understood is that what Britain needed most from him was not another successful season of blockaded American trade, but a restoration of what it felt to be its rightful share of competitive prestige among nations. He also knew that earning that prestige necessitated a victory over an American force "in even combat."

Broke's letter not only presents us with a noteworthy expression of honor, but also exemplifies how considerations of honor are typically weighed against other practical reasons we have, especially those of authority. Broke was officially under Admiralty orders to smother American trade, not to restore British honor. And although unofficially he was quite right that a victory over an equally (or ideally, more) powerful American would indeed be the "most grateful service" he could perform for his country, he would automatically be court-martialed for the loss of any of his ships, with a negative outcome likely if the Americans fared better by the encounter. And as an authority himself, he had a pastoral responsibility to his sailors, whom he was clearly putting in extra jeopardy by dispersing his squadron in order to invite a very preventable battle.

It might be wondered how considerations of "honor" and "authority" could be as distinct as all that. Surely, both authority and honor concern rankings, status, and social hierarchy? And if we view Broke's strange behavior as an ethologist might, we cannot help but interpret it in light of the striving for high position observed in many species, where competition for supremacy in (what biologists call) a "dominance hierarchy" can be fierce, especially for males. One might contend that Broke *had* power and dominance over his lieutenants, midshipmen, and sailors, and *sought* power over Lawrence and, by extension, the Americans. What does all this talk of "honor" add, other than to gild the lily?

This chapter's discussion begins by explaining why honor-governed competitions for prestige are indeed morally and psychologically distinct from authoritarian hierarchies. After characterizing honor psychology in humans, we turn to the question of whether honor-typical behaviors are found in nonhuman animals. I argue that paradigmatically honor-typical behavior is apparent in some nonhuman species, and it takes little specialized skill to recognize it or to distinguish such behavior from the primitive authoritarianism of our closest evolutionary relatives. Honor raises many exciting questions about human-animal normative continuity. The most radical proposal in this direction would be that some nonhumans not only behave in honor-typical ways, but are in addition honorable *agents*. I find that claims for "beastly honor" must wait upon philosophical consensus on the nature of moral agency, on the one hand, and additional empirical research into the distribution of honor-typical behavior in higher social animals, on the other. In an effort to help frame such research, I conclude by offering conditions of honor-agency that are general enough to apply to any species and any standard of moral agency.

HONOR VS. AUTHORITY

Honor is enjoying a renaissance, both as a topic of study and as a value worth rehabilitating.[1] What honor actually *is* remains a point of great dispute. Some scholars see it as equating to esteem, high regard, public praise, prestige, or social standing and respect.[2] Others see it as a *right* to these things, which is importantly different, since one may be honor*ed* without being honor*able*.[3] I have no objections to either scholarly tradition, since "honor" is undoubtedly used in those ways. However, I focus on a third item that also is discussed in terms of "honor" and its translations: a particular normative system that says *how*, *when*, and *why* prestige is deserved—in the philosophical jargon, a philosophy "of right" as opposed to a theory of "the good." To avoid any confusion this ambiguity may cause, I will use "prestige" to refer to honor *qua* a good, and will reserve the term "honor" to denote the moral value that legitimizes the normative system of honor, or "honor ethos."

Authoritarianism

The honor ethos, then, concerns the constraints on distributing, pursuing, and respecting prestige. Prestige connotes comparative rank—of some being superior to others. But so does authority. Does the honor ethos differ enough from the authoritarian moral system to justify its being thought of as a distinct ethos? Yes; and explaining why is the goal of this section.

For our purposes here, authoritarian norms concern *hierarchies*. In an ideal human hierarchy, rank is proportional to responsibility and control. Insofar as we are superiors in a hierarchy, we are responsible for the smooth functioning of our subordinates, and discharging this obligation justifies our control over them. On the other hand, insofar as we are inferiors, we must obey the commands of our superiors, and our obedience to their orders justifies our claim to continued status as subordinates.

In some hierarchies, mobility between ranks is impossible: examples include feudal societies, or the celestial hierarchy consisting of God and the angelic orders. But in hierarchies that allow mobility, individuals ideally move up or down only through promotion or demotion from above by virtue of how well they obey and discharge their rank-centered duties. In the authoritarian system of Judeo-Christian morality, for instance, God "raises up" the righteous, and the descendants of Abraham are "placed above" other nations because of Abraham's obedience. "Promotion cometh neither from the east, nor the west, nor the south," we are told, but from the Lord, who "putteth down one, and setteth up another" (Psalms 75:7). A believing centurion is praised by Jesus for his grasp of divine authority, for the centurion too was "a man under authority, having soldiers under me: and I say to this man, 'Go,' and he goeth; and to another, 'Come,' and he cometh; and to my servant, 'Do this,' and he doeth it" (Matthew 8:9). Like the Roman legions, our modern military is also authoritarian, as are our corporations: subordinates are promoted only if they obey orders and do their job well, and they are demoted or terminated if they do not.

When it comes to demotion and termination, it is important to separate poor performance from code offenses. *Poor performers* are merely incompetent: a well-intentioned middle manager may be unable to meet reasonable profitability expectations for his unit, say. Poor performers won't be promoted and may be demoted or even fired, but they won't usually be met with hostility. *Offenders* in hierarchies, on the other hand, are rebellious or insubordinate, which is seen by superiors as violating the basic assumptions of the authoritarian scheme. Offenders are met with hostility; and if they are given a chance to remain in the group at all, they must abase themselves in some way to demonstrate their renewed commitment to authoritarian structure.

Authoritarianism recognizes that poor leaders sometimes need replacing. A nominal authority who has failed his duties may be legitimately overthrown by the inferiors themselves if no superior does so—this is especially true if that leader is not only incompetent but violates his pastoral duties and thus offends against the very code that legitimizes his authority. Nonetheless, rebellion is typically the gravest of offenses, and ambition—a vice on authoritarianism—is a wholly unacceptable reason for turning against one's superiors. For instance, when Milton's Satan rebels against God, he does so not for any good authoritarian reason, but rather, as he admits,

> Pride and worse Ambition threw me down
> Warring in Heav'n against Heav'ns matchless King:
> Ah wherefore! he deservd no such return
> From me, whom he created what I was
> In that bright eminence, and with his good
> Upbraided none; nor was his service hard.
> . . . .
> O had his powerful Destiny ordaind
> Me some inferiour Angel, I had stood
> Then happie; no unbounded hope had rais'd
> Ambition.

Centuries of readers have found Satan's rebellion to be heroic. But as social psychologists Jonathan Haidt and Jesse Graham point out, questioning authority is not admirable in this model: "From [the authoritarian] point of view, bumper stickers that urge people to 'question authority' and protests that involve civil disobedience are not heroic, they are antisocial."[4]

The Honor Ethos

In contrast to authoritarian hierarchies, we have honor-governed *prestige rankings*. I noted above how the sense of "honor" I intend here is the one referring to a normative system that distributes prestige. We must now be more accurate: strictly speaking, the honor ethos regulates rankings of *competitive* prestige.

To see the difference between mere prestige and competitive prestige, note that in some cultures people enjoy high prestige and social rank because of various qualities, such as being high-born, charismatic, beautiful, tall, funny, light-skinned, or athletic. These qualities are not competitive. Take athleticism: whereas an excellent runner happens to run more quickly than most people, an excellent competitive runner runs quickly *and* has the virtues of being a good competitor. When pitted against others, a merely excellent runner may panic, cheat, lose sorely, win ungraciously, or simply decline to compete, whereas the excellent competitive runner will not do any of these things. Honor as a normative system, then, keeps tabs and encourages not excellence as such, but competitive excellence. In this way honor moralizes regular prestige in the same way justice moralizes material goods and welfare: although justice on any contractarian tradition is ultimately about a cooperative distribution of these things, someone with a justice mind-set comes to see unjustly gained goods as positively bad and not reason-providing (e.g., the pleasure of the rapist does not at all weigh in favor of rape). Likewise, honor is about prestige, but the honor-minded person will moralize prestige and thus come to regard only honorably gained—i.e., competitively gained—prestige as reason-providing and good.

In a well-functioning ranking of competitive prestige, rank comes with a proportional amount of competitive prestige (not control), and unequal prestige is justified by the unequal distribution of competitive excellence (not responsibility). The most obvious example of competitive prestige rankings is found in sports: a high-ranked tennis player has more competitive prestige than low-ranked ones, but she has no control of, responsibility for, or authority over her rivals. Nor does she seek any.

The basic aim of the honor-minded person is not to reach the top by any means possible, but to ensure that the public ranking of competitive prestige reflects true competitive excellence. That said, since it would distort the ranking just as badly to accept a lower rank than one deserves as to accept a higher rank than one deserves, honorable people must strive for a higher rank if they feel they can win it—there is no room for false modesty in an honor system. Likewise, lest one occupy a higher rank than one deserves, honorable people must welcome challenges from likely up-and-comers. However, since not all would-be challengers have a plausible claim to one's rank, one shouldn't accept challenges from much-lower-ranked competitors or challenge much-higher-ranked competitors. Finally, since one's claim to higher status isn't proven by besting lower-ranked opponents, the honorable avoid challenging those who are weaker or somehow lower in ranking than themselves. "Bullying" lower-ranked or weaker competitors suggests to others, if anything, that one sees oneself as deserving a *lower*, not a higher, place in their esteem. This is because honorable people demand fair contests for status, since obviously enough unfair competitions do not result in rankings that reflect true competitive excellence. We can codify these thoughts with the following principles:

Rank Ambition: One must seek the highest status one deserves, so one must challenge those who are ranked slightly higher if one thinks one can defeat them.

Rank Humility: But one mustn't challenge those who are ranked much higher, and parties who are ranked much higher cannot accept challenges from those who are ranked much lower.

No Ducking: One must not decline legitimate challenges to one's rank.

No Bullying: One mustn't aggress upon/challenge those of lower rank.

Fair Play: Competitions must be fair, and extraneous advantages (e.g., wealth, rank, superior networks, etc.) must be eliminated, set aside or voluntarily handicapped.

These are some of the rules that, if adhered to, make one fully honorable; similarly, violating them makes one dishonorable. According to this system, "honor" in the sense of competitive prestige is supposed to be apportioned in greater or lesser degree according to rank among those playing by the rules of the game; bystanders have no honor-standing.

The performance/offense dichotomy we noted in authoritarian hierarchies is also evident in the honor-governed rankings of competitive prestige. Poor performers in rankings of competitive prestige merely have low prestige. They may not be highly regarded, but they nonetheless are fully honorable because they compete correctly and give and demand rank-appropriate respect. Code offenders, on the other hand, are positively dishonored. The punishment directed at the dishonorable offender is not abasement, as it is in authoritarianism, but rather takes the form of social death: insignias are torn off of uniforms, names are erased from record books, e-mails are ignored, faces are not recognized in hallways.[5] Shame and contempt—the widely recognized self- and other-critical affects attending judgments of dishonorable conduct—prepare us to dole out and accept just these sorts of punishments.[6]

As Broke's letter exemplifies, honor's boyish and playful spirit was commonly applied to war—or, more precisely, battle. The First World War supposedly taught us that war was not a game, and to look pityingly on those naive British soldiers kicking along footballs as they charged German trenches. But in seeing battle as dangerous play, those young men were channeling an ancient and widespread human impulse. In his seminal work on play, *Homo Ludens*, Johan Huizinga describes the "play quality" of aristocratic warfare, which pitted equal antagonists against each other to prove who was "the better man."[7] Thus, underhanded forms of fighting (ambush, punitive expeditions) and "base" motives for conflict (conquest, domination, and material gain) are naturally repellent to this ethos. As Huizinga notes, in honorable war or play antagonists compete not out of a "desire for power or a will to dominate, [but rather] to excel others, to be the first and to be honoured for that."[8] This is why Achilles—who deliberately chose glory over life, prosperity, and authority—is the paradigm warrior, and not the wily Odysseus, whose less-than-honorable stratagem actually defeats the Trojans.

Theoretical Payoffs

The distinction between authoritarianism and honor and their corresponding sorts of rankings is relevant not only to ethics and political theory, but also to ethology, evolutionary psychology, comparative psychology, and behavioral ecology. For instance, in an influential article,[9] biologist Sandra Vehrencamp distinguishes between "egalitarian" animal societies and "despotic" ones, arguing that a main force in creating despotic animal societies is the inability of lower-ranked individuals to pull up stakes and leave the group.[10] Verhencamp defines a despotic society as one where "benefits accrue disproportionately to a few individuals in the group at the expense of others" and the egalitarian one to be "where benefits are divided roughly equally or in proportion to the risk or effort taken." Egalitarian societies are (for some unexplained reason) "cooperative," whereas despotic ones are "competitive."[11] Clearly, Vehrencamp's one-dimensional continuum cannot accommodate the distinction between authoritarianism and honor. On the one hand, honor-governed rankings of competitive prestige are clearly competitive. Furthermore, honor-based rankings of competitive prestige are surely ones in which "benefits accrue disproportionately to a few individuals at the expense of others," since prestige is a zero-sum commodity and can only be gained by one if lost by others. On the other hand, honor groups are also quite voluntary and egalitarian: the prestige that high-ranked players enjoy is voluntarily given by their rivals and their audience, and that prestige is instantly withdrawn the moment it is decided that it was won dishonorably—even God wouldn't be powerful enough to *coerce* competitive prestige. So are honor-based rankings of competitive prestige competitive and despotic (because prestige is distributed unequally and at the expense of others) or cooperative and egalitarian (because all involved voluntarily compete and bestow their prestige voluntarily)? There seems no sense to be made of the question, because Verhencamp presents us with a false choice. It is an abuse of the notion of "despotism" to think that Roger Federer, even in his prime, was a despot in the world of tennis simply because he had more prestige and won it competitively. Whereas authoritarian despots *compel*, honorable winners *attract*, their benefits.

I am not the first to note the important distinction between rankings of prestige and rankings of dominance. For instance, in a widely cited article, psychologists Joseph Henrich and Francisco Gil-White distinguish between prestige, which for them concerns ranks based on attraction, and dominance rankings, which are based on "agonism" or "force."[12] Prestige rankings for Henrich and Gil-White are based upon some excellence; and our attending to the excellent, high-status people is adaptive, they speculate, since this process helps us transmit important cultural knowledge. Their way of carving things up is revealed by an instructive example:

> In humans . . . status and its prerequisites have often come from *non-agonistic* sources—in particular, from excellence in valued domains of activity, even without any credible claim of superior force. For example, paraplegic physicist Stephen Hawking—widely regarded as Einstein's heir, and current occupier of Newton's chair at Cambridge University—certainly enjoys very high status throughout the world. Those who, like Hawking, achieve high status by excelling in valued domains are often said to have "prestige."[13]

So to Henrich and Gil-White, the enfeebled Hawking couldn't plausibly be said to have won his status agonistically. Rather, he is eminent because he's excellent at what he does. However, in light of the theory advanced above, precisely the reverse is true. Of course Hawking didn't rise to prominence through muscular exploit. But his area of endeavor is physics, not athletics or war, and in the academy excellence is distinguished through *intellectual* competition. Academia is in fact a fiercely competitive realm. As researchers, we must win our share of a limited amount of prestige by taking someone else's ideas down. The more popular and successful the theory we convincingly undermine or (better yet) replace, the better for our status. As professors, we generally do not demand that students agree with us, as happens in authoritarian educational systems, but rather we encourage our students to challenge our ideas and theories. As conference organizers, editors, and reviewers, we take measures to militate against the advantages of "old boy" networks and the disadvantages faced by those we have unconscious biases against. Moreover, the proliferation of grants and prizes is so extraordinary that the day-to-day labors of teaching and research often take a backseat to work created by those competitions. The competitiveness we observe at the professorial level is writ large on the level of our universities: the only measure of success for any dean, provost, chancellor, or college president is how well their "peer institutions" are doing, against whom schools compete for students, government and private funding, talent, and college rankings. *This* is the milieu in which Hawking rose to eminence. So to claim that Hawking gained his status non-agonistically is gravely mistaken.

That said, there is much to recommend Henrich and Gil-White's distinction. Certainly it is the case that prestige can be gained non-competitively, as it is with Indian castes. And even excellence itself can garner prestige non-competitively: the prestige of being musical may well encourage young people to become musicians. So I have no dispute with their claim that mere prestige may promote cultural transmission of successful practices. My point is that there are *agonistic* prestige-based rankings, and these agonistic rankings are nonetheless very much to be distinguished from the sort of strongman, authoritarian-style rankings that Henrich and Gil-White wish to separate from prestige-based ones. Their basic misunderstanding, as their example of Hawking reveals, is that they take "agonism" to include "aggression, intimidation, violence, etc."[14] But lumping agonism together with other sorts of violence is an abuse of the term. The focal meaning of the agon is a contest of equals, not just any old exertion of force, much less that of bullying aggression or enforced control of inferiors (even biologists, who are somewhat promiscuous with the term, won't refer to predation as "agonistic"). Whether the contest is physical or not isn't important—from the time of the Greeks we have used "agon" to describe non-physical contests, too. Hopefully, the account of the honor ethos offered here makes it clear that even a mild-mannered academic such as Hawking lives by a code that is structurally the same as the warrior's: both seek prestige through competitive excellence, both understand that this excellence can be revealed only through fair contests, and both seek from their high status not domination but recognition of their deserved place in the competitive ranking.

In summary, then, individuals in authoritarian hierarchies are connected by control, responsibility, and obedience. Individuals in contests for competitive prestige have no such ties, but are responsible for ensuring that the ranking reflects true competitive excellence. Prominent among the duties entailed by this overarching obligation is an imperative to compete fairly.

HONOR-TYPICAL BEHAVIOR IN ANIMALS

The authority- and honor-based models of rank described above are ideal types. Real cultures and real people are messy, and any particular human ranking will be influenced by a host of quirky historical and environmental factors, including factors that resist rankings altogether, as egalitarian tendencies do. There might even be *additional* normative systems suited for other sorts of rankings, for all we have said. Nonetheless, these two normative systems of honor and authority exert a considerable pull in our disassociated moral minds, and paradigmatic examples of each manifest themselves in the right contexts. Corporations, governments, and modern militaries are good places to look for authoritarianism. Warrior castes, athletics, and "competitive" academic institutions are good places to look for honor-typical behaviors. For various reasons, these subcultures create ecologies that make such systems likely. Might there be ecologies in non-human nature that are also conducive to authoritarian and honor-typical behaviors?

Chimpanzee Authoritarianism

Male chimpanzees present us with perhaps our best, but still a very imperfect, example of animal authoritarianism. Generalities are dangerous here. Chimpanzees are highly intelligent creatures with distinct personalities. And there are behavioral differences even among troops of them.[15]

Furthermore, different males will pursue different strategies in negotiating their local hierarchy: for instance, some alphas—and, it has been suggested, the smaller ones—employ a softer leadership style, which includes lots of grooming of the lower orders, whereas others—and perhaps the biggest alphas—use a more domineering approach.[16] Nonetheless, a composite picture of chimpanzee males suggests a somewhat authoritarian social structure.

Male chimpanzee rankings are decided by challenges, but these challenges are not completely predictable or rigidly ritualized. Challenging aggression is usually premeditated (a male might heft a stone before his target even appears), and is typically not a one-off action but part of a sustained effort to dominate the targeted male.[17] Males cannot achieve the highest ranks without forming alliances with other males and without gaining the support of females: indeed, chimpanzee dominance hierarchies are not well ordered in part because A may dominate B if allies are around, whereas B may dominate A in isolation.[18] Alphas sensing a troublesome alliance may form "alliance breaking" coalitions of their own, with lieutenants who not only help them physically coerce lower-ranked males but even alert them to potential upstarts.

When squabbles erupt among low-ranked individuals, alphas often play the populist and support the weaker of the two belligerents ("loser support"), and this is thought to help cement their status with the troop. On the other hand, social-climbing young challengers tend to adopt a "winner support" strategy, presumably to gain powerful allies in their future bid for supremacy. Generally, pacification behavior is seen as part of a "control role" that attaches to high status, and a clever male sometimes interferes with a rival's attempts to break up squabbles, as if challenging the rival's right to interfere. It is possible that the troop understands the political implications of all these behaviors and assesses the dominance ambitions and skills of males performing them.[19] For instance, Frans de Waal describes how an aspiring male, Luit, abused females in the presence of the dominant Yeoren, as if to demonstrate to the females that Yeoren was unable to protect them. When Luit became dominant, his behavior changed and he became a protector of the females.[20] In human terms, the idea would be that an ideal alpha doesn't so much *equalize* the weak and the strong as *protect* the weak against the excessive abuses of the strong.[21] Furthermore, he claims the right to do so solely for himself; so if another male successfully lobbies for grassroots support, he is in essence declaring himself to be the true alpha.

Chimpanzees have a variety of ways to communicate deference to dominant individuals, including special grunts, postures, and patterns of approach and avoidance. But for some alphas, the usual amount of dominance is not enough. Researchers routinely describe some alphas as "bullies," "brutes," "thugs," or "disagreeable" and "nasty."[22] And some researchers claim that particularly despotic alphas, who are selfish groomers and rule by terror, are deposed by subordinates more quickly and violently than average.[23] These moralistic evaluations are significant to the question of beastly morality, for they indicate a sense among researchers of the role a chimpanzee alpha is "supposed" to play. For instance, Jane Goodall is reported to have remarked to attendees at a leadership conference that chimpanzee "tyrants" last about two years, whereas a "real chimpanzee leader" lasts about ten years. This is because a leader "is one who leads because the others respect him and want to follow him. If he sets off on a boundary patrol the others will follow because they want to. Whereas if the tyrant sets off the others won't follow on boundary patrol because they don't like him very much."[24]

De Waal contrasts chimpanzee alphas with the much more despotic baboon and rhesus monkey alphas, observing that whereas most chimpanzee males take sides when they interfere in squabbles, those assuming a control role (and thus perhaps taking on the mantle of an alpha) are "impartial" and, as it were, "place themselves *above* the conflicting parties" (emphasis in the original). These observations lead de Waal to ruminate on a sort of egalitarianism among chimpanzees, insofar as these more "impartial" interventions—even to the point of favoring the weaker parties—may serve to level the hierarchy below an alpha, thus creating a "gap" between him and possible rivals. Moreover, the benefits of this populist strategy aren't to be despised by those at the bottom rungs.[25] An individual behaving in this authoritative but non-despotic way is in some sense an ideal chimpanzee alpha.

So although chimpanzee behavior presents us with an imperfect analogue to authoritarianism as described above, we do see some aspects of authoritarianism in their societies. Chimpanzees sort themselves into rankings, and those rankings come with control of those below. This control isn't brute domination, but has something like a primitively pastoral or "leadership" quality to it. Low-ranking chimpanzees expect and demand something from their dominants, and overweening alphas who rule by force alone pay a heavy price when, during a challenge to their reign, the lower orders of the troop turn on them. Coalition forming is rampant in conflicts; and in both intra- and inter-tribal conflict, we see no inkling whatsoever of a "fair fight" sensibility in these, our closest relatives.[26] Instead, we see a scheming, opportunistic, guileful "politicking" that is a credit to the social intelligence of the species, but hardly anything we would call noble or honorable. This is not to condemn chimpanzees morally, of course. Plausibly, all this strategizing and coalition building is a good way to select for alphas who will themselves be sensitive to the needs, interests, motives, and personalities of the troop they are to dominate.[27] Nonetheless, we will have to look elsewhere for beastly honor as such.

Honor-Typical Behavior in Nonhumans

But where? Well, given the theory of honor described above, we should start off by looking for honor-typical behavior in species where rank

(a) is fought for;
(b) is fought for "fairly"; and
(c) is not correlated with responsibility or control.

"Fair fighting" is somewhat common among "tournament species," or species in which a small number of males do most of the mating and their mating access is determined by their success in male-male competitions influenced, to some extent, by female choice.[28] This mating pattern creates highly dimorphic, ornamented, and weaponized males. For instance, elephant seals are a paradigmatic tournament species. They are highly sexually dimorphic, with males often four times the size of females. This is because bull size is highly correlated with sexual success, given that the most dominant "beachmasters" control the best stretches of beach and the largest harems, while smaller males lurk around the periphery, lucky to sneak in some sex here and there. And their male-male competition behavior—in which they rear up and smash themselves down against each other in a particularly ungainly form of combat—is as iconic an example of fair fighting in the animal kingdom as any. Elephant seal fights are fair because we do not see multiple bulls joining together to oust a more dominant male. The fights are also fair because challengers engage beachmasters only if they feel up to it. Thus, actual encounters between elephant seal bulls pit males of roughly equal size against each other. Finally, dominant elephant seals do not stand in any control relationship to the smaller males they fight off.[29] So are elephant seals demonstrative of honor-typical behavior?

No. Although elephant seal bulls are one of the species delimited by criteria (a)–(c) above, they do not present an ideal instance of honor-typical behavior because there is a strong element of "resource defense" in their mating system. Bulls arrive on the rookery before cows, and they fight to establish their dominance on the beaches that are most attractive to prospective mates (they also fight more often on breeding beaches than on non-breeding beaches). Once the cows arrive, bulls aspire to defend their stretch of beach against encroaching males. Granted, cows have a great deal to say about whom they mate with: they are more sexually receptive to dominant males, they are particularly receptive to bulls who have just won encounters, and they even alert dominant bulls if they are being mounted by a lesser male. So it may be that females are receptive to bulls who can maintain a beach not only because they dominate the *beach*, but because they *dominate*, period.[30] Nonetheless, the sexual success of bulls is substantially influenced by their ability to control an area that females want. According to our theory of honor, however, pure competitive prestige is about being attractive for what you *are*, given your victories in fair contests, not for what you will *provide* for your admirer. So we should add to (a)–(c) that we're looking for species for whom

(d) contestants are desirable because they defeat rivals, not because they dominate resources.

Criterion (d) thus directs our attention to species with "non-resource-based" mating strategies—that is, species for whom the competing sex provides nothing useful to the choosy sex except their gametes. The prime examples of such species are those in which males gather together in a lek, or grouping for the purposes of competitive display. (Pleasingly, the biological term "lek" is shortened from the Swedish *lek-ställe*, which literally means "sport-place," "playground," or "playing field.") Some grouse species, for instance, gather together in the spring to strut, vocalize, and fight "fairly" under the watchful gaze of highly selective females (10 percent of the males account for 80 percent of the matings).[31] Males provide nothing to the females other than their desirable genes. The exact cause of male desirability in species with non-resource-based mating systems is not fully understood. It may be that highly ornamented and weaponized males prove their genetic hardiness by surviving despite the extra costs of their ornamentation, which makes them easy targets to predators.[32] Or perhaps certain traits are attractive because they reveal a resistance to parasites.[33] It may also be that the trait is attractive to females precisely *because* it is attractive to females, making the prospect of having "sexy sons" from this male highly advantageous for a picky female.[34]

Various deer species also provide an excellent example of honor-typical behavior in nonhumans. As with grouse, in red deer we have a highly dimorphic, polygynous species with males who do not care for offspring or provide resources for females. Stags compete for harems through overt agonistic contests (locking horns), which explains their weaponry as well as their size dimorphism. And although stags do try to "herd" hinds into their harems, it would be an exaggeration to say that females do not have any say in the matter: females are attracted to dominant stag roars, and can escape one harem for another if they wish to.[35] During the rut, stags size each other up through roars and parallel walking rituals. Often, a prospective challenger realizes that he's bitten off more than he can chew, and trots off. But when he feels his chances are good enough, he will lock horns and battle things out in sometimes deadly encounters. Stags will challenge males who are only slightly higher-ranked than themselves, since this strategy strikes the ideal balance between risk and reward (fighting a much higher-ranked male is too risky, and defeating a roughly equally-ranked or lower-ranked male is not advantageous enough): animal equivalents of the "Rank Ambition" and "Rank Humility" principles.[36] It is also worth noting that when it comes to actual fights, stags clearly pass up opportunities to gore or kick their antagonists. Since stags do gouge and kick predators when they can, it doesn't seem as though this "fair fight" behavior with other stags is attributable to their being too unintelligent to realize the deadliness of their antlers or hooves. For instance, on one BBC video, a stag named Percy returns from an expedition to round up more females only to find a challenger, Titus, roaring right amidst his (Percy's) harem. As Percy charges, Titus's flanks are plainly exposed, but Percy trots *around* to Titus's front and locks horns with him in furious encounter. After about a minute, the two disengage and roar, parallel walk, and Titus retreats.[37]

Fallow deer present us with an even more interesting case of honor-typical behavior in animals. Fallow stags use two mating strategies. During the rut, some males use a resource defense strategy, and try to dominate large territories on the edges of glades with oak trees whose acorns does find desirable. But the stronger stags tend to form leks in the center of a rutting area that offer negligible benefits to females in terms of resources. However, females are more attracted to the lek, and greatly prefer mating with dominant lekking males. Thus the weaker males engage in a low-risk, low-reward strategy that may earn them a small number of copulations, whereas lekking males pursue a high-risk, high-reward strategy by fighting things out in the lek. For females, the lek provides a chance to efficiently evaluate males, but this choosiness is of course to be balanced against the costs of mating with males in areas that offer more resources.[38]

So in some grouse and deer species we have good analogues to honor-typical behavior in humans. As with chimpanzees, these animals create ranks and are acutely sensitive to who's stronger and weaker. Yet unlike chimpanzees, these creatures settle rank through "fair fights," even though they are physically capable of injuring opponents in other ways. Furthermore, it is highly probable that these victories serve to impress mobile, choosy females looking less for resources or protection than they are an excellent genetic contribution. Finally, these males take on no responsibility or control role by rising up the ranks.

Thus, whether we are speaking of animals or humans, it is plausible that certain sorts of ecologies promote authoritarian and honor-typical behaviors. Sometimes leadership is beneficial: when a group of highly social individuals with various interests need to coalesce for some reason, for instance. In that case, it makes sense to select popular and dominant individuals as leaders, since they are more likely to do a good job of satisfying or shaping the desires of the fractious group. Democratic election is one way to select such individuals. Another way is to create a system that promotes ambitious, charismatic, effective coalition builders (which self-made monarchs—and chimpanzee alphas—are). On the other hand, sometimes we're not looking for a leader, but we want to know who's best at something. Maybe we want to know which musician to make first chair. Or maybe we need advice about global warming, and need to know who the best climatologists are. Or maybe we enjoy some sport, and we can't help wondering who is best at it. Or maybe we want to know who will provide us with the healthiest offspring or the sexiest sons. In such cases we need competitive mechanisms to sort out who's best. Admittedly, this process does weed out some excellent individuals who are simply poor competitors—we all know immensely talented and capable people who could not handle the competitive aspects of their excellence's corresponding "game." But our need for objective proof of excellence forces us to use competitive success as the measure of even non-competitive excellence. Since the results of those contests illuminate the desired quality—i.e., are what biologists call "honest signals"—only if the contests are fair, we have a vested interest in ensuring fairness and condemning cheaters (see Bekoff, chapter 7 in this volume).

AGENCY AND MORAL MULTIPLICITY

Some sort of moral pluralism—at least on the psychological level—is increasingly probable: a recent "consensus statement" by a number of empirically informed moral psychologists affirms Jonathan Haidt's hypothesis that there are multiple building blocks of morality, each with its own evolutionary history.[39] On a version of this view I favor, there are multiple normative systems, each consisting of distinct principles and justified by different values. There may be a value we call *justice*, which validates an ethos that sees rightness in terms of cooperation and wrongness in terms of free-riding, and which legitimizes punishments designed to correct distortions to the distribution of the extra benefit gained by cooperating.[40] There may be a value we call *purity*, which justifies an ethos that sees rightness in terms of purity and wrongness in terms of contamination, and which legitimizes cleansing punishments, such as exile.[41] As seen above, there seem to be values of *authority* and *honor*, with their codes and characteristic punishments surveyed above. And so forth—how many of these moral systems influence human behavior is an open question.

Multiplicity

If this picture is correct, then our twentieth-century talk of "moral intuitions," "moral principles," and "moral judgments" is too coarse-grained, and in some contexts should be replaced with more-informative language along the lines of "honor intuitions," "principles of justice," and "purity judgments." And, apropos to the theme of this book, similar thoughts apply to "moral agency": it will be possible and advisable in many discussions to be more specific about what sort of moral agency we're talking about, so we should sometimes speak of *justice*-agency, *authority*-agency, *honor*-agency, and so on.

The multiplicity of moral systems complicates the question of whether an animal is a "moral agent." To see why, consider how most authors sympathetic to animal moral agency put forth heartwarming cases of animals acting kindly. A widely discussed instance is that of the self-sacrificing behavior of some captive macaques who preferred to go hungry rather than see an unrelated conspecific, sitting behind a one-way mirror, suffer from electrical shocks (macaques who had themselves been shocked were even more averse to being fed at the expense of the other's suffering).[42] We are moved by stories of elephants mourning dead loved ones, and accounts of dolphins who nudge weakened swimmers to the surface (recently, researchers filmed a handful of long-beaked common dolphins forming a "raft" to keep a paralyzed podmate afloat for hours before she finally succumbed).[43] Perhaps these are cases of "care-agency." However, there is no a priori reason to think that an individual who is agentive in one respect will be agentive in all respects. For example, de Waal's comments about "competent" male alphas who can stop a fight by "raising an eyebrow or with a single step forward" might suggest authority-agency in such individuals (holding fixed your favored view of what agency requires), but in and of itself such behavior gives us little indication of a caring agent.[44] So even if some nonhumans pass the threshold of "moral" agency because they are moral agents in certain ways, it is quite possible that these individuals lack other sorts of moral agency. In some cases, this moral inability results from lack of training or other environmental contingency. But in most cases the absence of some particular sort of agency is due to the makeup of the individual animal. If we magically made the asocial and non-maternal squid as intelligent as ourselves, surely it would nonetheless be hopeless as a caretaker, leader, and competitor, and it would be silly to blame intelligent squid for these qualities.

Thus, since moral agency may be realized in some moral modes but not others, we must keep distinct the qualities making an individual a moral agent generally from those making one an agent in some particular moral respect. Not everyone is as fastidious at separating the general conditions of moral agency from particular moral capabilities. For instance, in his discussion of animals and morality, de Waal writes at one point that "evolution has produced the prerequisites for morality: a tendency to develop social norms and enforce them, the capacities of *empathy* and *sympathy*, *mutual aid* and a sense of *fairness*, the mechanisms for *conflict resolution*, and so on."[45] De Waal is certainly not alone in thinking that the roots of human morality are to be seen in proto-moral qualities of caring and cooperative behavior in animals.[46] And in an important early essay on animal agency, philosopher Lawrence Johnson concludes that "in general, a being acts as a moral agent when it respects the interests of (some) others as well as, or to some degree, in preference to its own."[47] But it does not seem that honor (or, for that matter, authority) requires empathy, sympathy, mutual aid, or altruism. And it doesn't seem that altruism or authority requires fairness. So if creatures must have all these qualities to be agents, then no matter how intelligent and morally conscientious they are otherwise, they won't be moral agents if they lack any of these particular capacities. This strikes me as implausible. Take the case of honor-agency. *Star Trek*'s Klingons may serve as a thought experiment here: an intelligent species whose defining characteristic is their innate love of honor and its agonistic norms, but who have trouble understanding and abiding by "human" (read: Starfleet) norms, which are biased in favor of altruism and cooperation. Klingons are certainly agents. And although they lack agency in some moral respects (let us grant), they doubtless are honor-agents. In at least this way they are moral agents. Therefore sympathy, an interest in giving mutual aid, altruism, etc., are not necessary to moral agency.

Honor as a Moral Value

Of course, this argument assumes that honor is a *moral* value. Philosophers are divided on the question of whether honor is a moral quality, and I cannot make the full case for that assumption here.[48] Nonetheless, a few words on the moral status of honor should be sufficient for establishing the plausibility of the claim.

First, it is worth noting that the etymology of our words for moral praise—*virtus* (literally, "manliness") and *arête* (something akin to battlefield excellence)—testify to the widespread notion among pagan Europeans, at least, that agonistic qualities were once centrally important to our fundamental appraisals of people. We may have improved our notions of what is centrally important, of course. But progress in figuring out *what really matters morally* (a substantive normative discovery) is a different thing from progress in *what it means for something to matter morally* (a meta-normative, or formal, discovery).

Also worth thinking about is whether honor-psychology satisfies mainstream formal criteria of "moral" phenomena. We should be impressed by the way honor's demands are seen by many (sub)cultures as "trumping" all other concerns, as demonstrated by the shocking sacrifices that honor adherents, such as Captain Broke, are prepared to make. The nature of these sacrifices also suggests that duties of honor are being interpreted in a disinterested way: recall Broke's commitment to fight fairly with Lawrence under terms that Lawrence also would find acceptable—Broke was hardly "making an exception of himself." Furthermore, the honor ethos also portrays honor's principles as universally binding and inescapable. In his letter to Lawrence, Broke graciously apologized on behalf of Commodore Rogers for the latter's refusal to meet Broke on even terms, the suggestion being that Rogers's slipping out of Boston harbor under fog risked violating the "No Ducking" rule. Rogers didn't have the option, in Broke's mind at least, of simply rejecting the norms of honor.[49] Finally, honor's principles are certainly social, insofar as they regulate the social interactions, and they are practical, insofar as they claim to norm actions. So honor's principles are treated as trumping, universal, impartial, social, and practical.

These five qualities aren't sufficient for honor's principles to count as *in fact* moral: moral norms must also be reasonable—there must be some *reason* to follow a moral rule. Some readers will find competitive prestige to be valuable, and some won't. The latter group may reject the honor ethos because they find it otiose, given the irrelevance of competitive prestige or prestige generally. But most readers will grant that competitive prestige *is* valuable; indeed, few readers who are honest with themselves will find that they do not strive greatly for it, and I trust these readers will have a difficult time finding fault with honor's principles for distributing it.

Doubts might linger, of course: many audiences reject honor because the examples I and other scholars give of honor-typical behavior—duels, medieval tournaments, tribal contests, athletics—smacks of an ethically toxic brew of masculinism, bellicosity, aggressiveness, and inegalitarianism. Certainly my discussion of honor-typical behavior in strutting male grouse and sexually frustrated stags battling to impress females will do little to mitigate these concerns. Nonetheless, audiences who find honor bewildering or downright nasty must keep in mind two points. First, we must separate what *is* honorable from what people *think* is honorable. I doubt many friends of justice would want to defend ancient or medieval punishments executed for the sake of justice, or the many bad things that continue to be done in our "justice system," including inhumane forms of capital punishment and the widespread prosecution of people for morally permissible acts. So why must a friend of honor be committed to defending the immoral acts done in the name of honor? It is our job as philosophers to help improve humanity's sense of these values, not to dismiss them because of popular misconceptions of what they require. On the other hand—and this is the second point—we must grant the possibility that, even after giving honor a fair hearing, a critic may see no reason to act honorably in her pursuit of competitive prestige. After all, honor would not be a *unique* moral system if it was reducible to other moral values; so it stands to reason that if someone is quite (stubbornly?) satisfied with her present set of moral values, she will be bound to reject the addition of honor (or any other value that does not reduce to her preferred set of values). Suppose such a critic is right, and there really is no reason to be honorable. Even so, good philosophical practice nonetheless suggests we avoid begging questions against first-order views—especially against views cherished by large segments of humanity—in advancing formal conditions for the moral realm. Kantians and utilitarians disagree, and their disagreement at least partially reduces to disputes over what is reasonable or not. But each must concede that both sides are advancing *moral* theories, and thus each side must characterize the "moral" so as not to beg the question against the other. The same lesson applies to formulations of "moral agency" vis-à-vis honor.

Happily, most accounts of moral agency do not beg first-order moral questions. Some say an individual A is a moral agent if and only if A can apprehend moral reasons, and act accordingly.[50] Some say this is not enough—A must also understand that the moral reasons are *moral* ones, fulfilling the diverse (and contested) criteria for what counts as a specifically "moral" reason.[51] Some offer a much lower standard, according to which A is a moral agent if A merely acts virtuously (where "act" seems to imply voluntariness and the ability to have chosen otherwise).[52] For the purposes of this chapter, I wish to remain uncommitted on the general criteria for moral agency or the question of whether any animals are agents. My contribution is to say what must be added to "beastly" agency (supposing there is such a thing) to get us beastly honorableness.

Beastly Honor

We begin by noting that if one is to have any hope of being honorable, one must be able to identify her *honor group* (among whom it is appropriate for her to compete) and have some sense of the prestige rankings of individuals within that group (including herself). For animals, the honor group may be the conspecific males or females of a certain age and/or locality competing for mates, or perhaps it will be the other dogs at an agility competition. It may be possible to call a creature who is deprived of an honor group "honorable" if she *would* have been honorable if given the opportunity. Nonetheless, such a creature would have been prevented from acting honorably, since honor is (as is justice or authority) a social norm, and cannot be exemplified by isolated individuals. So there may be a third precondition on beastly honorableness: the creature in question must *actually* have the opportunity to negotiate a competitive prestige ranking.

With these preconditions met, we can use the principles of honor discussed earlier to guide our thoughts about what it would take to make an animal honorable. According to "Rank Ambition," the individual should be competitive. Again, by "being competitive" we do not mean the desire to monopolize some resource or to control others, but rather a drive to win. With respect to animals, it is not uncommon to hear horseracing professionals claim this on behalf of some horses. Perhaps the greatest thoroughbred ever, Secretariat, was said by many to be not only markedly intelligent but also keenly competitive. His trainer, Charlie Davis, claimed Secretariat moped after losses early in his career, and

Secretariat's owner Penny Chenery lends some credence to Davis' story. "I do think we humanize the animals we love," admits Chenery. "But Secretariat was like that. After he got beat, he wouldn't come to the webbing (the barrier across the stall door). He wouldn't be consoled, saying, in effect, 'I know I messed up.'" After each of those losses, Davis says he and groom Eddie Sweat knew exactly what to do: Nothing. They let their big horse work things out for himself. "We'd just leave him be the next couple days," Davis explains. But when Secretariat returned to the track to train for his next race, Davis would be ready. "I'd just hold on tight and let him do what he wanted to do," says Davis. "I knew I couldn't hold him. He'd be thinking, 'Now I've got to get this out of my system, and be ready next time.' When Onion beat him in the Whitney he was a mad horse. Mad. And then he came back and set a world record. When Prove Out beat him, I'd say, I know he wants to get big. He'd work fast and I'd say, 'Oh man. Oh, man. They better look out.' And sure enough he went right to the front—and was gone."[53]

Second, the individual should also be averse to challenging weaker parties in his/her/its honor group ("No Bullying"). Stags will challenge only higher-ranked individuals. Stags presumably act this way not because of some commitment to an abstract principle, but ultimately because challenging lower- or equal-ranked males does not benefit their mating prospects enough to risk themselves. It takes only a little imagination, however, to imagine a species that comes to care about competing for prestige for its own sake, even if the roots of that impulse lay in competition for mates. Third, the individual should challenge those just above it in the ranking ("Rank Humility"). As we saw, a red deer stag will challenge only slightly higher-ranked stags because its chances of losing to a much higher-ranked stag are significant enough to make it not worth the danger and effort. And once again, this pattern is a sound strategy not only when it comes to fighting for mates; it also makes sense for any ranking of competitive prestige, since only slightly lower-ranked challengers have proven that they have a plausible claim to some rank.

Fourth, an honorable agent should be receptive to challenges. A sort of desperate courage is common in animals defending their offspring. But the courageousness of an honorable agent arises in part by her refusal to decline a legitimate challenge in a fair fight ("No Ducking"). In ecologies in which we have good evidence for mate choice driving intrasexual competition, there is little possibility of an animal declining legitimate challenges without losing its status. If females of a species use male-male competition as a way to ensure honest signaling of male desirability, then they will ignore males who do not compete at all. Reproduction for most female creatures is far too costly to find charming any male who not only fails to provide resources and protection, but also refuses to prove the quality of his genes. If fights are the mechanism that females of some species have to evaluate the quality of males, then males hoping to mate must agon-ize, literally: they must fight.

Finally, the individual in question must have some sense of the desirability of fair play or fair fights ("Fair Play"). Of all the traits that are characteristic of honor, this is actually the one most commonly observed in nature (see Bekoff, chapter 7 in this volume). Species in which individuals use coalitions to overmaster rivals, such as male lions and chimpanzees, are the exception, not the rule: males (and in species where males care for offspring, females) compete in fair contests in many species of insects, fish, birds, reptiles, and mammals. And if we turn our attention from outright fights to other contests, we find that self-handicapping is a very common element in "agonistic play" across species.[54] "The basic rules for fair play in animals also apply to humans," Marc Bekoff writes, "namely, *ask first, be honest, follow the rules, and admit you're wrong.* When the rules of play are violated, and when fairness breaks down, so does play" (emphasis in the original).[55] So finding animals who play/fight fair is easy. Indeed, the behavior is so ubiquitous that it should be considered honor-typical only when *other* honor-typical behaviors and pressures are present, as we saw in our contrast of male elephant seals and stags.

Any individual creature found to express all five of these behaviors in whatever way we consider to be "agentive" would be honorable. Whether we should say any actual creatures are honor-agents must wait for further philosophical consensus about the nature of moral agency in general, and additional ethological research taking seriously the notion of honor as a distinct normative category.

I will conclude this section with three philosophical observations with respect to ascribing honorableness to animals. First, as with any case of beastly agency, ascribing honor-agency does not mean we can expect or demand that an honorable creature be honorable at all times or in all ways. Its cognitive and affective limitations—like yours or mine—would limit its ability to discern precisely when and how to act honorably. Second, we must not hesitate to identify an animal as honorable just because we morally condemn the aims and violence of the contests in which honor-typical behavior is so often found. Many humans past and present have thought honor *requires* violent contest. But according to the principles advanced above, it does not—I have argued that academic and artistic agonistic practices are perfectly honorable, too. However, honor does *not rule out* violent contests, either. Now it may be morally wrong to engage in violent contests; if this is so, it is because of reasons having nothing to do with honor, and reasons that our imagined creature might not be able to comprehend. So even if a creature were to manifest its honorable behavior in contests that a *more* morally rational creature would reject (as Broke and Lawrence did in the completely unnecessary War of 1812), that fact does not impugn said creature's genuine honorableness in the slightest. Third and finally, we must not infer that an honor-agent has acted wrongly just because it has acted dishonorably, even by its own local or species-based standards, and according to its own (sometimes meager) cognitive limits. This is because the individual may well be acting in response to another type of moral reason, and may have judged (rightly or wrongly) that this non-honor consideration outweighs its honor-based reasons. This point generalizes to any sort of moral condemnation of a creature: an individual might have an inclination to act cooperatively (justly), but may nonetheless act uncooperatively because of a greater kin-altruistic concern. If pluralism is true, the obvious difficulties of morally judging animal behavior are compounded by the challenge of discerning whether an act that failed to respect some sort of moral principle was nonetheless done conscientiously, out of respect for another sort of moral value. The epilogue (chapter 13) in this volume explores such questions, too.

CONCLUSION

Hobbes, himself an important critic of honor and defender of a sort of authoritarianism, wrote that "among men there is a contestation of honour and preferment; among beasts there is none."[56] Hobbes was dead wrong, if by "honor" we mean honor-typical behavior, which is characterized by fair contests for status. Hobbes thought it unreasonable to care about prestige for its own sake, and thus viewed the aristocratic concern for honor as foolish and detrimental to the cause of a "rational" ethic built upon a concern for life and property.[57] Whether competing for prestige is silly for humans is an issue that I have tried to set to one side. But competing for mates is emphatically not a trivial matter for animals, and I have argued that tournament species with non-resource-based mating systems have just the sort of ecology in which we should expect honor-typical behavior, since in such systems there is significant pressure for one sex to compete fairly among its own members in order to attract choosy mates who demand not food, shelter, or paternal investment, but good genes, which are proved by the "honest signal" of victories in fair fights. So in honor, as with other moral values such as justice and care, we observe a remarkable continuity between ourselves and other animals.

NOTES

1. In anthropology, Peristiany and especially Stewart are most influential; see J. G. Peristiany, *Honor and Shame: The Values of Mediterranean Society* (Chicago: University of Chicago Press, 1966); James Henderson Stewart, *Honor* (Chicago: University of Chicago Press, 1994). In political science, I am particularly guided by Laurie Johnson, *Thomas Hobbes: Turning Point for Honor* (Lanham, MD: Rowman and Littlefield,

2009), and Sharon Krause, *Liberalism with Honor* (Cambridge, MA: Harvard University Press, 2002). In intellectual history, see Peter Olsthoorn, *Honor in Moral and Political Philosophy* (Albany: SUNY, 2015); Paul Robinson, *Military Honour and the Conduct of War: From Ancient Greece to Iraq* (Oxford: Routledge, 2006); Bertram Wyatt-Brown, *Southern Honor: Ethics and Behavior in the Old South* (New York: Oxford University Press, 1982/2007); and Wyatt-Brown, *Honor and Violence in the Old South* (New York: Oxford University Press, 1986). In literary studies, see James Bowman, *Honor: A History* (New York: Encounter Books, 2006); George Fenwick Jones, *Honor Bright: Honor in Western Literature* (Savannah: Frederic C. Bell, 2000); William Ian Miller, *Bloodtaking and Peacemaking: Feud, Law, and Society in Saga Iceland* (Chicago: University of Chicago Press, 1990); Miller, *Humiliation* (Ithaca, NY: Cornell University Press, 1993); and Alexander Welsh, *What Is Honor?* (New Haven, CT: Yale University Press, 2008). In foreign affairs, see especially Ned Lebow, *A Cultural Theory of International Relations* (New York: Cambridge University Press, 2009); and Barry O'Neill, *Honor, Symbols, and War* (Ann Arbor: University of Michigan Press, 1999). In cultural psychology and social psychology, the most notable contribution is Richard Nisbett and Dov Cohen, *Culture of Honor: The Psychology of Violence in the South* (Boulder, CO: Westview Press, 1996) (although the account of honor in this chapter differs dramatically from Nisbett and Cohen's: see Dan Demetriou, "What Should Realists Say about Honor Cultures?" *Ethical Theory and Moral Practice* 17, no. 5 (2014): 893–911. Concerning the overlap of honor and economics, see Geoffrey Brennan and Philip Pettit, *The Economy of Esteem* (New York: Oxford University Press, 2004); and Robert Frank, *Choosing the Right Pond: Human Behavior and the Quest for Status* (New York: Oxford University Press, 1985). Discussion by ethicists in the past few decades has been comparatively sparse, but see the following: Kwame Anthony Appiah, *The Honor Code: How Moral Revolutions Happen* (New York: Norton, 2010); Peter Berger, "On the Obsolescence of the Concept of Honor," in *Revisions: Changing Perspective in Moral Philosophy* (Notre Dame, IN: University of Notre Dame Press, 1983); Anthony Cunningham, *Modern Honor* (New York: Routledge, 2013); Dan Demetriou, "Honor War Theory: Romance or Reality," *Philosophical Papers* 42, no. 3 (2013): 285–303; Demetriou, "The Virtues of Honorable Business Executives," in *Virtues in Action: New Essays in Applied Ethics*, ed. M. Austin (New York: Palgrave Macmillan, 2013); Shannon French, *Code of the Warrior* (Lanham, MD: Rowman and Littlefield, 2003; Lad Sessions, *Honor for Us* (New York: Continuum, 2010).

2. Brennan and Pettit, *The Economy of Esteem*; Olsthoorn, *Honor in Moral and Political Philosophy*.

3. Appiah, *The Honor Code*; Stewart, *Honor*.

4. Jonathan Haidt and Jesse Graham, "When Morality Opposes Justice: Conservatives Have Moral Intuitions That Liberals May Not Recognize," *Social Justice Research* 20, no. 1 (2007): 105.

5. O. Patterson, *Slavery and Social Death* (Cambridge, MA: Harvard University Press, 1982).

6. Appiah, *The Honor Code*; Allan Gibbard, *Wise Choices, Apt Feelings* (Cambridge, MA: Harvard University Press, 1990), 138–39.

7. Johan Huizinga, *Homo Ludens* (Boston: Beacon, 1950).

8. Ibid., 50.

9. Sandra Vehrencamp's "A Model for the Evolution of Despotic versus Egalitarian Societies," *Animal Behavior* 31 (1983): 667–82, is made much use of by the in-turn

very influential Christopher Boehm, *Hierarchy in the Forest* (Cambridge, MA: Harvard University Press, 1999), which in turn has influenced Jonathan Haidt, *The Righteous Mind* (New York: Pantheon, 2012).

10. Vehrencamp, "A Model for the Evolution of Despotic versus Egalitarian Societies."

11. Ibid., 667.

12. Joseph Henrich and Francisco Gil-White, "The Evolution of Prestige: Freely Conferred Deference as a Mechanism for Enhancing the Benefits of Cultural Transmission," *Evolution and Human Behavior* (2001): 165–96.

13. Ibid., 167 (emphasis added).

14. Ibid., 160.

15. Christopher Boesch, "Cooperative Hunting Roles among Taï Chimpanzees," *Human Nature* 13, no. 1 (2002): 27–46.

16. M. W. Foster, I. C. Gilby, C. M. Murray, A. Johnson, E. E. Wroblewski, and A. E. Pusey, "Alpha Male Chimpanzee Grooming Patterns: Implications for Dominance, 'Style,'" *American Journal of Primatology* 71 (2009): 136–44.

17. Jane Goodall, *The Chimpanzees of Gombe: Patterns of Behavior* (Cambridge, MA: Harvard University Press, 1986), 324–25.

18. Ibid., 409–10.

19. Frans de Waal, "Sex Differences in the Formation of Coalitions among Chimpanzees," *Ethology and Sociobiology* 5 (1984): 239–55.

20. Frans de Waal, *Chimpanzee Politics* (Baltimore: Johns Hopkins University Press, 1982/2007), 118.

21. Frans de Waal, *Good Natured: The Origins of Right and Wrong in Humans and Other Animals* (Cambridge, MA: Harvard University Press, 1996), 130–31.

22. Steve Ladd, "Pimu's Murder," *Vimeo* video, 4:10, April 16, 2012, http://vimeo.com/40444106; Mike Wilson, Jane Goodall Institute, "Reflections from Gombe," last modified July 8, 2010, accessed September 3, 2014, http://www.janegoodall.org/gombe50/reflections/mike-wilson.

23. De Waal, *Good Natured*, 132.

24. Caitlin Fitzsimmons, "Leading through Human Instincts," *CIO*, August 8, 2011, http://www.cio.com.au/article/396365/leading_through_human_instincts/?.

25. De Waal, *Good Natured*, 129.

26. Goodall, *The Chimpanzees of Gombe*, chap. 17.

27. As was suggested at least as early as T. Nishida, "Alpha Status and Agonistic Alliance in Wild Chimpanzees," *Primates* 24, no. 3 (1983): 318–36.

28. Robert Sapolsky, "Human Behavioral Biology: Behavioral Evolution," YouTube video, 1:36:56, posted by "Stanford University," March 31, 2010, http://www.youtube.com/watch?v=Y0Oa4Lp5fLE.

29. Burney Le Boeuf, "Male-Male Competition and Reproductive Success in Elephant Seals," *American Zoologist* 14 (1974): 163–76; Burney Le Boeuf and Richard Laws, "Elephant Seals: An Introduction to the Species," in *Elephant Seals: Population Ecology, Behavior, and Physiology*, ed. Burney Le Boeuf and Richard Laws (Berkeley: University of California Press, 1994).

30. Cathleen Cox, "Agonistic Encounters among Male Elephant Seals: Frequency, Context, and the Role of Female Preference," *American Zoologist* 21 (1981): 197–209.

31. Sandra Vehrencamp, Jack Bradbury, and Robert Gibson, "The Energetic Cost of Display in Male Sage Grouse," *Animal Behaviour* 38, no. 5 (1989): 885–96.

32. Amotz Zahavi, "Mate Selection: A Selection for a Handicap," *Journal of Theoretical Biology* 53, no.1 (1975): 205–14.

33. W. D. Hamilton and M. Zuk, "Heritable True Fitness and Bright Birds: A Role for Parasites?," *Science* 218 (1982): 384–87.

34. P. J. Weatherhead and R. J. Robertson, "Offspring Quality and the Polygyny Threshold: 'The Sexy Son Hypothesis,'" *American Naturalist* 113, no. 2 (1979): 201–8.

35. Karen McComb, "Female Choice for High Roaring Rate in Red Deer," *Animal Behavior* 41 (1991): 79–88; Benjamin Charlton, David Reby, and Karen McComb, "Female Red Deer Prefer the Roars of Larger Males," *Biological Letters* 3, no. 4 (2007): 382–85; T. H. Clutton-Brock, F. E. Guinness, and S. D. Albon, *Red Deer Behaviour and Ecology of Two Sexes* (Chicago: University of Chicago Press, 1982); David Reby, Mark Hewison, Marta Izquierdo, and Dominique Pépin, "Red Deer (*Cervus elaphus*) Hinds Discriminate Between the Roars of Their Current Harem-Holder Stag and Those of Neighbouring Stags," *Ethology* 107 (2001): 951–59.

36. Linton Freeman, Sue Freeman, and Kimball Romney, "The Implications of Social Structure for Dominance Hierarchies in Red Deer," *Animal Behavior* 44 (1992): 239–45.

37. Matt Walker, "Stags Locked in 'Moral Combat,'" *BBC Earth News* video, 2:00, October 6, 2009, http://news.bbc.co.uk/earth/hi/earth_news/newsid_8291000/8291710.stm.

38. T. H. Clutton-Brock, D. Green, M. Hiraiwa-Hasegawa, and S. D. Albon, "Passing the Buck: Resource Defence, Lek Breeding, and Mate Choice in Fallow Deer," *Behavioral Ecology and Sociobiology* 23, no. 5 (1988): 281–96.

39. Roy Baumeister, Paul Bloom, Joshua Greene, Jonathan Haidt, Sam Harris, Joshua Knobe, and David Pizarro, "Consensus Statement: A Statement of Consensus Reached among Participants at the 'Edge: The New Science of Morality' Conference," Edge. rg (2010), http://www.edge.org/3rd_culture/morality10/morality_consensus .html; Haidt, *The Righteous Mind*.

40. John Rawls, *A Theory of Justice* (Cambridge, MA: Harvard University Press, 1971); R. L. Trivers, "The Evolution of Reciprocal Altruism," *Quarterly Review of Biology* 46 (1971): 35–57.

41. Dan Demetriou, "There's Some Fetish in Your Ethics: A Limited Defense of Purity Reasoning," *Journal of Philosophical Research* 38 (2013): 377–404; Daniel Kelly, *Yuck! The Nature and Moral Significance of Disgust* (Cambridge, MA: MIT Press, 2011); Alexandra Plakias, "The Good and the Gross," *Ethical Theory and Moral Practice* 16, no. 2 (2013): 261–78; Paul Rozin, Linda Millman, and Carol Nemeroff, "Operation of the Laws of Sympathetic Magic in Disgust and Other Domains," *Journal of Personality and Social Psychology* 50 (1986): 703–12.

42. Stanley Wechkin, J. H. Masserman, and W. Terris, "Shock to a Conspecific as an Aversive Stimulus," *Psychonomic Science* 1, no. 2 (1964): 47–48.

43. Michael Marshall, "Dolphins Form Life Raft to Help Dying Friend," *New Scientist* (January 25, 2013), http://www.newscientist.com/article/dn23108-dolphins -form-life-raft-to-help-dying-friend.html#.UeF4odJOTng.

44. De Waal, *Good Natured*, 128.

45. Ibid., 39 (emphasis added).

46. For a survey of the topic, see Richard Joyce, *The Evolution of Morality* (Cambridge, MA: MIT Press, 2007).

47. Lawrence Johnson, "Can Animals Be Moral Agents?," *Ethics and Animals* 4 (1983): 50–61.

48. Appiah, *The Honor Code*; Steve Gerrard, "Morality and Codes of Honour," *Philosophy* 69, no. 267 (1994): 69–84; Sessions, *Honor for Us*.

49. Sometimes it is said that honor cannot be moral because its prescriptions are not universal (cf. Sessions, *Honor for Us*, chap. 4). I think this mistakes local conventions that help fix what is expected in some community with the general and abstract principles of honor. What matters is that honor adherents generally expect others to be honorable too, in exact parallel to how we expect everyone to be just, even though we recognize that local conventions help determine whether or not a particular action is just.

50. Evelyn Pluhar, *Beyond Prejudice: The Moral Significance of Human and Nonhuman Animals* (Durham, NC: Duke University Press, 1995).

51. Immanuel Kant, *Foundations of the Metaphysics of Morals*, trans. L. Beck, 2nd ed. (Upper Saddle River, NJ: Prentice Hall, 1997).

52. Paul Shapiro, "Moral Agency in Other Animals," *Theoretical Medicine and Bioethics* 27 (2006): 357–73.

53. Bill Doolittle, "Secretariat: Super Genius," Secretariat.com, http://www.secretariat.com/fan-club/writers-forum/secretariat-super-genius/, n.d.

54. Marc Bekoff, *Animals at Play: Rules of the Game* (Philadelphia, PA: Temple University Press, 2008).

55. Marc Bekoff, "The Need for 'Wild' Play: Let Children Be the Animals They Need to Be," *Psychology Today Blog*, February 25, 2012, http://www.psychologytoday.com/blog/animal-emotions/201202/the-need-wild-play-let-children-be-the-animals-they-need-be.

56. Thomas Hobbes, *Man and Citizen*, ed. B. Gert (Indianapolis, IN: Hackett, 1991).

57. Johnson, *Thomas Hobbes*.

Part Three **Reading Animal Morality**

Nine Reading, Teaching Insects

ANT SOCIETY AS PEDAGOGICAL DEVICE IN RABBINIC LITERATURE

Harrison King

WHEN IT COMES TO INSECTS, we remain awkward. What is it about these creeping things that bugs us?

In cultural productions of both ancient and contemporary civilizations, insects often represent that which is radically other and, therefore, unsettling, even grotesque. They are, in this sense, some loathsome intrusion discussed with disgust; we are inclined to smash, swat, and exterminate them with impunity, or failing that, draw away from them. Yet the spatial and behavioral proximity of human and insect bodies constantly undermines any attempt to ignore these entomological others or avoid contact with them. This closeness is most clearly reflected in the vocabulary commonly employed to describe some eusocial species: queen, colony, worker, soldier—a cluster of words we casually apply to nonhuman bodies that nevertheless have clear referents in human behavior and relationships. Further, recent scientific research has shed light upon the complex moral behavior of many insects, concluding, for example, that ants demonstrate a remarkable capacity to learn from individual experience, recognize the identities of others, and communicate with and teach one another.[1] Thus, a dialectical image emerges in which insects are transfixing in their otherness, arresting in their beautiful strangeness—otherness and strangeness in which we might glimpse a reflection of our uncertain gaze, of our inability to comprehend ourselves, much less another form of life.

This dialectical image of aversion and fascination helps explain the wide rhetorical range of insect metaphors. From the expressly political to the intensely personal, the insect can serve as the terminal reduction, the deleterious inhumanity that remains when the gift of humanity itself is rubbed off, stripped away.[2] At the same time, the eusocial insect in particular can be fashioned into the instrumentalized object of didactic or pedagogical discourse: ancient and contemporary authors alike have modeled human behavior and technological innovation with reference to insect society.[3]

Surely the rhetorical diversity noted here derives in part from the nearly unimaginable diversity of the biological class Insecta, which, after all, includes both butterflies and mosquitoes.[4] Yet even in limiting one's focus to an individual species, such as the ant, one observes the same ambiguities in representation.[5] Two familiar examples drawn from cinema will illustrate this. On the one hand, *A Bug's Life* (1998), an animated film produced by Pixar, plays with the many similarities between human and ant social organization to structure an idealistic tale about collective action overcoming oppression and exploitation. The use of cute anthropomorphized ants heightens the film's affective power and renders the story easily accessible to a broad audience that includes both children and adults. On the other hand, insects form an important visual motif in David Lynch's *Blue Velvet* (1986), including the memorable, Daliesque image of many ants crawling upon a severed human ear in a grassy vacant lot. Here, the relentless, ravenous insects in their writhing masses expose the viewer to the falseness of Reagan-era suburbia and its edenic promises. Each film inscribes a distinct rhetoric of ant-ness; indeed, both place a great deal of symbolic weight upon those chitinous bodies, which are, of course, well accustomed to carrying much more than their small statures and spindly legs would seem to allow. But even if it is fairly clear what the ants in *A Bug's Life* and *Blue Velvet* are being used to teach, it is less clear what these ambiguities say about our ability to think about the moral being of a life-form that serves equally well as an example of social cooperation and an all-consuming horde.

I do not wish to make a mountain out of an anthill, but such representations of ants and their potential for estrangement deserve further investigation. The pedagogical usage of the ant, with its attendant ambiguities, will be the focus of this essay, granted in an entirely different cultural context. Specifically, I take relevant insights from animal studies scholarship and focus them upon (and bring them into conversation with) two rabbinic texts from Late Antiquity.[6] Deuteronomy Rabbah 5:2 and Chullin 57b reference Proverbs 6:6–9 to utilize ant society as a positive pedagogical device by which human ethical behavior is to be modeled—putting the "ant" in "anthropology," so to speak.[7] Starting with the practically idyllic depiction of ant community (indeed, commonwealth) in the biblical text, the rabbis sought to interpret the ant's behavior as in some way ethically normative for humans, and in doing so, they located a discreet impetus for and naturalization of the rabbinic project—that is, the reproduction of rabbinism and rabbis through the production of authoritative discourse upon Torah. This rabbinic investigation into ant life poses a theoretical challenge to animal studies scholarship in its attempt to understand the operation of "animal pedagogy," in which different species, in different ways, teach "us" to be "human" (or, at least, a different kind of species— and, in principle, a better species for it).[8]

I argue here that by using ant society as a pedagogical device for modeling human ethical behavior, the authors of these related passages explore and even challenge the moral otherness of social insects. The authors' exploration of the porous boundary between human and insect climaxes with a striking narrative of physical contact between rabbi and ant in Chullin 57b. This contact is mediated by the semiotic marks that allow the rabbis to come to terms with human and ant bodies—those marks that allow bodies to be represented, conceptualized, and preserved in the very text itself.

The passages under analysis potentially evidence an awareness of the moral agency of animals as at once disruptive and constitutive of the rabbis' "homiletic distinction"[9] between human and animal. Yet, by pursuing such questions through the rabbinic idioms of commentary and writing, the authors simultaneously reinscribe this originary distinction between the human and the insect in the selfsame process of text creation, maintaining the crucial difference even as they subvert it. In other words, the ontological gap between human and ant morality is narrowed primarily as a function of literary representation, thus reaffirming this distance by repositioning the reader into a textually mediated interaction with a textualized ant colony; yet this textual encounter has the potential to reorganize one's perceptions of the space beyond the borders of the page and bridge the gap between utterly distinct ways of knowing.

In all this, I do not want to bite off more than I can chew; rather, it should be enough to nibble little crescent shapes into the margins of these texts, like a beetle or silverfish among the moldering books of a library slowly consuming the starchy pages, masticating and digesting the proteins thoughtfully, pondering all the while the different ways these texts can inform the current volume's discussion of nonhuman morality.

ANT TEACHING

Proverbs 6:6–9 reads as follows:

> Go to the ant, you lazybones;
> consider its ways, and be wise.
> Without having any chief
> or officer or ruler,
> it prepares its food in summer,
> and gathers its sustenance in harvest.
> How long will you lie there, O lazybones?
> When will you rise from your sleep?
> (NRSV)

The author of this proverb utilizes ant society as a practical pedagogical device for modeling an agrarian society.[10] The use of agrarian imagery would have resonated with the patterns of ancient Israelite life, in particular the rhythmic tread of verse 8, which produces the couplings "prepares/gathers," "food/sustenance," and "summer/harvest."

A later proverb among the Sayings of Agur similarly uses the figure of the ant to extol the virtue of hard work, here, as above, bonding the ant (again typified as a collective agent) to the human agrarian cycle: "The ants are a people without strength, yet they provide their food in the summer" (Prov. 30:25), and therefore, like badgers, locusts, and lizards, they are considered "small" yet "exceedingly wise" (vv. 24, 26–28).[11]

Given the biblical interest in the ant as a collective food-gathering instrument, it is noteworthy that the rabbinic text Deuteronomy Rabbah 5:2 mostly dispenses with the agrarian context and instead explores the proverbs in relation to the interdiction in Deuteronomy 16:18 ("You shall appoint judges and officials throughout your tribes . . ."). In this way, the rabbinic author offers a reading that expands upon the original biblical proverb, adding to the original writing the concerns of a later, distinct community.

The rabbinic text, a *sugya* organized similarly to the Socratic model of question-and-answer, begins by asking why Solomon, the traditional author of Proverbs, would draw a lesson from an ant. The author goes on to marvel at the ant's peculiar behavior. One such peculiarity is that the ant stores more food than she can possibly eat in her short life span, for which the rabbis allot six months at most:

The Rabbis say: The ant has three stories [in her house]; she does not store food in the top story on account of the drippings from the roof; nor in the bottom story on account of the moisture of the soil but only in the middle story; and she lives only six months. Why? Because any creature which has no sinews and bones can live for six months only. Her food consists of one and a half grains of wheat, and throughout the summer she goes about gathering all the wheat and barley and lentils she can find.

Significantly, the author begins by depicting human and ant dwellings and, more importantly, *bodies* as fundamentally unique assemblages of incompatible materials.

The obvious infrastructural differences in their respective dwellings and bodies allow the author to draw some preliminary conclusions about the ant's intelligence—she, like humans, knows to store her food where it will last the longest, in a dry, cool place—as well as pinpoint a fundamental incongruity in her behavior: since she cannot live longer than six months, it is unnecessary for her to store so much grain. This incongruity in turn allows for a radical reinterpretation of the passage in Proverbs. While the biblical text would originally have been directed at humans engaged in behavior comparable to that of the ants (the production and cultivation of food), with no specific reference to more far-reaching ethical implications than the singular importance of that mundane, worldly responsibility, the rabbis effect a symbolic transformation by which the foraging behavior of ants is repositioned to become the ground for human ethical behavior as a whole. According to the text, the ant is such a prolific creature

because she says: "Perhaps God will grant me [more] life and then I will have food in readiness." R. Simeon b. Yohai said: Once in the hole of one of them were found three hundred kor of wheat which she gathered in the summer for the winter. Therefore Solomon said, "Go to the ant, you sluggard; consider her ways and be wise." So do you too prepare for yourselves religious deeds [*mitzvot*] in this world for the World to Come.[12]

While it is tempting to write off this rather imaginative depiction of ant behavior as another instance of premodern anthropomorphism in which nonhuman animals are endowed with impossible moral characteristics, such a dismissive attitude toward premodern representations as irrational or nonscientific jeopardizes the opportunity to explore the alternate temporalities preserved in various classical texts, and, just as importantly, this gesture obscures the possibility that anthropomorphization is always already an animalization of the human—since these texts explore, to some degree, the coincidence of "what is considered human" and "what is considered animal" in the same bodies. In this instance, the viewpoint of the rabbis absolutely contrasts with the modern conception of nonhuman animals as mere unreflecting products of a given set of ecological processes, but I want to argue that the rabbinic representation of insects as creatures endowed with moral agency can be approached in a more productive way.

In the rabbinic formulation above, the ant does not necessarily teach the human what behavior is important and necessary for the flourishing of the human community; instead, in a more profound way, her exemplary behavior teaches the human how to be human and how to practice rabbinic Judaism. The qualitative shift from *what* to *how* serves to illustrate what Kelly Oliver calls "animal pedagogy," or the ways in which animals enter discourses to "teach us to be human."[13] In her wide-reaching monograph, Oliver follows various threads in modern continental philosophy for the ways in which animal behavior serves to naturalize certain forms of human behavior, usually by way of the negative bonds that humans draw to distinguish themselves from undesirable, beastly behaviors.[14] And certainly in the case of the rabbinic commentary, the ant's behavior serves as the ground for imagining the correct behavior of humans—but in a decidedly positive valence, for this is a text that to some extent admonishes humans to act like ants: to follow the commandments the way an ant accumulates surplus grain in her den.

Similarly, the focus on devotional behaviors (human *and* nonhuman) invites one to reflect upon what Susan McHugh calls the "unnatural histories of species"—or, the literary representation of animal agency.[15] Even as discourses serve to naturalize, as it were, the cultural arrangements of human speakers, they cannot escape the input of their animal interlocutors. For the ant's behavior, though textually clothed, is shown to be her own.

To that effect, it is significant that the text continues with a brief example of the ant's peculiar behavior, as if drawn from observation, that invites the reader to see further parallels in the "unnatural histories" of insect and Jew:

> The Rabbis say: Consider her [the ant's] good conduct, how she keeps away from robbery. R. Simeon b. Halafta said: Once it happened that an ant

dropped one grain of wheat and all the ants came and sniffed at it and yet not one of them took it, until the one to whom it belonged came and took it. Consider her wisdom and all her praiseworthiness inasmuch as she has not learnt [her ways] from any creature. She has no judge or officer over her, as it is said. . . . Then you, for whom God has appointed judges and officers—how much more should you hearken unto them. Hence, judges and officers shalt thou make thee in all thy gates [Deuteronomy 16:18].

In addition to the industriousness of ants, Rabbi Simeon gives evidence that the moral behavior of ants also is beyond reproach—a fact that is difficult to explain, given that ants do not take orders from any other ant and ant society is not organized hierarchically.[16] Because the rabbis conceive of the ant, like many nonhuman beings, as a creature endowed with some form of agency (as well as, perhaps, its own path to righteousness), the above discussion of ant morality offers a unique form of reflection upon nonhuman life through which the individual creature's character and possible motivations can be discerned.

Inasmuch as nonhuman forms of moral agency (imagined or not) can serve as normative guides for human behavior, one can begin to articulate a strategy of reading rabbinic literature that focuses on interspecies interactions in which human and nonhuman textual agents are superimposed and, consequently, values and authority are derived.[17] In the above source, for instance, the rabbis use the medium of the ant's body to negotiate their own authority—indeed, the identity of the judges and officers in the post-Temple context can hardly be mistaken for anyone else—by noting an intrinsic parallel in human and nonhuman behaviors. However, this move comes with a strong critique of human society, for if the cooperative anarchism of ants has produced such a profound example of both industriousness and ethicality, how much more accomplished and righteous should humans be, given that they do have such governance! In this formulation, the human is less morally responsible than an ant (thus requiring more regulation) but at the same time held to even higher moral standards (by virtue of that increased measure of regulation). So in the above text, the naturalization of the rabbinic project through animal pedagogy is inextricably linked to the attempt to confirm the authority of rabbis, and vice versa.

ANT READING

Yet as we move on to Chullin 57b, we find that the representation of animal agency is more than just a means to naturalize the rabbinic project; dialectically, animal agency serves to undermine any attempt at constructing unqualified human authority over other humans or the natural world. For the literary awareness of animal agency is always an awareness of the unpredictability of the animal that inhabits even the represented, representable world. This means that when one discusses the construction of rabbinic authority as in some way linked to the cultural artifacts that have gained some measure of "permanence," as in their writings, one can do so only with the acknowledgment of some subaltern force that cannot be fully brought under this expansion of power. The ants cannot be grasped in a fist but rather crawl around the crevices and curves of the open palm, as in the well-known imagery of Salvador Dali. In Chullin 57b, the ants simply will not stay put: they are not the furniture or furnishings of a static textual ecology but are operative constituents whose subjectivity crisscrosses that of the human to produce the fluidity of that world. The ant can be instrumentalized in service of the human, but this can occur only at the risk of turning the human into an instrument of the ant.

I recognize that in saying this I may be accused of effacing the fact that human dominance over animal life, though dialectical, has led to terrible violence against animals, and that discourses which instrumentalize animal life often work to naturalize these patterns of domination and violence. But in no way do I want to minimize or obscure this fact. Rather, it seems to me that recognizing the potential for such discourses to be turned inside out—to recognize, in other words, their potential for radicalization—is an important step in scholarship and ethics, not to mention "ethical scholarship."

To return to the vocabulary of pedagogy, it would seem that the animal always has two lessons to teach: the first lesson, the invited lecture, is the lesson on which we base our concept of human morality, deducing, either positively or negatively, the behavior proper to human beings; the second lesson, the unexpected interruption, is that lesson which constantly calls human morality into question and, perhaps, takes human readers to task for the epistemological assumptions inscribed in a given text. That Deuteronomy Rabbah 5:2 can be so effectively paired with Chullin 57b is one illustration of the way in which the second, subliminal, or sublimated lesson is so often paired with the first.

Rabbi Simeon, whose observation opened the gates to the above discussion, also appears in the related Talmudic source at Chullin 57b; indeed, his proto-scientific explorations of the natural world are the topic of this text, which, like the above passage, grapples with the issue of kinglessness in the ant kingdom. Chullin 57b, however, contains a grotesque representation of insect otherness that rather contrasts with the idealism of the previous passage, just as the monstrousness of *Blue Velvet*'s insect motif disturbs the pleasant utopianism of Pixar's *A Bug's Life* when the two films are juxtaposed.

This passage uses a jarring, violent rupture to argue an ethical point about the need for (rabbinic) authority. The text begins when Rabbi Simeon seeks to verify experimentally the biblical claim about the lack of hierarchical structure in ant society:

> It was said of R. Simeon b. Halafta that he was an experimenter in all things . . . He said: I shall go and find out whether it is true that they [ants] have no king. He went at the summer solstice, and spread his coat over an ant-hill. When one [ant] came out he marked it, and it immediately entered and informed the others that shadows had fallen, whereupon they all came forth. He [R. Simeon b. Halafta] then removed his coat and the sun beat down upon them. Thereupon they set upon this ant and killed it. He then said: It is clear that they have no king, for otherwise they would surely have been required to obtain royal sanction![18]

As before, the rabbinic author assumes that the ant acts freely or, at least, exerts some modicum of individual will in response to her environment; but in this case, that agency is used to construct a view in which one is perpetually reminded of the violence that is made possible by a lack of valid authority (rabbinic or otherwise). Specifically, the gruesome death of the deceived ant as she is set upon by her own kind recalls the horrifying narrative of gang rape, death, and dissection that closes the Book of Judges (chapters 19–21), a narrative that is bookended, like many of the violent narratives in Judges, with the following refrain: "In those days, there was no king in Israel" (19:1; 21:25). Both narratives take place outside, but only just, leaving the victim exposed but within view of her abode. The similarities are more poignant when one considers the way ants customarily kill other ants—by dismemberment.[19]

The text goes on to make this echo more audible by inserting a second rabbi's voice, who examines Rabbi Simeon's "experiment" in light of ancient Israelite myth (explicitly referencing, as he does so, the final verse of Judges):

> R. Aha, son of Raba, said to R. Ashi: But perhaps the king was with them, or they had royal authority, or it was during an interregnum [when they were under no law], as it is written: In those days there was no king in Israel: every man did that which was right in his own eyes [Judges 21:25]! Rather must you take the word of Solomon for it.

If the passage in Deuteronomy Rabbah served to naturalize rabbinic deliberative authority by utilizing ant society as a pedagogical device, Chullin 57b serves to highlight the unstable landscape on which this power is constructed. After Rabbi Simeon's inconclusive experiment, discursive authority is returned to the traditional author of the Proverbs, meaning that knowledge, and to some extent judgment, cannot be located squarely within the domain of the rabbis.

As such, placing Chullin 57b alongside Deuteronomy Rabbah 5:2 allows the former to comment upon and complicate the latter's representation of moral agency. In Deuteronomy Rabbah 5:2, ants refuse to pick up the grain of wheat dropped by one of their fellow laborers as a matter of course, and for this act, they are singled out for the rabbis' praise. In this way, this text offers a moral vision akin to virtue ethics: one avoids unrighteous behavior for the very fact that it is unrighteous and therefore conflicts with one's virtuous character. However explicitly Deuteronomy Rabbah models human virtue on the actions of ants, perhaps it is Chullin 57b that offers a better illustration of morality in its raw complexity (despite or perhaps because of its subtlety). The well-meaning trickery of Rabbi Simeon, which inadvertently leads to the death of an innocent ant, demonstrates that moral choices are often overdetermined by actors and actions beyond one's control or even recognition. Chullin 57b thus describes an alternate form of morality that begins with the undecidability of the ethical event as such, in which multiple actors and their proximate relations trouble categories we might otherwise expect to see as separate, even unrelated, entities.

In sum, though both texts support a view in which individual ants constitute moral agents—the intertwining of culpability and punishment in Chullin 57b seems to me to evidence a perspective in which any ant constitutes a moral agent capable of making the "right" and "wrong" decisions—I would argue that the vision of moral agency in Chullin 57b demonstrates the degree to which morality is not an abstract category but a process intricately bound to interactive events. The question of how and under what circumstances an animal (such as a human, such as an ant) constitutes a moral agent becomes crisscrossed with the question of moral otherness: beastly morality is, in the current context, a netlike, reticular tissue that mediates between and has profound implications for such categories as self and Other, human and nonhuman, culpability and punishment, and, in the final analysis, the reader and the text.

To pursue the way in which moral content might emerge in the context of creaturely contact, I would like to conclude this discussion by reflecting upon the specific actions that frame Rabbi Simeon's confrontation with the ants. I would argue that at the heart of Chullin 57b are Rabbi Simeon's two seemingly contradictory acts: first, he covers the anthill with his coat to simulate darkness; second, he marks his ant. These acts are as difficult to come to terms with materially as they are suggestive symbolically, for if Rabbi Simeon is able to "mark" the first ant that emerges, it must mean that he himself is under the coat—face to the earth, soft breath falling upon the dirt. While it is unclear to me whether Rabbi Simeon's "mark" is a literal or figurative one, the significance of this gesture can hardly be missed: to mark an otherwise unidentifiable ant is to adorn the creeping thing with some sort of knowability; it is to insinuate one's own way of signifying, of seeing, onto the other, to render meaningful or meaningless with the stroke of a pen. But most importantly, it is a way to come to terms with the moral being of another animal, for in this context, writing this particular ant into the text requires the author to know an individual body as something more than an abstraction, as an actually existing alterity. Thus, from a position of power—over text, over life—the human author of Chullin 57b might be said to sympathize with another way of existing in the world.

From my vantage, this striking narrative of contact between rabbi and ant appears doubled by the meeting of reader and text—and indeed, I am not the first to note the similarity between a keen interest in insects and close reading. In an essay on the American author William H. Gass, Bertrand Gervais speaks of the reader's encounter with the text as such an encounter of irreducible alterity in which self meets Other, human meets insect. "Reading," Gervais writes, "is an encounter between a reader and a fundamental otherness"—it is "an encounter with an insect, an arthropod, a being with which we share neither the same body structure nor the same subjectivity,"[20] and in handling this delicate creature, the reader comes close to another being who, with a language that is and is not one's own, opens upon another world. Gervais derives this metaphor from the short story "Order of Insects," narrated by a woman who, like Rabbi Simeon, becomes entranced by the strange anatomy of bugs: she pores over their dead bodies in intimate detail, not unlike a reader poring over the particularities of a page. The eyes, in following the path of signs carefully laid out for them, sweep over the preserved words and assemble the segmented bodies of meaning, and in so doing remind one of the instructive orthographic proximity of "etymology" and "entomology," which May Berenbaum rightly calls "a fortuitous resemblance."[21]

Gervais's unusual interpretation of the reader-text relationship is an instructive one, even for the current discussion, since we are presently coming into close contact with a religious text from another world, so to speak; by poring over the pages that have come down to us through the many twists and turns of history, we are attempting to bridge the gap between multiple possible ways of knowing the world, knowing the self, and knowing the animal that is deemed other. Hunched over an open book, making a mark here or there, we find ourselves to be in quite the same position as Rabbi Simeon, whom I like to imagine hovering above an anthill only inches away from the carnage he incited.

CONCLUDING REMARKS

In the introduction to a short-story collection, J. M. G. Le Clézio writes, "I don't much believe in lofty sentiments. In their place I see an army of insects or ants, nibbling in all directions."[22] To Le Clézio, this essentially amoral, insectoid world of passionate consumption and the ultimately fragile moral conceits of humankind are necessarily juxtaposed. This simple, not to say simplifying, view of insect life is familiar; it is certainly echoed in the insect images of *Blue Velvet*, discussed above. But the rabbinic texts Deuteronomy Rabbah 5:2 and Chullin 57b suggest an alternate way of knowing these entomological others. Specifically, they challenge the stark moral binaries that position humans as authors of their own moral worlds and nonhumans as, at best, passive recipients of human beneficence or, at worst, collateral damage. The first text invites the reader to consider the moral being of ants, utilizing ant society as a model for human behavior, while the second can be used to conceptualize morality itself as a product of interspecies contact, not located within either domain but the result of the essential imbrication of human and nonhuman worlds.

In encountering a pair of texts like this, with unfamiliar words and alien temporalities, one cannot help but be struck by the estranging otherness of reading. The otherness of reading is such that the Other's words give the reader transient access to the Other's world—but not unrestricted access, never permanent access. One's interaction must be mediated by the text in which this encounter is played out, allowing the segmented body of the book to become a kind of exoskeleton; to this effect, the text also acts as a wall—albeit a paper-thin wall—that restates the essential difference between mutual informants of otherness and confirms the intelligible distinction of a reifying "mark." But this separation makes a different kind of learning possible.

While being confronted or comforted with the limits of knowing, is it possible to see the marked ant from the vantage of the rabbi, any more than it is possible to see the rabbi from the vantage of the marked ant? Like Rabbi Simeon and the marked ant, the rabbis of Late Antiquity and the contemporary reader-critic inhabit different worlds—not "worlds apart," but touching worlds, like the antennae of two ants, communicating. But I speak not of speaking, as if the unaided voice of one alone might bridge the temporal abyss that separates one from the other, but of knowing; I speak of bridging the gap between two distinct ways of knowing, through the fleshy contact between the reader and the page.

My interest in the relationship between social insects and the formation and organization of various concepts of "the human" and "the animal" has guided my reading of these texts. In tracing such open questions, which have served as openings into the rabbinic writings, I have attempted to make a contribution to animal studies scholarship regarding the textual representation of animal agency and historical constructions of human-animal difference, finding that these texts renew our sensitivity to nonhuman morality, even that of insects, and its importance for understanding human morality.

What ancient and contemporary authors alike must find so transfixing yet unsettling about the insect especially must be the closeness of something so alien or the alienness of something so close. Hence, the covering and re-covering of that indecent exposure in garments of text and language.

NOTES

1. See Michel Chapuisat, "Social Evolution: Sick Ants Face Death Alone," *Current Biology* 20, no. 3 (2010): 104–5; Alexandra Achenbach and Susanne Foitzik, "First Evidence for Slave Rebellion: Enslaved Ant Workers Systematically Kill the Brood of Their Social Parasite *Protomognathus Americanus*," *Evolution* 63, no. 4 (2009): 1068–75; Fabien Ravary et al., "Individual Experience Alone Can Generate Lasting Division of Labor in Ants," *Current Biology* 17, no. 15 (2007): 1308–12; Duncan E. Jackson and Francis L.W. Ratnieks, "Communication in Ants," *Current Biology* 16, no. 15 (2006): 570–74; Nick Bos and Patrizia d'Ettorre, "Recognition of Social Identity in Ants," *Frontiers in Psychology* 3, article 83 (2012), http://www.ncbi.nlm.nih.gov /pmc/articles/PMC3309994/, accessed June 2, 2014; and Nigel R. Franks and Tom Richardson, "Teaching in Tandem-Running Ants," *Nature* 439 (2006): 153.

2. Consider, for instance, Rafael Eitan's controversial statement likening Palestinians to "drugged cockroaches in a bottle" (quoted in Steven Erlanger, "Rafael Eitan, 75, Ex-General and Chief of Staff in Israel, Dies," *New York Times*, November 24, 2004, http://www.nytimes.com/2004/11/24/obituaries/24eitan.html, accessed April 12, 2012), or Franz Kafka's novella *Metamorphosis*. See also Christopher Hollingsworth, "The Force of the Entomological Other: Insects as Instruments of Intolerant Thought and Oppressive Action," in *Insect Poetics*, ed. Eric C. Brown (Minneapolis: University of Minnesota Press, 2006), 262–77.

3. For some modern examples, see such popular works as Thomas D. Seeley, *Honeybee Democracy* (Princeton, NJ: Princeton University Press, 2010), or Peter Miller, *The Smart Swarm: How Understanding Flocks, Schools, and Colonies Can Make Us Better at Communicating, Decision Making, and Getting Things Done* (New York: Avery, 2010). Also worth considering would be the development of Swarm Intelligence algorithms and the related field of ant colony optimization, which base artificial intelligence on the swarm behavior of insect colonies and other biological patterns of organization and movement. For an accessible overview of the advances and applications in such areas, see Dario Floreano and Claudio Mattiussi, *Bio-Inspired Artificial Intelligence: Theories, Methods, and Technologies* (Cambridge, MA: MIT Press, 2008). An excellent critical overview of the interplay between technology and insect intelligence, including the modern cultural foundations of their association, can be found in Jussi Parikka, *Insect Media: An Archaeology of Animals and Technology* (Minneapolis: University of Minnesota Press, 2010).

4. This ambivalent fascination is beautifully exemplified in the volume *The Management of Insects in Recreation and Tourism* (Cambridge: Cambridge University Press, 2013), a multidisciplinary collection edited by Raynald Harvey Lemelin, which focuses on the insect recreation industry and select encounters between human and insect.

5. For a helpful overview of cultural attitudes toward the ant, see especially the work of Charlotte Sleigh in *Ant* (London: Reaktion, 2003), and *Six Legs Better: A Cultural History of Myrmecology* (Baltimore: Johns Hopkins University Press, 2007).

6. While a growing body of literature explores conceptions of the animal and animality in rabbinic literature, there have been few engagements with rabbis in relation to insects. Aside from some of the more obvious work on famine-inducing hoppers, one short but exceptional article is Allen Feldman's "The Gnat and the Sovereign," *Social Text* 26, no. 2 (2008): 107–10.

7. The passage drawn from Deuteronomy Rabbah (a homiletic commentary on the biblical Book of Deuteronomy divided into twenty-five discrete sections) is distinct from the passage drawn from Chullin, which belongs to the Kodashim order of the Mishnah (a written redaction of the Oral Torah). The goal of this study is not to demonstrate conclusively the relationship between these two sources, nor to make any speculative arguments about their authorship or integrity; rather, as I hope is obvious from the foregoing, I want to bring the two sources into conversation with each other to draw some preliminary conclusions about rabbis' perceptions of insects and their importance to imagining the rabbinic project while also leaving room for reflections about animal studies theory and possible contemporary valences.

8. Though numerous scholars and philosophers have theorized the ways in which concepts of "the animal" or "animality" are central to any normative concept of "the human" or "humanity" (see, for instance, Erica Fudge, *Perceiving Animals: Humans and Beasts in Early Modern English Culture* [Urbana and Chicago: University of Illinois Press, 2000]) and thus form part of the intellectual context of the current study, I receive the term "animal pedagogy" specifically from Kelly Oliver, *Animal Lessons: How They Teach Us to Be Human* (New York: Columbia University Press, 2009).

9. For this conceptualization of the human-animal relationship in rabbinic literature, I am indebted to conversations with Julia Watts-Besler. She uses the phrase "homiletic distinction" in an unpublished essay, "Suffering Rabbis and Other Animals: Women, Wickedness, and the Construction of Rabbinic (In)Humanity in Bavli Baba Metsia 83b–85a" (forthcoming), 3–5. A version of her argument was also presented at the Society for Jewish Ethics 2012 annual meeting.

10. Tova L. Forti has provided a careful reading of this and other biblical proverbs in light of cultural and linguistic context in her study *Animal Imagery in the Book of Proverbs* (Boston: Brill, 2008), 101–6. See also the brief discussion of animals and biblical didacticism in Katherine J. Dell, "The Use of Animal Imagery in the Psalms and Wisdom Literature of Ancient Israel," *Scottish Journal of Theology* 53, no. 3 (2000): 283–84.

11. The applied wisdom of seemingly inexhaustible ant labor is a common trope in ancient literature, though it has only tangential relevance for the current study as an additional illustration of the moral complexity with which ancient authors viewed various creatures of the natural world. For example, several of Aesop's well-known fables, such as "The Ant and the Fly" and "The Ant and the Grasshopper," use personified ants to praise initiative, self-reliance, and productivity while lambasting procrastination, over-dependency on others, and laziness.

12. Similarly, the Qur'an contains a passage in which the ant's cautiousness and sense of community become an occasion for Solomon to reflect on the righteous path more generally. According to M. A. S. Abdel Haleem's translation: "When they [Solomon and his hosts] came to the Valley of the Ants, one ant said, 'Ants! Go into your homes, in case Solomon and his hosts unwittingly crush you.' Solomon smiled broadly at her words and said, 'Lord, inspire me to be thankful for the blessings You have granted me and my parents, and to do good deeds that please You; admit me by Your grace into the ranks of Your righteous servants'" (27:18–19). This passage gives the 27th *sura* its name ("The Ants") and dates to roughly the same period as the rabbinic text (the seventh century CE, with Deuteronomy Rabbah probably following in the tenth century).

13. Oliver, *Animal Lessons*, 5.

14. Ibid., 66.

15. Susan McHugh, "Literary Animal Agents," *PMLA* 124, no. 2 (2009): 488.

16. The inappropriate identification of the mated female ant as "the queen" says more about the infelicitous terminology in relating models of social organization for insects than about revealing anything specific to "the queen's" role within the colony. Current research suggests that ants fulfill their responsibilities to the colony by communicating with one another and from individual learning experiences rather than by taking orders from "the queen." See Deborah M. Gordon, *Ant Encounters: Interaction Networks and Colony Behavior* (Princeton, NJ: Princeton University Press, 2010), 45–74. All of this is in no way to suggest that the rabbinic discourse somehow anticipates contemporary myrmecological research. The agreement between the ancient rabbis and contemporary scientists, though fascinating, is only accidental, and is played in vastly different discursive scenarios with radically different intent.

Perhaps it would be more instructive to compare and contrast the rabbinic perspective with the writings of Aristotle. In the *History of Animals*, Aristotle notes, like the rabbis, that ants are social creatures with a common objective but apparently lack a ruler or form of governance (I.1, 488b). In *De Anima*, however, he argues that ants, like bees and worms, do not seem to have an imagination (III.3, 428a11); perhaps, he argues, this is why ants can function without a ruler: lacking imagination, ants lack individual will. The rabbis, on the other hand, seem to grant ants a sense of community *and* imagination, making Rabbi Simeon's investigations into ant morality all the more compelling.

17. The essays in *Judaism and Environmental Ethics: A Reader*, ed. Martin D. Yaffe (Lanham, MD: Lexington Books, 2001) are an excellent source for locating and making sense of this articulation. Another excellent sourcebook for understanding representations of animals and animal agency is Elijah Judah Schochet, *Animal Life in Jewish Tradition: Attitudes and Relationships* (New York: Ktav Publishing House, 1984).

18. An additional textual tradition of the moral accountability of individual insects can be found in the Islamic milieu. In one hadith (a saying or deed ascribed to the Prophet Muhammad that functions as a tool of jurisprudence in the Islamic tradition), the Prophet relates a story of an earlier prophet who is bitten by an ant while resting under the shade of a tree. After the prophet orders the anthill to be destroyed by fire, God asks whether it wouldn't have been more appropriate to burn the individual offender who bit the prophet instead of retaliating blindly against all the ants that live in the anthill (Sahih Bukhari IV.54, 536). Since an individual ant would be practically impossible to single out amongst her community, this story appears to be related to a further hadith that lists the ant (along with bees, hoopoes, and sparrowhawks) as one of four creatures the Prophet prohibited killing (Sunan Abu-Dawud 41, 5247). Like the rabbinic text, the hadith makes it clear that individual ants are responsible for their own actions, and punishment (whether an inter- or intra-species event) ought to be carried out on that basis.

19. Andre Stipanovic, in his careful reading of two insect similes from the *Aeneid*, notes that Virgil portrays ants as intrinsically more violent and aggressive than bees ("Bees and Ants: Perceptions of Imperialism in Vergil's *Aeneid* and *Georgics*," in *Insect Poetics*, ed. Brown, 13–28); following R. D. Williams, Stipanovic also notes that the passage in question (4.401–7) is one of only two similes drawn from ants in all extant Greek or Latin epics (26n2). Whatever the respective destructive capacities of the two species, Virgil's depiction of the ant as a "ravager" who coerces

other ants into labor demonstrates a similar human suspicion about insect morality to Chullin 57b.

20. Bertrand Gervais, "Reading as a Close Encounter of the Third Kind: An Experiment with Gass's 'Order of Insects,'" in *Insect Poetics*, ed. Brown, 179.

21. May Berenbaum, "On the Lives of Insects in Literature," in *Insect Poetics*, 3.

22. J. M. G. Le Clézio, introduction to *Fever*, trans. Daphne Woodward (London: Penguin, 2008), vii.

Ten Jakushin's Dogs
and the Goodness of Animals

PREACHING THE MORAL LIFE OF BEASTS IN
MEDIEVAL JAPANESE TALE LITERATURE

Michael Bathgate

What would dogs know about their past lives?
—*KONJAKU MONOGATARISHŪ* 19:3

HISTORIANS RECOGNIZE YOSHISHIGE NO YASUTANE (d. 1002) as an accomplished litterateur and as a formative figure in the development of Japanese Pure Land Buddhism.[1] The twelfth-century story collection known as *Konjaku monogatarishū* (Collection of Tales from Times Now Past), however, remembers him by his religious name, Jakushin, and recounts his exploits as an outspoken, if eccentric, holy man.[2] When traveling on the road, we are told, he allows his horse to stop and graze as it wishes, angering the groom, who is eager to reach their destination. When the groom tries to whip the horse, however, Jakushin confronts him, saying:

> What are you thinking, behaving like this? Are you beating him so contemptuously because an old monk like me is riding him? Couldn't this horse have been reborn again and again as one of your parents in previous lives? Do you despise him, thinking this was not the case? Couldn't he, having been born many times as one of your parents, have suffered out of love for you, being reborn as an animal, and descending into any numbers of hells or the Realm of the Hungry Ghosts?[3]

Later in the same account, he applies the same logic to a stray dog; as a gesture of filial respect, he offers it a proper meal rather than leaving it to sniff around the latrine. But when another dog approaches, a fight ensues, and Jakushin attempts to correct them in the same way he did the groom, with a sermon about the laws of karma and the cycle of rebirth: "Please don't behave so disgracefully," he tells the dogs. "I will provide more food, so please enjoy it together. You have received these unfortunate animal forms precisely because of such cruelty!"[4] While the groom was moved by Jakushin's argument—and promised to treat the horse in a manner befitting a former parent—the dogs seem less impressed. In the end, Jakushin is forced to withdraw, to spare himself the terrible sight of such wanton brutality (and, one suspects, to avoid being bitten). An eyewitness to the event can only laugh at the holy man's folly. The story concludes with the comment that however noble his concern for animals, he had been absurdly ignorant of his audience.

If the narrator appears critical of Jakushin's naïveté, it is at least in part because they likely shared a common moralizing enterprise. With more than a thousand extant tales, the *Konjaku monogatarishū* (hereafter simply *Konjaku*) is the largest, and arguably the most ambitious, example of a genre of didactic tale literature known as *setsuwa bungaku*. Its twenty-eight extant scrolls, divided into three geographic sections, draw on Indian, Chinese, and Japanese sources in order to demonstrate the totality of forces that shape our lives and thus encourage us to act accordingly.[5] It should therefore not be surprising that among its accounts of kings and peasants, of warriors and wizards, of ghosts, demons, and tricksters a significant number of the *Konjaku*'s tales concern themselves, like the story of Jakushin, with nonhuman animals.[6]

In many of these stories, animals appear not only as objects of moral concern but as moral agents in their own right. Indeed, it is easy to find the two notions closely bound up with each other, an affirmation of moral community that is based not only on our shared capacities for suffering but also on our common disposition toward loving-kindness. Yet, as Jakushin discovered to his chagrin (and the narrator's amusement), we are also marked by qualities—our shared gift for unthinking cruelty, for example—that mitigate against an easy sense of moral solidarity. The diversity of ethical, cosmological, and narrative logics that a collection like the *Konjaku* brings to bear offers ample warning against positing any univocal Japanese or Buddhist "attitude" toward the moral life or the moral standing of animals, whether medieval or modern. It may also require us to consider the extent to which the imagination of animals' moral life in such contexts is, in fact, about morality at all.

FELLOW TRAVELERS: IMAGINING ANIMALS AND
HUMANS ON THE SIX PATHS

Like Jakushin, the authors of *setsuwa* narratives often call for moral consideration of animals based on an image of animal life as one of the Six Paths of Rebirth (*rokudō* in Japanese). In this vision of the cosmos, all beings (gods and titans, humans and animals, hungry ghosts and the damned who suffer—and inflict suffering—in hell) are caught up in an unending cycle of rebirth, determined by the law of karmic cause and effect. What Jakushin preached in theory, however, the compilers of the *Konjaku* took pains to demonstrate in practice. A number of accounts, for example, reveal animals to have been human beings in a past life, having earned their animal form thanks to some basic character fault. Among the most common stories of this type, attachment (to wealth, to sex, or even to one's favorite tree in the garden) causes one to be reborn as a snake, while beasts of burden (cows, oxen, or horses) serve to repay the debts they left behind as human beings by laboring for their former creditors.[7]

In other tales, it is human beings who discover that their lives have been fundamentally shaped by their past lives as animals. A number of monks, for instance, learn that their affinity for a particular scripture is the result of a past rebirth as a cow, ox, or horse tasked with carrying the document, while others learn that their frustrating inability to memorize a particular passage is caused by their past life, say, as a bookworm, who had dined on that very section of a scroll.[8] In one tale, a blind man learns that in his previous life he had been a snake living on the grounds of a temple. Every day, he listened to the monks reciting the scriptures, and every evening, he crept into the temple to lap at the oil in the lamps. The former, he learns, earned him rebirth as a human being, while the latter (essentially the theft of temple property, a sin condemned in many *setsuwa* accounts) cost him his sight.[9]

Together, such stories serve to undermine any sense that human life and animal life are fundamentally distinct, demonstrating both the intersections between them and the laws of karmic cause and effect that govern them. Although Jakushin seems to have been too kindhearted to suggest it, other Buddhist preachers drive home this message by pointing out the terrifying karmic consequences of cruelty to animals. Jakushin himself may well have been familiar with one tale reproduced in the *Konjaku*, which tells the story of a melon farmer named Iwawake, who, like

Jakushin's groom, had a penchant for beating horses. Overloading his wagon, he would savagely whip his animals until tears streamed from their eyes. One day, when looking into a pot of boiling water, his own eyes simply fell from his head into the water.[10] In other stories, a thief who cuts out the tongues of sheep to prevent them from bleating has his own tongue shrivel, while a man who took perverse pleasure in skinning rabbits alive develops terrible sores, as if he too had been skinned.[11] Those who enjoy eating boiled eggs are presented as object lessons in more than one tale, when their legs blister as if they too had been dipped in boiling water.[12] If such grisly karmic consequences are well designed to dissuade us from making similar mistakes—at least one story is careful to describe the reaction of witnesses, who wisely take up vegetarianism—they also make a tacit claim about our shared capacity for suffering.[13] After all, if karmic consequences resemble their causes (as a fruit resembles its seed or an echo resembles the sound that caused it), then clearly the suffering caused by these physical transformations must be grounded in a comparable suffering experienced by the animals themselves.

Lest such subtleties be lost in our horror at these events, however, the *Konjaku* offers a number of stories that seem designed specifically to provoke our sympathies by drawing explicit parallels between human suffering and animal suffering. One impoverished samurai, for example, kills a drake to feed his wife and family, and is amazed to find that a duck has followed him home, refusing to leave the side of her dead mate. Seeing this, the samurai laments: "Even though she is a beast, she risked her life to come here out of concern for her husband. And even though I am a human being, I killed a bird out of concern for my wife. How can I offer its flesh to be eaten?"[14] In a similar tale, a falconer experiences a vivid dream in which he is the bird caught in a hunt; he watches in impotent terror as, one by one, his family are caught and killed, and wakes just as the falcon's talons find him.[15] Shaken by their realizations, both the samurai and the falconer not only give up hunting, but eventually leave secular life (and their families) altogether to become monks.

Still other tales close the circle of moral community completely. Like Jakushin, they suggest that animals not only may love their families, but may in fact have been our beloved relatives in a past life. In some accounts, the protagonist is quick to accept the past-life identity of a cow, an ox, or a sheep, saving it from the butcher's knife and treating it with all the loving care appropriate to a dearly departed parent or child. More often, however, the revelation of the animal's past identity as a family member is not sufficient to save it from death at the hands of its former son or father, or takes place only after the animal has been killed. So, for example, a man dismisses a dream that his departed mother had been reborn as a deer; it is only while hunting, when the doe he shoots cries out in his mother's voice, that he realizes the terrible truth. In another tale, a man ignores a dream vision in which his deceased father informs him that because of his misuse of temple property, he had been reborn as a catfish. When a huge catfish is discovered under the eaves of the temple, he helps his children catch it and make it into stew. Later, while mocking the concerns of his pious wife (afraid of the consequences of what is essentially a form of patricide), he begins to choke on a fish bone and dies in agony. That is not to say that all signs of past life connections are reliable—one account pokes fun at a fellow who mistakes a turtle for the rebirth of his dead wife—but one dismisses them at one's peril. In one story, a man learns that his deceased father had been reborn as an animal, not once but many times. In only one of those forms, however, did the son do his filial duty and offer him food.[16] The lesson, it seems, is clear—far better to treat all animals with the respect due past-life family members than run the risk of unwittingly killing, abusing, or simply disrespecting a loved one.

The notion that an animal may have been one's parent in a past life has a long history in the Buddhist tradition. As one scripture has it: "It is not easy, bhikkhus, to find a being who in this long course has not previously been your mother . . . your father . . . your brother . . . your sister . . . your son . . . your daughter."[17] Indeed, the sheer number of *Konjaku* stories that play on this idea would seem to confirm Jakushin's instincts as a preacher.[18] As Lori Gruen has perceptively argued,

> Kinship or closeness is a very important element in thinking about virtually every feature of our daily lives. To deny the reality of the influence this factor has on our decision-making, in favour of some abstraction, like absolute equality, may be considered saintly, but probably is not possible for most mortals faced with complex decisions.[19]

If Jakushin fails, it is not because of his efforts to evoke the bonds of sympathy between humans and animals, but because his efforts fall on the uncomprehending ears of hungry dogs. In this respect, the story evokes a long-standing tension in the Buddhist imagination of animals. For all our commonalities—our shared capacity for suffering, for example, or the laws of karmic cause and effect to which we are both subject—humanity remains a distinct (and, for the purposes of achieving salvation, distinctly privileged) form of rebirth. Located in the middle ground between the bliss of heaven and the torments of hell, with lives long enough and minds perceptive enough to appreciate the Buddhist teachings, we are uniquely suited to the pursuit of the Buddhist Path.[20] As fellow travelers on the round of rebirth, even as family members, animals may well deserve our loving-kindness, especially insofar as the very actions that led to their animal rebirth may have been committed on our behalf. That sense of kinship, however, does not make them any less animals, nor any more likely to be moved by a lecture on Buddhist doctrine.[21] Without the marvelous revelations that appear in other tales of animal rebirth—and attended less by the shock of sudden realization than by mirth—Jakushin's call to remember our place in the cycle of rebirth loses a good deal of its rhetorical force, and the differences that separate us threaten to outweigh the capacities that unite us.

SHALL WE NOT REVENGE? THE AMBIVALENCE OF OBLIGATION

Given Jakushin's singular lack of success in encouraging ethical reflection in stray dogs, it is interesting to note that the *Konjaku* is otherwise replete with tales in which animals are portrayed, not only as moral but as ethical agents, capable of recognizing as well as acting upon their responsibilities. Indeed, while depictions of past-life family connections and the terrible karmic consequences of animal abuse are limited to the Chinese and Japanese sections of the text, images of animals as conscious moral agents appear in every section of the collection.[22] A tale from the Indian section, for instance, describes a man who buys a turtle in order to release it. Years later, the man is startled to find the turtle by his bedside—the nearby river, it warns him, is about to flood. Securing a boat, the man escapes the disaster with his family, washing up on a tumulus where the water had exposed ancient treasures, all part of the turtle's repayment of his debt.[23] Similarly, a story from the Chinese section tells of a young man sent abroad as his father's purchasing agent; on the way, he encounters a man with five large turtles and offers to pay for their release. In the end, the young man spends the entire fortune with which his father had entrusted him, but when he returns home to explain, his father tells him that he had been visited by five mysterious men, who had returned the funds he had sent with his son. "The money they gave me," he tells him with some confusion, "was damp."[24] In the Japanese section, too, we can find the story of the monk Gusai, who encountered a fisherman with four large turtles at the port of Naniwa. Rather than let them become someone's dinner, Gusai paid for their release before embarking on his own sea voyage. When his ship is captured by pirates, they toss him overboard, yet he is saved from drowning by the very turtles he had set free.[25]

That is not to say that turtles are the only creatures represented in tales of this kind: elephants, monkeys, and insects also make expressions of gratitude to the humans who save them.[26] Yet sea creatures predominate in these accounts, likely because of their connection with the ritual liberation of captive animals, a practice that continues to be performed (for better or worse) by Buddhists today.[27] As one tale concludes, "The release of animals should be the primary practice of all sensible people."[28] The collection's advocacy of this practice, however, depends on imagining the moral life of humans and animals as taking place within a larger web of reciprocity, a vision of moral community shaped as much by the moral principle of indebtedness (*on* in Japanese) as by the law of karma. More than one tale concludes with the lesson that if even animals have the sense to repay their obligations, then surely we humans should have the sense to do the same.[29] The Indian tale of the turtle who saves his rescuer from a flood goes further still, stating that "animals recognize their obligations, but human beings do not."[30]

Despite the latter claim, animals do not always appear as moral exemplars, nor does the fulfillment of their obligations always unfold in an entirely salutary fashion. One account, for instance, tells the story of a father and daughter whose compassion for animals embroils them in a drama in which animals appear as both hero and villain. One day, we are told, the daughter (a pious and kindhearted devotee of the bodhisattva Kannon) encountered a man carrying a live crab home for dinner. She convinced the man to give her the crab, and released it into the nearby water. Not long after, the father found himself in a similar situation while working in the fields. Seeing a huge snake about to swallow a frog, he begged the snake to free its prey, offering it the only thing he thought it might want: his lovely daughter.[31] Looking the man in the eyes, the snake released the frog and slithered away. The father immediately regretted what he had done, and although his dutiful daughter asked him not to worry, she nevertheless hid herself in a hastily fortified outbuilding and fervently prayed to Kannon. Taking on human form, the snake arrived in the evening to collect his bride, but when he saw her so securely locked away, he flew into a rage. Reverting to his original form, he coiled himself around the structure and battered it with his tale. Huddled in her enclosure in the dark, the girl was unable to see anything, but around midnight she heard the snake cry out, and then silence. The next morning, she emerged to find the snake dead—a large crab (presumably the very one she had freed earlier) had led an army of its smaller fellows against the monster, leaving it in pieces in the yard. The tale concludes with the father and daughter burying the snake and erecting a temple on the site, both for the repose of the snake and to expiate the karmic consequences of what the crabs had done on her behalf.[32]

This tension between the principles of moral obligation and karmic cause and effect is perhaps nowhere as clear as when the principle of indebtedness manifests itself in acts of vengeance. One tale—describing a swarm of bees that repaid a merchant's care and protection by stinging a gang of robbers to death—concludes with the comment that animals have the sense to repay a kindness, but will just as surely repay an injury.[33] In some stories, animals act out cycles of revenge from earlier lives, as in the case of a dog who attempts to maul a girl in the neighborhood whenever he sees her. When neither the girl nor the dog is seen for a few days, people go to the girl's home, and find that the two had bitten each other to death. Clearly, the author concludes, the dog and the girl had nurtured a grudge from a previous life.[34] In other tales, the spirits of dead animals return to haunt those who killed them, as a hunter discovers when his sudden illness is revealed to be caused by the angry spirits of a thousand headless birds, who flock around him in his fevered state demanding the return of their heads. When he promises to perform Buddhist memorial services for them, they depart, and he recovers from his sickness.[35]

But the desire of animals for vengeance is most clearly and frequently heard in court, when human beings are called upon to answer for their crimes before the Judge of the Dead.[36] In one story, a certain Zhang Ju-dao is suddenly struck down by illness, only to find himself brought before the King of the Underworld at the formal petition of a boar, a sheep, a duck, and a goose he had killed to feed his wife and children. In it they argue: "We received the bodies of beasts because of the sins we committed in our past lives. Nevertheless, we enjoyed a certain life span.

Ju-dao, however, has unjustly taken those lives."[37] Throwing himself on the mercy of the court, Ju-dao promises to copy all four scrolls of the Sutra of Golden Light (a text that advocates the rite of liberating captive animals) and have memorial services performed on behalf of the animals. Mollified, the animals withdraw their complaint, and Ju-dao is permitted to return to the land of the living, where he shares his story and thenceforward leads a life of piety.

Not all animals are as quick to forgive, however. When a man named Sui An-gong finds himself called to answer the charges of five dogs that his minions had slaughtered to feed his hawks, he also attempts to appease them by offering memorial services. But one of the dogs recalcitrantly insists on vengeance, proclaiming, "I was killed though I had committed no crime. As I lay dying, you carved my flesh, and I suffered unendurable agony. I cannot forget my resentment. How can I offer forgiveness when I remember how I was treated?"[38] Only when the court reminds the dog that a Buddhist memorial service would benefit it far more than any fleeting satisfaction it might gain from watching An-gong suffer does it withdraw its claim and allow the man to return to life. Another story tells of a wealthy man brought to the underworld to hear the charges of seven oxen he had killed as part of a sacrificial cult intended to placate an angry deity. The oxen identify the man as their assailant, stating, "We will chop him into mincemeat and eat him. This will repay him for our murder."[39] The man, however, claimed to have seen the error of his ways, and he had spent the past seven years diligently liberating animals to make amends for his misguided actions. Before the cleaver-wielding oxen can act, ten million witnesses appear for the defense. Untying him, the multitude (spirits of the animals the man had freed) reminds the court that the oxen had been sacrificed to appease an evil deity; surely, they argue, it is the deity who is to blame. In the end, the court is moved by their testimony and releases the man back to the land of the living, but not before the oxen make one final threat: licking their chops in anticipation of the gory feast to come, they tell him, "We won't forget this. One day, we will have our revenge."[40]

The dread of animal vengeance is a pervasive theme, a disturbing corollary to evocations of sympathy for animal suffering. If animals' moral status—symbolized here by their legal standing as plaintiffs in the Court of King Emma—is bound up with their capacity (like us) to suffer, they also share with us the ability to feel outrage at their treatment. It is a sense of moral commonality, however, that serves to mitigate against a sense of moral solidarity. Like Shakespeare's Shylock in *The Merchant of Venice*, the posthumous courtroom dramas of the *Konjaku* present us with an ambivalent image of the Other that is, for better or worse, much like ourselves. "If you prick us, do we not bleed? If you tickle us, do we not laugh? If you poison us, do we not die? And if you wrong us, shall we not revenge? If we are like you in the rest, we will resemble you in that."[41]

In these stories, the moral logic of the characters' arguments seems to be in tension with the narrative logic of the overall plot. Like Shylock, whose implacable drive for justice renders him the play's antagonist, the angry dogs and cleaver-wielding oxen of King Emma's court appear as villains rather than victims. As such, the protagonist's escape—whether from the grisly terms of Shylock's contract or the gruesome retribution of angry animal spirits—is presented as a happy ending. If the effort to personify some animals as dutiful parents and loving spouses bolsters our sense of moral obligation, the personification of other animals as vengeful plaintiffs, pressing their claim beyond all reason (or, at least, beyond all sympathy) allows us to view the evasion of their demands as a welcome relief, rather than as a dereliction of justice. Indeed, the lengths to which these accounts go to effect this transformation are suggestive of the fundamental challenge posed by this vision of the moral life of Others, both to our imagination and to our ethics. In this view, animals are not only full participants in an economy of indebtedness that necessitates their inclusion in a radically reimagined social order, but they are also moral beings capable of choosing (rightly or wrongly) the terms of their inclusion.

THE ANECDOTAL IMAGINATION AND THE MARKETING OF RITUAL

At the most basic level, the *Konjaku* represents what might be described as an exercise in narrative pointillism, a collection of case studies on the intersection of principle and practice that serves to illuminate both. As Marian Ury has written: "The best anecdotes, revealing aspects of their subject that would otherwise have remained hidden, extend our knowledge. Massed together, they can form portraits which are complex and comprehensive. Boswell's *Life of Johnson* is anecdote depicting a man; *Konjaku monogatari shū* is anecdote depicting a world."[42]

The daunting size and comprehensive scope of this collection has challenged scholars seeking to identify the selection criteria and organizational principles of its compiler(s), an enterprise made all the more difficult by the lack of an authorial preface.[43] Despite efforts to impose a degree of uniformity on the material—each tale, for example, begins with the formulaic expression "a long time ago now" and ends with the statement "so it was told and so it was handed down"—the varied purposes and generic characteristics of its source materials often show through.[44] Many animal tales from the Indian section, for example, are drawn from Sanskrit past-life biographies (*avadāna*), a heavily anthropomorphized genre with close affinities to Aesop's fables.[45] Similarly, the Chinese section combines Buddhist miracle stories with passages drawn from Daoist philosophical classics like the *Zhuangzi*.[46] And in the Japanese section (the largest in the collection, with roughly twice the number of stories as the other two sections combined), accounts of past-life relationships and karmic retribution appear alongside more worldly stories celebrating the heroism of great men, in which violence against animals serves to demonstrate their strength and skill rather than their cruelty.[47] If Jakushin preached against whipping horses, and the melon seller Iwawake demonstrated the terrible karmic consequences of doing so, these other stories marvel without apology at the exceptional courage of men who are able to "break" headstrong stallions.[48]

More than a simple matter of genre and textual influence, however, this diversity should be understood as a fundamental feature of the anecdotal enterprise itself, a narrative strategy that preserves disjunctions and tensions rather than collapsing them into a single coherent plot. In the process, it may well reveal the complexities of our efforts to imagine the moral life of animals (and the obligations they entail) in a way that can be obscured by more systematic accounts. The sheer heterogeneity of these stories renders them a kind of didactic archive, a reflection of the divergent foundations and contexts in which the medieval Japanese moral imagination (and, not infrequently, our own) unfolds.

In the tales discussed above, the reader encounters at least four distinct principles underlying the moral status of animals. First, animals appear (like all other beings on the Six Paths of Rebirth) as sentient beings, marked by a shared capacity for suffering that should elicit our most basic sympathies. Second, that shared capacity for suffering also renders them figures in tales of karmic retaliation, in which the harm we cause others is revisited upon us in disturbing specificity. Third, animals are shown to have been our relatives in past lives, and are thus deserving of at least the same respect and loving-kindness we offer to our human families. Finally, animals are described as bound up with human beings in webs of indebtedness and obligation, demanding the repayment of kindnesses as well as injuries.

Of course, these principles are closely related, and often intertwine to serve the rhetorical ends of a particular story. So, for example, despite the very different emotions on which they call, the threat of immediate karmic retribution works toward a conclusion quite similar to the idea that animals were once our family members: both self-preservation and sympathy for kin introduce a degree of immediacy to animals' status that might otherwise fade into ethical abstraction. After all, it is one thing to recognize that animals are capable of suffering pain, but another to know that the animal suffering pain was your beloved father in a past life and that you will yourself suffer a comparable pain for any harm you may inflict on him.

In a similar fashion, the imagery of karmic cause and effect, like the ethics of indebtedness and obligation, presents an image of just retaliation that is often as unnerving as it is poetic. In these stories, the prospect that we will inevitably "get what's coming to us"—whether from the spontaneous unfolding of cosmic forces or the carefully laid plans of others— typically appears less as a reward to be anticipated than a punishment to be averted.[49] And it is in this regard that we might best understand what is perhaps the most pervasive theme in *Konjaku* animal tales (indeed, in the collection as a whole): a call for correct action that is grounded as much in ritual as in pragmatic or ethical action.

Perhaps this may be seen most clearly in tales of animal vengeance, where ritual observances offer the chance to escape the (essentially just) retribution of creatures we have harmed. Like the story of Sui An-gong— charged with murder in the court of the underworld—or the girl promised as bride to a snake, the reader-audience of these tales is encouraged to offer Buddhist memorial services to assuage the resentment of the animals they have wronged. In other cases, ritual action (most notably the liberation of animals) provides a way to escape the consequences of their actions altogether, by building up a repertoire of positive action (and, in some cases, spiritual character witnesses) that permit the judge to overrule the claims of the plaintiff. The efficaciousness of such rituals is further underlined by stories in which hunters are saved from judgment even by halfhearted or inadvertent ritual gestures. In one such tale, for example, a hunter who chances upon a backwoods shrine to the bodhisattva Jizō cursorily doffs his hat to the image before galloping off after his quarry. When he later finds himself before a hellish tribunal for his sins, a manifestation of Jizō appears and succeeds in securing his release back into the land of the living.[50] The story of Ju-dao appears to combine these themes in what is perhaps the most explicit example of ritual as a form of legal maneuver in the Court of the Underworld: in that story, the vow to perform memorial services and copy the animal liberationist Sutra of Golden Light is made on the way to the dock, at the suggestion of one of the hellish guards tasked with bringing him to judgment.

If the trope of King Emma's judgment seems to invite images of legal loopholes (or even the miscarriage of justice—in one tale, the protagonist escapes judgment by bribing the demons sent to collect him with freshly slaughtered beef), the more mechanistic imagery of karmic cause and effect also appears open to ritual as a means of escape.[51] While some tales of karmic retribution end with the terrible consequences of harming animals—offering a negative object lesson for those who follow—many others suggest that Buddhist rituals may offer a potent means of counteracting those consequences. So, for example, the sheep thief who miraculously lost his own tongue after excising those of his ill-gotten gains experienced an equally miraculous recovery when he offers his victims Buddhist memorial rites. Similarly, the hunters who took the tonsure when faced with the harm they had done to animal families may have done so in part to escape the moral compromises of family life (and adopt the practice of vegetarianism), but also likely because the religious life permits the greatest access to efficacious rituals. One tale, for example, tells of a priest named Yakuen who continued to hunt animals after taking the tonsure, but who nevertheless achieved salvation in Amida's Pure Land thanks to his unfailing practice of the Hokke Repentance Rites, reciting the Lotus Sutra, and chanting the Buddha's name.[52] Indeed, stories of animal rebirth are themselves offered as signs, of the power of particular scriptures not only to bestow knowledge of past lives but also to offer escape. In these stories, animals achieve human or heavenly rebirth simply by hearing the scriptures recited,[53] or even commission rituals on their behalf, speaking through dreams or spirit mediums to request the recitation or copying of scriptures.[54] In one particularly striking tale, a parrot from Persia asks not for the stereotypical cracker but for invocations of the name of Amida Buddha.[55]

In these tales, the moral agency or ethical status of animals appears less as a principle guiding our treatment of those animals than as a means to

affirm the efficacy and authority of rituals capable of averting the consequences of our actions. As Arne Kalland and Pamela Asquith have argued,
the "ritualization" of our relationships with the nonhuman natural world
provides a source of cultural and religious power, but bears no necessary
connection to sustainable ethics. The ritual pacification of animal spirits,
for example, has little appreciable impact on the well-being or ecological
viability of animals, and may actually serve to perpetuate their poor treatment by offering a means of compensating the animals we harm rather
than avoiding harm altogether.[56] Indeed, it would be easy to view this
aspect of the *Konjaku*'s didacticism as a matter of economics as much
as ethics. Insofar as these stories introduce the reader-audience to some
heretofore unsuspected peril in order to present a solution that rests solely
within the purview of professional ritualists, they represent what is in essence a form of religious marketing.[57]

Whatever the case, the sheer pervasiveness of ritualized responses to
the suffering (or the vengeance) of animals in the *Konjaku* never amounts
to univocality. The diversity of the anecdotes collected in this text means
that for virtually any position there are alternative voices that serve to
point out its weaknesses. For example, returning to the story with which
we began, we find that Jakushin did not earn the laughter of bystanders
and the disdain of the narrator because of his fundamental devotion to the
web of moral commitment that joins humanity and animals. Rather, he is
mocked for precisely the sort of naive anthropomorphism that characterizes many stories in the collection, particularly those that advocate ritual
responses to animals' moral standing. The narrator's condescension in
asking "What would dogs know about their past lives" presents a pointed
response to the self-assuredness with which those tales purport to describe
the ethical deliberations of dogs (and other animals), and their willingness
to be placated by ritual action. If his efforts (and those of the collection
as a whole) to imagine a wider moral community fall short, it may be less
because of a failure of imagination—attributable to simple hypocrisy or
the lamentable failure of ordinary people to live up to their own highest
principles—than because the very strategies of imagination that they (and
we) employ can undermine their (and our) efforts.

NOTES

1. He is the author of the *Chiteiki* (Record of a Pond Pavilion), an influential exemplar in the classical genre of miscellany (*zuihitsu*), as well as the *Nihon ōjō gokurakuki*

(Japanese Record of Rebirths in the Pure Land of Utmost Bliss), the first Japanese collection of Pure Land hagiography (*ōjōden*). Before taking the tonsure in 986, he was also a founding member of the *kangakue* (Society for the Promotion of Learning), a group of monks and lay scholars from the capital that met regularly to compose poetry and discuss Chinese learning and Buddhist doctrine. It was in this context that he likely became associated with the Pure Land thinker Genshin, whose seminal treatise on Pure Land doctrine (*Ōjōyōshū*, or Essentials of Rebirth in the Pure Land) commends Yasutane's work.

2. In what follows, I draw on the Nihon Koten Bungaku Taikei (NKBT) edition of the *Konjaku monogatarishū* , ed. Yamada Yoshio et al., vols. 22–26 (Tokyo: Iwanami Shoten, 1959–63). A complete translation of the collection can be found in Yoshiko K. Dykstra's six-volume *The Konjaku Tales* (Osaka: Kansai Gaidai University, 1986–2003).

3. KM 19:3 (NKBT 25:62).

4. Ibid. (NKBT 25:64).

5. Perhaps the best summary of the *setsuwa* didactic project remains William LaFleur, *The Karma of Words: Buddhism and the Literary Arts in Medieval Japan* (Berkeley: University of California Press, 1983), 26–59. On the links between *setsuwa* and Buddhist preaching, see Charlotte Eubanks, *Miracles of Book and Body: Buddhist Textual Culture and Medieval Japan* (Berkeley: University of California Press, 2011), 62–96.

6. A comprehensive count of such stories is complicated by the differences between medieval Japanese and modern zoological understanding. Not only do animals in the KM perform a variety of feats that we would be inclined to consider supernatural (assuming human form, growing to enormous size, breathing fire, etc.), but they may also prove to be gods, buddhas, bodhisattvas, or dragon kings in disguise. Excluding clearly imaginary creatures (like dragons and the therianthropic bird-goblins known as *tengu*), but including those tales in which animals are credited with marvelous powers, I estimate that animals play a part (as characters or as symbols) in 188 of the 1,059 extant tales in the collection, amounting to 18 percent of the total.

7. KM 13:42–43, 14:1–4, 20:23–24, 12:25, 14:37, 20:20–22.

8. KM 7:4, 14:13–25.

9. KM 14:19.

10. KM 20:29. The tale originally appears in the ninth-century *Nihonkoku genpō zen'aku ryōiki* (Record of Marvelous Karmic Retribution for Good and Evil in Japan) or *Nihon ryōiki* 1:21.

11. KM 9:23, 20:28.

12. KM 9:24, 20:30.

13. KM 9:24.

14. KM 19:6 (NKBT 25:75).

15. KM 19:8.

16. KM 9:19, 12:25, 14:37, 9:18, 19:7, 20:34, 28:33, 20:16.

17. Mata Sutta (Saṃyutta Nikāya 15:14–19) in *The Connected Discourses of the Buddha: A New Translation of the* Saṃyutta Nikāya, trans. Bhikkhu Bodhi (Boston: Wisdom Publications, 2000), 1:659.

18. With a dozen tales (KM 6:45, 7:46, 9:17, 9:30, 12:25, 12:36, 13:43, 13.44, 14:37, 19:7, 20:16, 20:34), this is one of the most frequently repeated tropes in the *Konjaku*'s animal tales.

19. Peter Singer, ed., "Animals," in *Companion to Ethics* (Oxford: Blackwell, 1991), 350.

20. Ian Harris makes note of this tension (including the notion that a given animal may, indeed, have been one's parent in a past life) in "'A vast unsupervised recycling plant': Animals and the Buddhist Cosmos," in *A Communion of Subjects: Animals in Religion, Science, and Ethics*, ed. Paul Waldau and Kimberly Patton (New York: Columbia University Press, 2006), 208–9.

21. Some tales in the *Konjaku* do describe animals who listen receptively to scripture recitations, and even make offerings to the holy men who do so (KM 12:34, 12:40, 13:2, 13:4). Yet, as Barbara Ambros notes, the nature of animals in much Buddhist literature is clearly described as bestial (*chikushō*)—see *Bones of Contention: Animals and Religion in Contemporary Japan* (Honolulu: University of Hawai'i Press, 2012), 35–38. These tales should therefore perhaps be viewed as the exceptions that prove the rule, demonstrating the power of the Buddhist teachings (especially when conveyed by holy men) to reach even the minds of brutes.

22. The lack of these stories in the Indian section of the collection would seem to correlate well with the argument of Lisa Grumbach, who locates the development of Buddhist rhetoric against meat eating in the Chinese engagement with Confucian and Daoist dietary restrictions ("Sacrifice and Salvation in Medieval Japan: Hunting and Meat in Religious Practice at Suwa Shrine" [Ph.D. diss., Stanford University, 2005], 50–85).

23. KM 5:19.

24. KM 9:13 (NKBT 23:203).

25. KM 19:30.

26. KM 5:27, 29:35–36.

27. On the scriptural precedents and Japanese history of the rite, see Jane Marie Law, "Violence, Ritual Reenactment, and Ideology: The 'Hōjō-e' (Rite for Release of Sentient Beings) of the Usa Hachiman Shrine in Japan," *History of Religions* 33, no. 4 (1994): 325–27. As Duncan Ryūken Williams notes, the ritual of releasing captured animals was ironically (and, insofar as it was intentional, perversely) predicated on the capturing of those animals in the first place, many of which would perish before the completion of the ritual ("Animal Liberation, Death, and the State: Rites to Release Animals in Medieval Japan," in *Buddhism and Ecology: The Interconnection of Dharma and Deeds*, ed. Mary Evelyn Tucker and Duncan Ryūken Williams [Cambridge, MA: Harvard University Press, 1997], 149–62).

28. KM 20:15 (NKBT 25:173).

29. KM 29:35–36.

30. KM 5:19 (NKBT 22:380).

31. Elsewhere in the collection (see, for example, KM 24:9, 29:39–40), snakes appear as lascivious creatures, pursuing women (and, in one case, a man) for sexual purposes.

32. KM 16:16.

33. KM 29:36.

34. KM 26:20; see also KM 14:2.

35. KM 9:25.

36. This theme appears in both the Chinese and the Japanese sections, including KM 6:35, 6:41, 9:22, 9:29, 17:26, 20:15.

37. KM 6:41 (NKBT 23:109).

38. KM 9:22 (NKBT 23:217).

39. KM 20:15 (NKBT 25:172). In literal terms, they threaten to "make him into *namasu*," a kind of cold meat salad composed of raw seafood and vegetables, marinated

in vinegar. Dykstra's choice of the term "mincemeat" (*The Konjaku Tales*, 5:188) seems the best idiomatic translation.

40. KM 20:15 (NKBT 25:173).

41. For animals as rightful litigants in court in the Abrahamic traditions, see Crane and Gross, chapter 12 of this volume; *Merchant of Venice*, Act 3, Scene 1.

42. Marian Ury, *Tales of Times Now Past: Sixty-Two Stories from a Medieval Japanese Collection* (Ann Arbor: University of Michigan Center for Japanese Studies, 1979), 10.

43. Unlike other *setsuwa* collections, the compiler(s) of the *Konjaku monogatarishū* remain unknown—the contemporary consensus holds it to have been the work of a committee, working at the behest of a well-funded patron; their motivations for embarking on such a daunting literary enterprise remain similarly unknown. A summary of scholarship on the text can be found in Michelle Osterfeld Li, *Ambiguous Bodies: Reading the Grotesque in Japanese* Setsuwa *Tales* (Stanford: Stanford University Press, 2009), 16–30.

44. The Chinese characters used for the first of these formulae can be read as "*ima wa mukashi*" or as "*konjaku*." It is the latter reading from which the collection derives its title.

45. See especially KM 5:13–14, 20–21, 24–25.

46. KM 10:11–13.

47. KM 23:22–23, 25:6. In one case, a samurai's ability to shoot a fox from a great distance is even credited to the assistance of the gods and buddhas (KM 25:6).

48. KM 22:4, 23:26.

49. This may, in fact, represent a characteristically East Asian motif. In his study of Chinese *zhiguai* tales (many of which served as source materials for the *Konjaku*), Robert Campany notes that for all their common desire to explicate the workings of karmic cause and effect, Chinese tales demonstrate a fundamentally different tone from their Indian predecessors, emphasizing the dire and immediate repercussions of evil acts rather than the sublime benefits of small acts of kindness and devotion unfolding over myriad rebirths (*Signs from the Unseen Realms: Buddhist Miracle Tales from Early Medieval China* [Honolulu: University of Hawai'i Press, 2012], 33).

50. KM 17:24. See also 6:11, 24.

51. KM 20:19.

52. KM 15:30; another tale (KM 6:18) describes a man who performs recitations of Amida's name in order to save his parents from the Crying Hell—where they had been born for the sin of eating meat—and secure their rebirth in Amida's Pure Land.

53. See, for example, KM 3:12, 4:19, 7:10, 7:13, 7:24, 13:17, 13.43.

54. See, for example, KM 12:36, 13:42, 13.44, 14:1, 14.3–6.

55. KM 4:36.

56. Pamela Asquith and Arne Kalland, *Japanese Images of Nature: Cultural Perspectives* (Richmond, Surrey: Curzon, 1997), 20.

57. The economic contexts of Buddhist ritual performances is a theme in a number of recent works on Japanese religion. Nam-lin Hur, for example, describes the importance of miracle stories advocating the efficacy of "prayer goods" and "prayer services" exchanged for "prayer fees" at Asakusa Sensōji in *Prayer and Play in Late Tokugawa Japan: Asakusa Sensōji and Edo Society* (Cambridge: Harvard University Press, 2000), 33–47; and Barbara Ambros devotes considerable attention to the economic implications and marketing strategies of memorial rites for animals in *Bones of Contention*. Perhaps the most striking example of such an approach remains Helen Hardacre's study

of the postwar development of memorial rites for aborted fetuses (*mizuko kuyō*), where she writes: "*Mizuko kuyō* was advanced as the 'answer' to a 'problem' created mostly by those purveying the rites in question" (*Marketing the Menacing Fetus in Japan* [Berkeley: University of California Press, 1997], 251). Not surprisingly, the entrepreneurial marketing of religious services of this kind is perhaps most easily traced in the modern and early-modern periods, although Ian Reader and George Tanabe touch on its premodern precursors in *Practically Religious: Worldly Benefits and the Common Religion of Japan* (Honolulu: University of Hawai'i Press, 1998), 209–11.

Part Four **Reconceiving Animal Morality**

Eleven Just Chimpanzees?

A THOMISTIC PERSPECTIVE ON ETHICS IN A NONHUMAN SPECIES

John Berkman

MY ARGUMENT FOR ASSERTING THAT it makes sense to speak of a chimpanzee ethics from a Thomistic perspective proceeds in five parts.[1] First, I will explain what I mean by "Thomistic" and situate this inquiry within that field of study, as well as explain what "ethics" means in Thomistic perspective. Second, I will outline common approaches to thinking about ethics in nonhuman animals that I will argue are unhelpful and should be avoided. In particular, I will criticize the "principle of parsimony" and also the tendency among many ethicists to generalize about the lack of "reason" and/or "ethics" in all nonhuman animals.[2] Thus I restrict my focus to "just chimpanzees." Third, I will characterize a Thomistic approach to thinking about the possibility of a chimpanzee ethic as an "ethics of continuity," namely that ethics arises out of the nature, telos, and desires of a particular species, and that the possibility of a morality depends on the capacity of the species in question to engage in practical rationality—that is, making choices about what it should do. Fourth, I will examine the kinds of characteristics that a Thomist will attribute both to chimpanzees and to human beings that are necessary substrata to attribute an ethic to a species. Fifth and finally, I will examine characteristics of what an Aristotelian-Thomistic framework considers to be the virtue of justice—that is, the virtue Thomas considers the most distinctly human of the cardinal virtues—then examine instances of practical rationality[3] that chimpanzees have been shown to engage in, and at last draw my conclusions as to whether one can fairly attribute justice to chimpanzees.

INTRODUCTION

In a contribution to an interdisciplinary volume, it should be noted that "Thomistic ethics" refers to the tradition of moral thought in continuity with the approach to ethics of Thomas Aquinas, the thirteenth-century theologian and philosopher.[4] Of course, a contemporary Thomist will not agree with all of Aquinas's views (any more than an Aristotelian will agree with all of Aristotle's views). For instance, aspects of Aquinas's ethics derive from views of the relationship between individuals and institutions that are generally rejected by contemporary societies. And many of Aquinas's views—e.g., his medical and embryological views—were based on premises now known to be scientifically false. However, Aquinas's views on human nature, his purpose-guided approach to human life, and his understanding of human actions, emotions, and virtues are all still highly important and influential, and it is to those views to which "Thomistic ethics" refers in this essay.

It has been typically assumed, though sometimes argued, that a Thomistic morality—with its apparently strong contrast between humans and nonhuman animals in the magisterial *Summa Theologiae*[5]—cannot have an account of ethics in any nonhuman animals. Furthermore, some Thomists seem to believe that Aquinas simply ruled out on metaphysical grounds the possibility of free choice, and thus ethics, among any other earthly animals.[6] Now, it is true that Aquinas *did* not have an ethics for nonhuman animals. In various places Aquinas asserts the view that nonhuman animals were unable to engage in the kind of practical rationality necessary for morality.[7] However, I take the view here that Aquinas's views of the amorality of nonhuman animals were instead based on the knowledge he had of the capacities of various "perfect" animals, and thus his views on this topic would be open to revision based on what one might know or come to know about such animals, for example, chimpanzees.[8]

Let me be very clear up front as to what I wish to argue here: an authentic Thomistic morality can be and must be open to the possibility that among all the other animals, there may be some species, or individual animals within a variety of species, whom one can legitimately refer to as having or embodying a "morality." Because my point is that one must have a sophisticated understanding of the form of life of members of a particular species of animal to make judgments about the capacity for morality, in this essay I will focus almost exclusively on chimpanzees. What I will argue is how—on a Thomistic approach—one can appropriately come to the judgment that at least some chimpanzees are "just."

It is worth noting that although I will refer to Thomistic (and even at times Aquinas's views regarding the emotions, intelligence, practical rationality, and virtues of chimpanzees), it is not clear whether Aquinas would have been familiar with the particular species we now know as chimpanzees (and certainly not under that name).[9] But he was surely familiar with a variety of primates, as monkeys and apes were extremely popular in medieval "animal shows," and they were also kept as (expensive) pets in many western European towns.[10]

Furthermore, Aquinas's teacher Albert was the greatest zoologist of the medieval period and wrote about a variety of species of simians—i.e., monkeys and apes—as the most intelligent of nonhuman animals. Albert notes that these simians show a "human likeness beyond all other animals" and that they "seem to have something like reason."[11] Thus, when Aquinas refers to the "perfect animals," he certainly included simians in that group, although he did not have an animal as intelligent as a chimpanzee in mind when he made his general comments about the sensitive and cognitive capacities of "perfect animals."

In addition to explaining "Thomistic," it will no doubt help if I also introduce his understanding of "ethics," and what it might mean to speak of a chimpanzee ethic or a virtuous chimpanzee. Broadly speaking, a Thomistic ethic is Aristotelian. As it is with Aristotle, ethics for Aquinas is primarily about the cultivation of the virtues or excellences of character necessary for them to flourish according to their nature as human beings.[12]

But we must be careful here, for flourishing is a necessary but not sufficient condition for "ethics" to be involved. A cabbage, a clam, or my cat may flourish according to its nature, but that does not mean that any "ethics" are involved. According to Aquinas, ethics pertains to human life insofar as a human being "is the principle of his actions, as having free-will and control of his actions."[13] So in a Thomistic account, if we are to speak of a chimpanzee ethic, we will have to be able to attribute some degree of "free-will and control of his or her actions" to a chimpanzee. As with a human ethic, the choices made by the chimpanzee must either contribute (or detract) from his or her flourishing. And by flourishing, we mean both its individual flourishing and (as a social animal) the flourishing of its wider kin group and/or troop.[14] Furthermore, if a Thomist is to speak of a "just chimpanzee," it entails the view that such a chimpanzee

develops a certain kind of character, and can be more or less just, coura-
geous, or wise.[15]

As I noted above, within a Thomistic framework we can speak of all
living creatures as either flourishing or failing to flourish according to
their kind, but that does not entail morality. Tulips and tarantulas may
successfully go through the life cycle that we attribute to healthy tulips or
tarantulas, but we don't think of either as making choices, nor of a moral
or immoral tulip or tarantula. And most modern Thomists (like most
moderns generally) up until recently seem to have thought that animals
such as chimpanzees or elephants are rather like tulips or tarantulas in that
their flourishing or failing to flourish is determined much in the same way
as the flourishing of tulips or tarantulas—through having good or bad
fortune in terms of purely external conditions allowing them to flourish
or preventing them from flourishing. Flourishing for such creatures has
nothing to do with free will and control.

On the contrary, human beings, while also subject to external conditions (e.g., disease, famine, war, etc.), what Aquinas called *fortuna*, are
also able through their actions and cultivation of character to increase
or decrease their likelihood of a flourishing existence. Both Aristotle and
Aquinas believed that cultivating excellences of character maximized the
likelihood that one would flourish as a human being, regardless of the
degree to which good or bad fortune accompanied a person in life. To
attribute an ethic to a chimpanzee, the Thomist will be committed to
the view that a chimp's being "just" or possessing other chimpanzee virtues will increase the likelihood of that chimp's flourishing, and if widely
practiced or practiced by key members of a chimpanzee society, will also
contribute to the flourishing of that society.

AVOIDING AN ERRONEOUS APPROACH

Chimpanzees live in close-knit societies, and yet there are bouts of aggression and discord among them. After extensive observation, de Waal
and his associates noticed a striking pattern among chimpanzees in which
former opponents in a squabble were "attracted to each other like mag-
nets! Much of the time, we registered contact rather than avoidance in the
aftermath of fights."[16] De Waal goes on to discuss the patterns of embracing, kissing, and grooming that so often occurred with former opponents
in a fight, sometimes immediately after the fight, but at other times hours

later. He notes that conflicts between two individual chimpanzees affected the whole group, that tension and hesitancy remained in the group until the differences between the opponents had been resolved and the former combatants made affectionate overtures to each other. De Waal then says:

> The obvious word to describe this phenomenon is reconciliation, but I have heard people object to it on the grounds that by choosing such terms chimpanzees are unnecessarily humanized. Why not call it something neutral like "first post-conflict contact," because after all that is what it is? Out of the same desire for objectivity, kissing could be called "mouth-mouth contact," embrace "arms-around-shoulder," face "snout," and hand "front paw." I am inclined to take the motives put forward in favor of dehumanized terminology with a pinch of salt. Is it not an attempt to veil in words the mirror that chimpanzees hold up to us? Might we not be sticking our heads in the sand to preserve our need for dignity?[17]

This brings us to the point that all observers of chimpanzees (or a variety of other nonhuman animals, for that matter) bring their preconceptions to their observations. Those more willing to see continuity and analogies between human and chimpanzee behavior tend to appeal to the principle of evolutionary parsimony. De Waal explains that "evolutionary parsimony" is the principle that if closely related species act similarly, then we should presume that the underlying sensory, emotional, and cognitive processes that lead to those actions are also similar.[18] On the other hand, those who tend to resist seeing continuity between chimpanzee and human behavior also appeal to a principle of parsimony, sometimes called cognitive parsimony, namely that one should not attribute cognitive processes to another creature without overwhelming evidence, presumably because for so long the reigning scientific doctrine has been that other animals do not think.

The Thomistic philosopher Marie George, in an otherwise interesting and insightful article, explicitly affirms the principle of cognitive parsimony. In the midst of discussing chimpanzee tool use to extract termites from logs, George adopts a non-cognitive explanation for it and concludes that "assuming that the [chimpanzee] thinks is contrary to the principle of parsimony."[19] Rather than simply noting or giving reasons why she finds the evidence for chimpanzee cognition unconvincing, she raises her objection to the level of preexisting epistemic principle.

But what, we may ask, is problematic about holding to the principle of "cognitive parsimony"? Is it not the right approach to doubt that animals can think unless we can clearly infer it from their behavior? Alasdair MacIntyre, another Thomistic philosopher, argues that this is exactly the wrong approach to take if one wants to understand the nature and capacities of chimpanzees or other nonhuman animals (in his work on the subject, MacIntyre focuses on dolphins and other cetaceans). Contrary to those philosophers who are deeply troubled by the problem of "other minds" (i.e., how can one *know* if any other human beings actually have minds) and those who apply the "principle of parsimony" to what otherwise appear to be signs of theoretical or practical intelligence in chimpanzees and/or other nonhuman animals, MacIntyre argues that human beings come to essential understandings of other human and nonhuman animals *only* through interactive interpretative experience of them. MacIntyre notes that it was Descartes's error to think "that our beliefs about the thoughts, feelings and decisions of others are wholly founded on inferences from their overt behavior and utterances."[20] In contrast, according to MacIntyre, our ability to understand other humans and nonhuman animals depends on a "more fundamental interpretative knowledge of the thoughts and feelings of others which does not have and does not need inferential justification."[21] Rather, interactive interpretive experience of other people and other nonhuman animals is absolutely crucial in coming to understand the practical rationality of them, for without it "we would be unable to ascribe thoughts and feelings to others, whether human infants or dogs or whatever."[22]

In other words, we can come to understand the capacities of chimpanzees only through extensive interaction with them and wise interpretation of what we experience with them—that is, the kind of interaction to which ethologists like Jane Goodall and Frans de Waal have devoted much of their lives. I say "ethologists like Jane Goodall and Frans de Waal" because we should be careful not to give equal weight to the experience of some who extensively interact with chimpanzees—i.e., those who for one reason or another are captured by a preexisting account of what chimpanzees "should" or "should not" be able to do.[23]

The upshot of all this is that to come to a fair judgment about the extent to which (if at all) chimpanzees exhibit practical rationality and the virtues, one must turn to the experience of those who have this experience, and thus Franz de Waal is a central interlocutor in the final section of this essay. It is reasonable to believe that Thomas Aquinas, in addition to his own direct experience of a variety of nonhuman animals, similarly depended on a "medieval Frans de Waal" as an authority for his judgments about the rational capacities of a variety of "perfect animals," namely his teacher Albert. While Albert the Great undoubtedly wrote the finest zoological text of the medieval period, and while he was well aware of some of the intellectual capacities of monkeys, apes, dolphins, and whales, his knowledge of those mammals was secondhand and limited.[24] It should not surprise us then if a contemporary Thomist diverges from Thomas on some of his judgments about "perfect animals."

AN ETHIC OF CONTINUITY

In the history of theology and philosophy, one can divide the understanding of the nature (and in some cases origins) of morality into two camps. On the one hand, there are those who believe that human morality is on a continuum with and/or develops out of characteristics that humans share with other nonhuman animals. In this camp one will find classic thinkers like Aristotle and Aquinas, Enlightenment philosophers like Hume, and Darwinians like Westermarck.[25] On the other hand, there are those who believe that morality is something in humans that reflects a fundamental disjunction from all other creatures. In this camp one will find ancients like the Gnostics, moderns like Descartes and Kant, and Darwinians like Huxley.[26]

For example, Albert the Great's *On Animals* includes an extended discussion of the bodily form of the human animal and its perfection and clearly relates the human's rational ability to its bodily form. In Albert's discussion of various other animals, he proceeds with the view that the degree of bodily likeness to humans is associated with the degree of mental likeness to humans. Thus, in his discussion of pygmies and monkeys, he classifies them in such a way that the descending scale of physical likeness to humans corresponds with their mental likeness.[27]

Now, while those in the "continuity" camp such as Aristotle, Albert, and Aquinas may not have been willing to attribute morality to simians, it would be because while they thought simians shared a variety of emotional and intellectual capacities with human beings, they did not view simians as sharing with human beings all the capacities necessary for "reason" or morality.

BUILDING BLOCKS OF A THOMISTIC MORALITY

Before discussing the characteristic that according to most Thomists divides humans from chimpanzees (and all other animals), let us first look
at what any Thomist should say about the capacities that humans and
chimpanzees share—that is, the elements of continuity between humans
and other primates in terms of the foundational building blocks of reason
and ethics. As noted earlier, when one speaks of ethics or morality in the
Thomistic framework, one is basically drawing on a largely Aristotelian
architectonic in ethics. Let me briefly summarize three key aspects of an
Aristotelian-Thomistic ethical framework:

First, a Thomistic ethic is committed to the view that all animals (including humans) have a nature and a telos. For Aquinas the telos of a
human being or a chimpanzee is to flourish *qua* human being or chimpanzee. Second, a Thomistic ethic is committed to the view that the building blocks of morality are (a) the knowledge obtained by the senses and
(b) the desires of the sense appetites. For Aquinas, simians and other
"perfect" animals as well as human beings have these building blocks
as the source of their activity. Third, a Thomistic ethic is committed to
the view that ethics requires will ("rational desire"). By rational desire is
meant the ability to reflect on the desires given by one's sense appetites,
determining whether they in fact serve one's individual good, and/or the
good of another, and/or the common good.

Each of these three building blocks requires more elaboration. In this
section I will discuss the first two, namely the telos for humans and the
senses (i.e., prerational sources), and in the following section I will discuss
the will.

The End for Humans and Chimpanzees

According to Aquinas, animals (humans and chimpanzees) are ordered
toward their *telos* or *flourishing* as humans and chimpanzees. That is, there
is the notion of a "good" for a chimpanzee that is good according to
its species, requiring the knowledge and actions that contribute to that
particular chimpanzee's flourishing as a member of the species. This is
what one contemporary Aristotelian philosopher refers to as the "natural
goodness" of animals like human beings and chimpanzees.[28] With chimpanzees as well as with humans, it is clear that both their eating and their

social habits are not merely "given" by their nature, but also involve the development of a non-universal "culture" that obtains only among some chimpanzee communities or only among a chimpanzee community at particular times.

With regard to chimpanzee eating habits, a chimpanzee must know what foods are good to eat and how to obtain them. While the need to eat is part of chimpanzee nature, the kinds of foods a particular chimpanzee community eats, and especially its use of various tools to get its food (e.g., termites out of logs or seeds out of hard shells), would seem to be a "cultural" development. Tool use by chimpanzees is clearly a learned behavior, either independently devised by a chimpanzee or learned from another chimpanzee. The fact that different communities of chimpanzees devise and develop different tool use depending on their habitat and/or ingenuity would seem to show that tool use is a "cultural" development and that these developments are part of a chimpanzee's flourishing.

With regard to chimpanzees as social and political creatures, the social and hierarchical nature of chimpanzees makes having an alpha chimpanzee part of their nature. However, the personality and characteristics of the alpha chimpanzee have significant impact on the degree to which the whole chimpanzee community flourishes or fails to flourish. For example, de Waal discusses at length the transition of the alpha status within the Arnhem community from Mama to Yeroen. He notes that the transition was important for the community as a whole because after the transition there was much less violence and fewer injuries suffered among the chimpanzees in the group.[29]

> There was a very urgent reason for wanting to curb Mama's power. . . . [Chimpanzees] were being injured at a rate of almost one a week and having to be kept apart for a while until they had recovered. The injuries were mainly Mama's work. Not only did she bite frequently, but she drew blood and sometimes ripped her victim's skin. . . . As far as the number of injuries in the group was concerned, Yeroen's rise to power was a relief. The lowest ranking individuals especially benefitted from the changeover. Instead of Mama's fierce attacks, there was Yeroen, who could be harsh, but who never went too far.[30]

The fact that one chimpanzee leader can be far superior to another in terms of serving the good of the community is in itself important for understanding that chimpanzee flourishing depends on the character of its leaders as well as on external conditions and natural desires and instincts. An even more important example (which I will return to later) is that of Luit, who led his chimpanzee community in a remarkably impartial manner, showing "a lack of correlation between his social preferences (measured by association and grooming) and intervention in open conflict. Only Luit showed this dissociation: interventions by other individuals were biased in favor of friends and family."[31] This is strong evidence indeed that the decisions by a chimpanzee leader contribute both to the individual good of chimpanzees and, more importantly, to the common good and communal flourishing of the chimpanzee community.

Prerational Sources of Human and Chimpanzee Knowledge and Action

For a human or chimpanzee to flourish, it must (a) recognize the various goods of its nature and (b) be able to pursue them.[32] According to Aquinas, all possibilities of *knowing* for a human or a chimpanzee begin with the *senses*, and all possibilities for *action* begin with *sense desires* (i.e., emotions or "passions"). In other words, at the most basic level, for both humans and chimpanzees the senses are the first source of all knowledge of their world and of various goods of their nature. Similarly, at the most basic level, for both chimpanzees and humans sensible desires are the first source of all actions. We will examine a Thomistic understanding of the senses and sense desires in turn.

Aquinas thinks that humans and simians can accomplish a lot by relying on their senses and sense desires. The everyday phrase for living according to common sense (which has medieval origins) is "living by one's wits." One Thomist describes a variety of contemporary life skills and arts as things that human beings do by their wits, such as tying one's shoes, learning to ride a bicycle, or cooking.[33] One would expect on this account that survival skills like crossing the road safely, or social skills like learning to get along with others at school or work, or arts and crafts like learning to hit a baseball, knit, play the piano, or memorize passages from Shakespeare or the Bible would also be considered skills that do not require a Thomistic understanding of rationality.

The centrality of the senses for knowing things for flourishing is easily demonstrated by limiting one. De Waal, for example, discusses Krom, a deaf female chimpanzee, who managed excellently as a community member despite her disability. However, Krom was unable to raise her offspring. She was unable to hear the auditory cues of her offspring, and each died within a few weeks of birth.[34]

According to Aquinas, both humans and simians have nine senses. Both have five exterior senses (sight, hearing, smell, taste, and touch) and four interior senses.[35] The four interior senses are the ways humans and chimpanzees make sense of and then make use of what they take in with their exterior senses. The *central sense* is the ability to make a gestalt, comprehend what one sees or hears or touches. Anyone familiar with Wittgenstein's duck-rabbit or Oliver Sacks's various case studies knows that this is a gradual and learned process from infancy onward. The *imaginative sense*, or imagination, is what allows a chimpanzee or a human to retain the seen or heard gestalt, storing it for future recollection. The *estimative sense* is a kind of practical rationality whereby a chimpanzee or a human apprehends intentions that do not come from the senses. In other words, the estimative sense allows the chimpanzee to recognize the lion not just as a lion but also as a threat that it should run away from, or allows a human being to recognize the chocolate cake as something delicious or the poison ivy leaves as not something with which to wipe its behind. Finally, the *memorative sense* allows chimpanzees and humans to retain the practical knowledge regarding lions and poison ivy for future use.[36]

It is worth saying a little more about the estimative sense, as it is the most complex of the senses. It is primarily concerned with a chimpanzee's finding effective means to fulfill his ends. One example from de Waal's community of chimpanzees is when the declining alpha chimp Yeroen, who is under siege from his upstart challenger Nickie for the position of alpha male, realizes that if he fakes an injury whenever he is around Nickie, Nickie will leave him alone for a period of time.[37] Whether the purpose is to get a larger snack or to get relief from a political challenger, through the estimative sense these chimpanzees achieve their purposes more efficiently and effectively. This ability of a chimpanzee to act with reason—whether it is to recognize and flee from a predator or fake a limp to buy time from a community rival—is what I will henceforth refer to as *basic* practical rationality. It is important to note that Aquinas does not consider the exercise of these sorts of practical rationality to constitute rationality proper; that, as we shall see, is restricted to what I will call reflective practical rationality.

In addition to sharing the nine senses, chimpanzees and humans also share the full range of sensible desires. Aquinas divides these sensible desires into concupiscible and irascible desires.[38]

The concupiscible desires are love and hatred, sensory desire and aversion, delight (or joy) and sorrow. These desires are essentially passive, in that they respond to external stimuli or conditions. A human or chimpanzee comes across some berries it loves, is attracted to them, and acts to get them. A human or chimpanzee may be delighted by a ball or other toy, playing with it at length. If a human or a chimpanzee is defeated in a conflict, it is likely to feel sorrow. These sensible desires also respond to internal stimuli such as hunger, thirst, or sexual desire.

The irascible desires are hope and despair, fear and daring, and anger. These irascible desires are more "cognitive" in that they are not an immediate response to stimuli but require a concerted effort by a human or a chimpanzee to possess them. De Waal provides numerous examples of chimpanzee activities that a Thomist could assign to these various passions or emotions, although perhaps these examples push the boundaries of what Aquinas thought a simian could do by its wits.

For example, de Waal relates a story about Dandy, an adolescent male chimpanzee who when in the midst of other chimpanzees does not reveal that he's spotted a cache of delicious grapefruits that have been half-hidden in their outdoor enclosure. It is only hours later, when the other chimpanzees are dozing and none are in sight of the cache of grapefruit, that Dandy rushes back to the spot to eat all of the grapefruit himself.[39] This story clearly shows Dandy's strong love of the grapefruit when he sees it. If it had been some other, less desirable food the chimpanzee might have notified others of it and shared it immediately. The example also shows the chimpanzee's memorative sense and presumably a very strong estimative sense (i.e., basic practical rationality). [40]

De Waal also shows the necessity of the irascible passion of hope in the many examples of when a maturing male chimpanzee begins to challenge the alpha chimpanzee. If the challenger did not have hope that he could eventually triumph, then he would abort his ongoing quest and settle in as another mid-ranking male in the community. Because the challenger's efforts have no guarantee of success, it can only be that he does what he does out of hope for success. In this way his hope is an irascible passion.

REASONING AND PRACTICAL RATIONALITY

When one comes to understand adequately Aquinas's view of reason, what is perhaps striking is not that he thinks that chimpanzees are incapable of it, but that he attributes so little of it to human beings. As we noted earlier, while Aquinas certainly thinks that chimpanzees participate in intelligence through the estimative sense and in basic practical rationality, he does not attribute to them reflective practical rationality, which he thinks is necessary for rationality and morality, strictly speaking.

For Aquinas, morality requires a particular kind of desire or appetite, namely "rational appetite," otherwise known as the will. According to Aquinas, the will is something that humans must use to flourish fully as human beings—that is, to find the happiness appropriate to human beings. The will gives humans the ability to question and reverse a decision based on their sense-desires.[41] If chimpanzees have the ability to choose freely, they would also be expected to use it and be held similarly responsible for their actions.

Now, the question is, can a chimpanzee do this? Can it first have a desire to do something, such as eat a particular food, but then deliberate about the goodness of the food and reverse course? We can certainly imagine a chimpanzee who typically has an unpleasant reaction to a food it very much likes (peanuts and chocolate candy are apparently favorites of chimpanzees), and then one day as it is about to consume the chocolate candy it remembers those unpleasant sensations in its gastrointestinal tract and decides to avoid this delicacy. Two steps would be necessary for the "rational" or moral perspective to arise. First, the chimpanzee would have to make the connection between eating the chocolate and his gastrointestinal issues (that's the chimpanzee's memorative sense). Second, at some point he would choose not to eat that particular food that he loved because he would realize it was not good for him on some deeper level.

Of course the problem with this possibility is that the skeptic will simply say that in this situation one desire—fear of abdominal pain—came to the chimpanzee's mind in a delayed fashion after it was initially planning to eat the treat, and so rather than that representing reflection on its choice, the chimpanzee is simply having one sensible desire necessarily "win out" over the other, and thus is not deliberating at all. Is there a way to avoid this kind of problem with any attribution of deliberation to a chimpanzee, short of the chimpanzee learning to speak and telling us the kind of mental process with which it is engaged? Does the chimpanzee merely possess basic practical rationality—that is, it has reasons for its actions? Or does the chimpanzee also at times reflect on its desires and reverse them—that is, can the chimpanzee exercise reflective practical rationality?[42]

The Kantian philosopher Christine Korsgaard, in her discussion of de Waal's work, wrestles with this problematic. For her, it is correct to say of a chimpanzee that it can entertain its purposes, and perhaps think about how to achieve those purposes. But Korsgaard denies that a chimpanzee can "choose to pursue those purposes."[43] Again, this seems to be accepting that chimpanzees have basic but not reflective practical rationality. She goes on to say that a chimpanzee's purposes are given to him by his sensible desires. She then gives the example of a chimpanzee who must choose between two purposes—say a male wants to mate with a female but a larger male is coming and he wants to avoid a fight—the choice is made for him by the strength of his affective states.[44] In other words, chimpanzees do not question the purposes given to them by their sensible appetites.

But the way Korsgaard sets up her example, it would seem difficult if not impossible to falsify it. Is this an example of Korsgaard's succumbing to the problematic principle of parsimony? Furthermore, both the Kantian Korsgaard and the typical Thomist seem to subscribe to the view that all nonhuman animals are "wantons," that is, they are all "defined as creatures vulnerable to whatever impulse strikes them."[45]

Let us construct a more interesting example. It is about Dandy, the grapefruit-loving male chimpanzee. A bit of background is needed first. De Waal explains that Dandy, the youngest and lowest-ranking of the four adult male chimpanzees in the Arnham community, is generally prevented by the dominant males in the group from having sexual intercourse with the adult females in the group. Nevertheless, Dandy—as with the grapefruit—periodically is able to furtively arrange discreet mating sessions with an interested female, out of sight and hearing of the other males. Mating sessions that go on behind the back of the alpha males (and/or other dominants) are known as "dates."[46]

In our example, Dandy is lounging in the afternoon—while the other dominant males are snoozing—and notices two attractive possibilities simultaneously. First, he notices that a female chimpanzee seems interested in a "date." He realizes that if he acts quickly and surreptitiously, he'll likely get his date. Second, he notices that one of his favorite foods has been put out to eat, and some of the other chimpanzees are going over to eat it. In Korsgaard's model, Dandy's "choice" will be determined by his affective state—does he date or does he eat?[47] According to those who see chimps as "wanton," it will be determined by Dandy's strongest impulse. Aquinas's and Korsgaard's Dandy will simply pursue one or the other. However, if there's one thing that de Waal's work seems to shows us, it is that chimpanzees are able to strategize about how best to achieve their desires. What if it were the case that Dandy regularly ordered his actions in ways that consistently increased his chances of getting both his food *and* his date? If an experiment were performed that showed that at least some chimpanzees consistently chose in ways that would increase the likelihood of both desires being fulfilled, would this be an example of reflective practical rationality? If it occurred, it would certainly appear to fit Aquinas's definition of choice or deliberation, which, as he notes, is not of the end, but of the means to achieve a given end, and not about the general good of the creature, but about particular goods for it.[48]

In light of the inherent difficulties with determining whether chimpanzees pass the "Thomistic test" for reflective practical rationality, it seems more promising to follow the route that MacIntyre suggests, noted earlier. That is, that we immerse ourselves in prereflective experiences of the capacities of chimpanzees that de Waal and other ethologist relate to us. Rather than considering whether they pass the standard Thomistic test, we instead examine whether chimpanzees in their actions seem to embody something analogous to particular Thomistic moral virtues (specifically justice and its various elements, including compassion). For if chimpanzees in fact possess the virtue of justice or something analogous to it, then one would have to conclude that they have the use of reflective practical rationality and hence have a morality. So at this point we turn to a variety of examples of the activities of chimpanzees to see the kind of practical rationality exemplified by them—specifically whether they seem to constitute merely *basic* practical rationality (having reasons for action) or also *reflective* practical rationality.

JUSTICE AND CHARITY IN HUMANS AND CHIMPANZEES

Although many different kinds of chimpanzee activity could be cited to illustrate a Thomistic sense of morality, I will focus on those activities that show something analogous to the human virtue of justice. When discussing the most fundamental inclinations of human life, Aquinas firmly locates the inclination to "live in society" (his brief description of the inclination that necessitates the virtue of justice) as a rational inclination. As he puts it:

There is in man an inclination to good, according to the nature of his reason, which nature is proper to him: thus man has a natural inclination . . . to live in society: and in this respect, whatever pertains to this inclination belongs to the natural law; for instance . . . to avoid offending those among whom one has to live, and other such things regarding the above inclination.[49]

In other words, justice is a particularly apt virtue to discuss with regard to chimpanzees because of Aquinas's four cardinal virtues (practical rationality, justice, courage, and temperance), Aquinas particularly emphasizes the rational character of justice (as seen in the quoted passage above). Whereas virtues like courage and temperance arise out of the proper ordering of the passions, "justice is about a man's relations with another, and we are not directed immediately to another by the internal passions."[50] In other words, for Aquinas, learning to "live in society" and to "avoid offending those among whom one has to live" are rational tasks![51]

However, Aquinas seems to be mistaken in his failure to recognize the emotional seeds of the virtue of justice. For there are a number of inclinations and emotions that very young humans share with chimpanzees and that seem to be seeds of the virtue of justice. For example, long before the "age of reason," children have an inherent sense of certain things not being "fair" (especially to them) and exhibit both positive and negative "retributive" emotions—yelling at or hitting those that offend their sense of fairness, and smiling at or sharing with those who do good things to and for them.

De Waal shows that a similar sense of fairness also exists in a variety of simians. While there are exceptions, most monkey species have what de Waal calls an "egocentric" notion of fairness—namely, they are very aware of how it is fair to treat them, but they have not developed much of a notion of how other monkeys should be treated. It would seem that some of the less capable species of monkeys have a notion of fairness similar to what we see in very young children.[52] But as de Waal notes, the sense of fairness has to start someplace, and it does indeed seem to be the necessary building block for a full-blown conception of justice.[53] At what point does this emotional sensitivity to fairness—or, for that matter, reciprocity (or retribution—both positive and negative)—develop into something analogous to the virtue of justice? This is of course a key question.

In order to determine the answer, we must pause from the discussion of the building blocks of justice to explicate at least some of what Aquinas means by justice. The purpose of justice is (quoting Cicero) "the association of humans with one another, and the maintenance of the life of the community."[54] Aquinas begins with the commonplace view that things are just "when they are made equal." The most fundamental form of justice is what he calls "natural right," by which he means justice that obtains "by its very nature, as when a man gives so much that he may receive equal value in return, and this is called natural right." At its most basic, the virtue of justice is the disposition that makes humans do just actions.[55]

But that is merely Aquinas's outline. In fact, Aquinas has a very high view of justice, in some places identifying justice with the human good more generally. Thus the virtue of justice, while involving a "will to observe what is due to others in all times and circumstances,"[56] in fact requires rather more, involving virtues like "liberality" (the proper sharing of one's excess possessions) and "compassion" (identifying with and aiding the suffering).[57]

Aquinas goes on to note that justice guides humans in their relations with others in two ways: first, in relation to another individual; and second, in a person's relations "with others in general, in so far as one who serves a community, serves all those who are included in that community." In other words, one should be just in relation to another individual, and also in relation to the good of all, i.e., the common good. Of these two, priority goes to the common good, since reason "judges that the common good is better than the good of one."[58]

And here we come to a very important point that differentiates an Aristotelian-Thomistic account of human nature and ethics from many modern accounts of ethics, including the account of human nature and ethics assumed by de Waal. De Waal seems to assume that being "ethical" requires altruism or some other pure other-regarding activity, and this I believe makes conceptual difficulties for him with regard to his otherwise typically acute observations about ethics and "goodness" in simians. On these modern accounts, the altruist is contrasted with the egoist, who in being purely (or overwhelmingly) self-regarding is unethical.[59] This conception of morality presumes a certain understanding of human (and chimpanzee) nature, namely that humans and chimpanzees are fundamentally and ineluctably divided in their inclinations and emotions. Some of these inclinations and emotions are self-regarding and some are other-regarding. If the other-regarding inclinations prevail (at least some of the time) over the self-regarding ones, then that human or chimpanzee is considered altruistic. If the self-regarding inclinations always prevail, then that human or chimpanzee is egoistic.[60]

A Thomistic account of human nature is rather different, denying that an ineluctable conflict between self-regarding and other-regarding inclinations is the crux of morality. While infants and children (and regrettably some adults) experience a constant conflict between egoistic and altruistic desires, that is not the situation with those who achieve moral maturity. As MacIntyre puts it,

> The task of education is to transform and integrate [conflicts between egoistic and altruistic impulses and desires] into an inclination towards both the common good and our individual goods, so that we become neither self-rather-than-other-regarding nor other-rather-than-self-regarding, neither egoists nor altruists, but those whose passions and inclinations are directed to what is both our good and the good of others.[61]

In other words, from a Thomistic perspective, morality is about flourishing, and since humans and chimpanzees are social animals, authentic flourishing necessarily integrates their individual good with the common good of their various communities. Thus, if a chimpanzee can in fact make "choices" that facilitate and promote both its individual flourishing and that of its community (that is, display practical rationality regardless of whether it "practically reasons" about either its individual or its community's flourishing), for it to act ethically is simply to act in ways that generally promote both its individual flourishing and the flourishing of its community. Correlatively, a virtuous (or vicious) chimpanzee would be one who in a regular and stable way makes choices that are conducive to (or destructive of) the authentic flourishing of that chimpanzee both as an individual and as a member of its chimpanzee society.

To sum up, the idea that a chimpanzee must be self-sacrificial or altruistic to be ethical is not a Thomistic viewpoint. Rather, an ethical or just chimpanzee is one who acts to promote the good of its society in ways that show this communal flourishing is an integral part of its own good. Of course, this may at times lead a chimpanzee to make minor or major sacrifices for other chimpanzees, but such is an element of—rather than the whole or essence of—a Thomistic understanding of the virtue of justice in a chimpanzee.

Having outlined a Thomistic conception of justice and having differentiated it from the "altruism" understanding of ethics with its very different understanding of moral maturity, we can now return to the seeds or building blocks of the virtue of justice that we can find in chimpanzees. We have already noted one building block of justice—a sense of "fairness" in children and chimpanzees. In the rest of the essay I will do two things: first, I will discuss three additional "seeds" of justice in chimpanzees, namely, *friendliness, reciprocity,* and *compassion*; second, I will discuss three examples of what I believe constitutes acts (and thus potentially the virtue) of justice in different chimpanzees, specifically in acts of *peacemaking, vengeance,* and *impartial leadership.*

The first seed of justice to be discussed is that of chimpanzee friendliness, the desire of chimpanzees to be helpful to other chimpanzees in general. There are innumerable examples of these behaviors among chimpanzees,[62] but I will discuss just one.

During one winter at the Arnhem Zoo, after cleaning the hall and before releasing the chimps, the keepers hosed out all rubber tires in the enclosure and hung them one by one on a horizontal log extending from the climbing frame. One day, Krom was interested in a tire in which water had stayed behind. Unfortunately, this particular tire was at the end of the row, with six or more heavy tires hanging in front of it. Krom pulled and pulled at the one she wanted, but couldn't remove it from the log. She pushed the tire backward, but there it hit the climbing frame and couldn't be removed. Krom worked in vain on this problem for more than ten minutes, ignored by everyone except Jakie, a seven-year-old that Krom had taken care of as a juvenile.

Immediately after Krom gave up and walked away, Jakie approached the scene. Without hesitation he pushed the tires one by one off the log, beginning with the front one, followed by the second in the row, and so on, as any sensible chimp would. When he reached the last tire, he carefully removed it so that no water was lost, carrying it straight to his aunt, placing it upright in front of her. Krom accepted his present without any special acknowledgment, and was already scooping up water with her hand when Jakie left.[63]

Here one chimpanzee (Jakie) assists another (Krom), wanting to help her realize her goals. Jakie's assisting his "aunt" Krom is an example of friendliness from one chimpanzee to another, and in this case may reflect a natural familial gratitude.[64] De Waal calls this "targeted helping": Jakie not only wanted to be of assistance to Krom but was also able to figure out Krom's (somewhat complex) goals. Although de Waal is particularly impressed by Jakie's intellectual ability to discern Krom's goals and the fact that this targeted helping is "rare or absent in most other animals" (at least that is what de Waal thought when he wrote this in 1982), what is of particular interest for our purposes is that Jakie shows a bond of gratitude to his kin, which would seem to be a building block for the virtue of justice.

A second building block of justice in chimpanzees can be seen in their sense of reciprocity. Reciprocity is related to friendliness in that both may in some instances show gratitude, but reciprocity seems to be moving closer to justice in terms of its approximation to "giving each their due." Although measuring food sharing would seem to be an obvious way to measure reciprocity (particularly since chimpanzees generally recognize food as "private property" and beg from one another when others have food), since there are many variables involved in food sharing, de Waal devised an experiment measuring a second expression of service among chimpanzees, namely grooming (a common and appreciated practice), to test whether there was indeed reciprocity among chimpanzees:

> The frequency and duration of hundreds of spontaneous grooming bouts among our chimpanzees were measured in the morning. Within half an hour after the end of these observations, starting around noon, the apes were given two tightly bound bundles of leaves and branches. Nearly 7,000 interactions over food were carefully recorded by observers and entered into a computer according to strict definitions. . . . It was found that adults were more likely to share food with individuals that who had groomed them earlier. . . . The data indicated that the sharing increase was specific to the previous groomer. In other words, chimpanzees appeared to remember others who had just performed a service (grooming) and respond to those individuals by sharing more with them. Also, aggressive protest by food possessors to approaching individuals were directed more at those who had not groomed them than at previous grooming partners. This is compelling evidence for partner-specific reciprocal exchange.[65]

Again, this sense of reciprocity and "fairness" in terms of sharing food is another fundamental building block for the virtue of justice.

The third seed of "justice" is compassion or empathy, which is identifying with the suffering of others and consoling those who are in distress.[66] We might see this as a transitional notion, since as Aquinas notes, compassion may be merely an emotional reaction, or, if it "is vouchsafed

FIGURE 11.1 A typical instance of consolation in chimpanzees in which a juvenile puts an arm around a screaming adult male who has just been defeated in a fight with his rival. *Source*: Photograph by Frans de Waal.

in such a way that justice is safeguarded,"[67] compassion may be an authentic virtue.

As with reciprocity, there is abundant evidence that chimpanzees show compassion to other distressed chimpanzees. De Waal calls this "consoling behavior," which he defines in one context as "reassurance by an uninvolved bystander to one of the combatants in a preceding aggressive incident."[68] De Waal notes that the act of consoling is to be contrasted with reconciliation, which he thinks could be for the self-interest of the one reconciling. There is no apparent benefit for the chimpanzee who consoles. His studies of these consoling behaviors also showed that losers of conflicts and those who had been more intensely attacked receive relatively more consolation. There are a variety of other examples of chimpanzees showing compassion, as when a chimpanzee will starve himself to prevent another chimpanzee from receiving a painful shock.

Aquinas defines compassion (*misericordia*) as "heartfelt sympathy for another's distress, impelling us to succor him."[69] As Aquinas notes, the term itself refers to a person's compassionate heart (*miserum cor*) for another's unhappiness. It arises when a person grieves another person's distress because he sees this distress as his own.[70] And why does he do that? According to Aquinas, it is through "union of the affections, which is the effect of love. For, since he who loves another looks on his friend as another self, he counts his friend's hurt as his own. . . . Hence [Aristotle] reckons 'grieving with one's friend' as one of the signs of friendship."[71] Aquinas also reckons *misericordia* to be the greatest of all the virtues that relate to another person, presumably making it both a part of and arguably the greatest part of justice.[72]

Aquinas does, however, offer a qualification. Compassion can refer to a movement of the sensitive appetite, in which case it is not a virtue but a passion. Yet if compassion is guided by reason, then it is a virtue. How can these be reconciled? It functions as a virtue if the action of compassion is done so that "justice is safeguarded, whether we give to the needy or forgive the repentant."[73] So if chimpanzees regularly direct compassion to the truly needy and to those who are wronged in the community, such compassion would indeed be a virtue.

What the above examples of friendliness, reciprocity, and especially compassion show at the very least is that chimpanzees, like human beings, are able to show care and concern for others in their communities. Whether or not these accounts of care and concern among chimpanzees are limited to the extended friend and family network of chimpanzees (or are at times displayed beyond these networks), the examples show seeds of (and analogies to) justice—fairness to other individuals within their chimpanzee community.

Finally, beyond the above three types of seeds of virtue among chimpanzees, I now turn to three examples of justice in chimpanzee communities: peacemaking, vengeance, and impartial leadership. What makes these examples *actual* instances of justice is that they so clearly and definitively promote the common good of the chimpanzee community.

The first example is what I call peacemaking. De Waal discusses how certain high-ranking female chimpanzees are able to mediate between and reconcile conflicts (of which they are not a part) between male chimpanzees:

Especially after serious conflicts between two adult males, the two opponents sometimes were brought together by an adult female. The female approached one of the males, kissed or touched him or presented towards him and then slowly walked towards the other male. If the male followed, he did so very close behind her (often inspecting her genitals) and without looking at the other male. On a few occasions the female looked behind at her follower, and sometimes returned to a male that stayed behind to pull at his arm to make him follow. When the female sat down close to the other male, both males started to groom her and they simply continued grooming after she went off. The only difference being that they groomed each other after this moment, and panted, spluttered, and smacked more frequently and loudly than before the female's departure.[74]

Here the goal of the peacemaking chimpanzee is to bring about harmony between other chimpanzees who are or have been in conflict that has not been resolved. One may speculate as to whether the motivation for the female chimpanzee in the above example is primarily to benefit the two males or to benefit the group as a whole (or both), but while interesting, that detail is largely irrelevant to the fact that either way, the female chimpanzee is serving the good of peacemaking (and hence of justice) in that chimpanzee community.

The second example is what I call chimpanzee vengeance, and I use it in the positive Thomistic sense of avenging a wrong against an individual or the community. In this example, a chimpanzee society is able to recognize violations of its community expectations and, well after a violation has occurred, functions as a vigilante group to punish offenders:

One balmy evening at the Arnhem Zoo, when the keeper called the chimps inside, two adolescent females refused to enter the building. The weather was superb. They had the whole island to themselves and they loved it. The rule at the zoo was that none of the apes would get fed until all of them had moved inside. The obstinate teenagers caused a grumpy mood among the rest. When they finally did come in, several hours late, they were assigned a separate bedroom by the keeper so as to prevent reprisals. This protected them only temporarily, though. The next morning, out on the island, the entire colony vented its frustration about the delayed meal by a mass pursuit ending in a physical beating of the culprits. That evening, they were the first to come in.[75]

In this case, a chimpanzee society avenged a wrong done to it by the two adolescent chimpanzees. While "vengeance" is not currently a popular notion, it is clearly part of Thomas's understanding of justice. The first requirement is that vengeance may be taken only upon those who wronged the community voluntarily. The second requirement is that those who avenge a wrong must do it for some good, specifically, "that the sinner may amend, or at least that he may be restrained and others be not disturbed."[76] While we can debate the voluntariness of the adolescent chimpanzees, de Waal gives plenty of examples of mischievousness among chimpanzees.[77] Furthermore, it would seem as if some good was done, as the two adolescent chimpanzees seem to have learned their lesson and no longer "disturbed others."

The third and final (two-part) example is of "impartial leadership," beginning with a truly remarkable example of how a male leader of a chimpanzee society is able to police the society, resolving disagreements between opposed individuals and establishing relative peace among its members. This is particularly interesting since before the ascent of this leader, the chimpanzee society was much more conflicted under a previous leader who seemed incapable of fairly resolving conflicts among the members of the chimpanzee society:

> Policing by high-ranking males show the same sort of community concern. These males break up fights among others, sometimes standing between them until the conflict calms down. The evenhandedness of male chimpanzees in this role is truly remarkable, as if they place themselves above the contestants. The pacifying effect of this behavior has been documented in both captive and wild chimpanzees. [In an attached footnote, de Waal goes on to note that] My popular books do not always present the actual date on which conclusions are based. For example, the claim that high-ranking males police intragroup conflicts in an impartial manner was based on 4,834 interventions analyzed by De Waal. One male, Luit, shows a lack of correlation between his social preferences (measured by association and grooming) and interventions in open conflict. Only Luit showed this dissociation: interventions by other individuals were biased in favor of friends and family.
>
> A recent study of policing in macaques has shown that the entire group benefits. In the temporary absence of the usual performers of policing, the remaining group members see their affiliative networks deteriorate and the opportunities for reciprocal exchange dwindle. It is no exaggeration to say, therefore, that in primate groups a few key players can exert extraordinary influence.[78]

In this two-part example of the chimpanzee leader (and some macaque monkeys) we see them demonstrate an ability to go beyond their immediate kin group and to act impartially among larger simian societies. Such lack of favoritism demonstrates a sense of justice. In a Thomistic perspective, it is remarkable enough that chimpanzees are able to show "right" or just behavior among their kin groups, which in itself would constitute a form of justice. But the ability of some chimpanzees to rise above their kin loyalties and display a sense of universal fairness in their society is truly extraordinary, and it would seem that the most reasonable explanation for that kind of action was that these chimpanzee leaders displayed the virtue of justice in their dealing with their communities.

The examples and the commentary presented above constitute a prima facie case for chimpanzee justice and thus a chimpanzee ethics, giving us good grounds to assert that at least some chimpanzees display at the very least something analogous to the virtue of justice. But this is just a start. Much more work needs to be done to develop a more adequate case.

NOTES

1. Thanks to Jonathan K. Crane for helpful comments on an earlier version, and to Fergus Kerr O.P. for much-appreciated encouragement.

2. Unless one had expert ethological knowledge of a wide range of animals, it would seem odd that one could assuredly assume that all nonhuman animal species—e.g., elephants, turtles, dogs, cats, rats, raccoons, dolphins, badgers, bonobos, pigs, chimpanzees, mongooses, or macaques, to name just a few—lacked "reason" or an "ethic." Unless, of course, one simply presumed that to be the case or had an a priori view that the only animal with reason or an ethic was the human.

3. Throughout this essay I prefer to use "practical rationality" rather than "practical reasoning." As Millgram notes, there are some approaches that seek to understand the former without developing a theory about the latter. According to some theorists (Millgram names Elizabeth Anderson's *Value in Ethics and Economics* [Cambridge, MA: Harvard University Press, 1993] as an example), "a desire is rational if it is one you would have if you knew or thought more about it." See Elijah Millgram, "Practical Reasoning: The Current State of Play," in *Varieties of Practical Reasoning*, ed. Elijah Millgram (Cambridge, MA: MIT Press, 2001), 2.

4. Aquinas's approach to ethics was influenced by Aristotle, and thus a Thomistic ethic is also in large part an Aristotelian ethic.

5. Thomas Aquinas, *Summa Theologica* (New York: Benziger Bros., 1947). Henceforth cited as *ST*.

6. Marie George provides a number of a priori arguments from Aquinas as to why humans are the only rational species. However, she does not see these as decisive, as she spends most of her article examining and rejecting the empirical evidence for rationality among any nonhuman animal. See Marie George, "Thomas Aquinas Meets Nim

Chimpsky: On the Debate about Human Nature and the Nature of Other Animals," *Aquinas Review* 10 (2003): 14–15.

7. E.g., *ST* I-II 12.3 ad.3; I-II 40.4 ad.1. See also Thomas Aquinas, *Summa Contra Gentiles*, (London: Burns, Oates, and Washbourne, 1923), II 82.

8. Aquinas uses the term "perfect animal" rather loosely, and it signifies a wider range of animals than, say, the modern notion of a mammal. "Other [animals] have the further power of moving from place to place, as perfect animals, such as quadrupeds, and birds, and so on" (*ST* I 18.2 ad.1).

9. The term "chimpanzee" enters the West only in the eighteenth century, and the first documented contact between Europeans and the particular species we now know as chimpanzees seems to have been in the sixteenth or seventeenth century.

10. See H. W. Janson, *Apes and Ape Lore in the Middle Ages and the Renaissance* (London: Warburg Institute, University of London, 1952), 30.

11. See Albertus Magnus, *On Animals: A Medieval Summa Zoologica*, trans. Kenneth F. Kitchell and Irven Michael Resnick (Baltimore: Johns Hopkins University Press, 1999), 1421. Furthermore, Albert discusses a species he calls "pygmies," which he claimed to be intermediate between simians and humans. The reference to "pygmies" in *On Animals* is unclear: was it a tribe of human beings? or a mysterious reference to chimpanzees or bonobos? or perhaps a mythological reference to one of the "monstrous races" that fascinated the ancients and medievals?

12. I see the project of this essay as being in continuity with Aristotelian naturalism, varieties (or at least aspects) of it being put forward by Elizabeth Anscombe, Larry Arnhart, Philippa Foot, Raimond Gaita, Rosalind Hursthouse, Alasdair MacIntyre, John McDowell, and Michael Thompson. For an overview of the various approaches, as well as a constructive account of the key tenets of Aristotelian naturalism, see Christopher Toner, "Sorts of Naturalism: Requirements for a Successful Theory," *Metaphilosophy* 39, no. 2 (April 2008): 220–49.

13. Aquinas, *ST* I-II, prologue.

14. At *ST* II-II 49.10 Aquinas takes up the question of whether practical rationality is concerned only with the individual or also with the common good. Aquinas (contrary to theorists about egoism vs. altruism) says that "he who seeks the good of the many, seeks in consequence his own good . . . because the individual good is impossible without the common good of the family, state, or kingdom. Hence Valerius Maximus says of the ancient Romans that they would rather be poor in a rich empire than rich in a poor empire."

15. Here I am of course presuming that these three "classic" cardinal virtues for human beings are also relevant for flourishing chimpanzees. But of course it would be highly unlikely that the list of human virtues and chimpanzee virtues would be the same.

16. Frans de Waal, *Chimpanzee Politics: Power and Sex Among Apes* (Baltimore, MD: Johns Hopkins University Press, 2007), 27.

17. Ibid., 28.

18. Frans de Waal, *Primates and Philosophers: How Morality Evolved* (Princeton, NJ: Princeton University Press, 2006), 61–62.

19. George, "Aquinas Meets Nim Chimpsky," 28.

20. Alasdair MacIntyre, *Dependent Rational Animals* (London: Open Court Press, 1999), 14.

21. Ibid.

22. Ibid., 17.

23. It is not just philosophers who are likely to be captured by modern epistemo-logical skepticism about animals such as chimpanzees having feelings and thoughts. Christine Korsgaard, commenting on the principle of parsimony (what de Waal calls "anthropodenial") puts the matter very eloquently: "It is important to remember that human beings have a vested interest in what de Waal calls 'anthropodenial.' We eat nonhuman animals, wear them, perform painful experiments on them, hold them cap-tive for purposes of our own—sometimes in unhealthy conditions—we make them work, and we kill them at will. . . . I think it is fair to say that we are more likely to be comfortable in our treatment of our fellow creatures if we think that being eaten, worn, experimented on, held captive, made to work, and killed, cannot mean anything like the same thing to them that it would to us. And that in turn seems more likely to the extent they are unlike us in their emotional and cognitive lives. . . . But once you correct for that vested interest there seems little reason to doubt that observations and experiments of the sort de Waal does and describes, as well as our own everyday interactions with our animal companions, show exactly what they seem to show: that many animals are intelligent, curious, loving, playful, bossy, belligerent creatures in many ways very much like ourselves" (Korsgaard, "Morality and the Distinctiveness of Human Action," in de Waal, *Primates and Philosophers*, 103–4).

24. On the other hand, Albert had a particular interest in falcons and hawks, and gives repeated and extensive discussion of them (in one section alone devoting more than fifty pages to an account of the various species and their veterinary care). Another excellent medieval source for zoological information is the *Rasa'il al-Ikhwan al-Safa*, a comprehensive encyclopedia written in tenth-century Basra, Iraq, especially epistle 22. For more on this source, see Crane and Gross, chapter 12 in this volume.

25. For a discussion of Westermarck, see de Waal, *Primates and Philosophers*, 17–21.

26. For a discussion of Huxley's views on morality as distinct from nature, see Frans de Waal, *The Bonobo and the Atheist: In Search of Humanism Among the Primates* (New York: Norton, 2013), 37–41.

27. As William Wallace notes in his forward to *On Animals*, books 21 and 22 of *On Animals* are the heart of Albert's integrative project, where Albert is discussing the hierarchy of perfections among the bodies (and thus minds) of various animals (including humans). See Albertus, *On Animals*, pp. xviii–xix. Aquinas also displays his understanding of the relationship between the perfection of the body and intellectual capacities when he notes that it is "necessary that man, among all the animals, should have the largest brain in relation to his body." See *ST* I 91.3 ad.1. For another example of such medieval morphological-mental connection, see epistle 22 of the *Rasa'il*, men-tioned in note 24.

28. See Philippa Foot, "Natural Norms," chap. 2 of *Natural Goodness* (Oxford: Oxford University Press, 2001), 25–37.

29. De Waal, *Chimpanzee Politics*, 46–50.

30. Ibid., 49.

31. De Waal, *Primates and Philosophers*, 171.

32. For an analogous account of morality, see Hess's chapter 2 in this volume.

33. George, "Aquinas Meets Nim Chimpsky," 21 ff.

34. De Waal, *Chimpanzee Politics*, 70.

35. *ST* I 78.3,4. There is some debate as to whether Aquinas enumerates four or five internal senses, but that is beyond the scope of this discussion.

36. See *ST* I 78.4; 83.1. Whereas the imagination allows a creature to retain an image created by the central sense, it is memory that allows a creature to actually do things appropriately with these images by understanding a past image as past. It is from the memory that a creature is able to trace an image to its point of origin, distinguish a past event from a present event, and have a sense of time. Memory creates in part experience and thus the possibility to learn from particular past events. Whereas the external senses and the imagination are passive, simply taking in and storing information, the memory is active, working on these images to benefit the creature that possesses this sense.

37. De Waal, *Chimpanzee Politics*, 34–36.

38. *ST* I-II 22–48.

39. De Waal, *Chimpanzee Politics*, 62.

40. Although I would add that it is certainly questionable whether Aquinas's understanding of estimative sense (what I am calling basic practical rationality) can adequately account for the young chimpanzee's ability to delay his gratification and act so sneakily to avoid sharing the grapefruit with others.

41. In more technical terms, Aquinas says that when humans act freely, they make a "comparison" in the reason, which he calls deliberation. Such deliberation is "second-order" reflection on one's initial inclination. In contrast to the deliberative capacity Aquinas grants humans, Aquinas notes that while nonhuman animals are capable of making a "decision of sorts," it is a decision from "natural instinct" rather than deliberation, precisely since they do not have the ability to critically evaluate their choice and possibly reverse their course. Thus in his stock example of the sheep seeing and fleeing from the wolf, Aquinas considers the sheep's response to be necessitated by its instinct, and not deliberating or making a deliberative choice. Aquinas continues by generalizing "and this is likewise true for every judgment made by brute animals" (*ST* I 83.1). Similarly, when birds build nests or a pig squeals with delight, their actions are determined "because they are unaware of the reason for their judgment" (Aquinas, *Truth* [Quaestiones disputatae de veritate. English.], 3 vols. [Chicago: H. Regnery, 1954], 24.2.

42. If the chimpanzee did this, it would certainly be more complex than Aquinas seems to allow a nonhuman animal. As Aquinas puts it, "An irrational animal takes one thing in preference to another, because its appetite is naturally determinate to that thing. Wherefore as soon as an animal, whether by its sense or by its imagination, is offered something to which its appetite is naturally inclined, it is moved to that alone, without making any choice. Just as fire is moved upwards and not downwards, without its making any choice" (*ST* I-II 13.2 ad.2).

43. Christine Korsgaard, "Morality and the Distinctiveness of Human Action," in de Waal, *Primates and Philosophers*, 110.

44. This is very similar to Aquinas's view. See note 42.

45. De Waal attributes this definition to Philip Kitcher. See de Waal, *The Bonobo and the Atheist*, 151. The philosophical use of "wanton" originates in Harry Frankfurt, "Freedom of the Will and the Concept of a Person," *Journal of Philosophy* 68, no.1 (1971): 5–20. In that article Frankfurt defines "wantons" as agents who have first-order desires but no second-order volitions. He goes on to say that the essential characteristic of a wanton is that "his desires move him to do certain things, without its being true of him either that he wants to be moved by those desires [i.e., "second-order" desires] or that he prefers to be moved by other desires. The class of wantons includes

all nonhuman animals that have desires and all very young children. Perhaps it also includes some adult human beings as well" (11). For Frankfurt, second-order desires are desires about our desires, that is, reflective self-evaluation. Second-order volitions are choices in response to second-order desires. As such, Frankfurt's use of "wanton" is very close to the Thomistic notion of the class of agents who are not "rational."

46. De Waal explains further that "when [a date] happens the female and Dandy pretend to be walking in the same direction by chance, and if all goes well they meet behind a few tree trunks. These 'dates' take place after the exchange of a few glances and in some cases a brief nudge. This kind of furtive mating is frequently associated with signal suppression and concealment. I can remember the first time I noticed it very vividly indeed, because it was such a comical sight. Dandy and a female were courting each other surreptitiously. Dandy began to make advances to the female. While at the same time restlessly looking around to see if any of the other males were watching. Male chimpanzees start their advances by sitting with their legs wide apart revealing their erection. Precisely at the point when Dandy was exhibiting his sexual urge in this way, Luit, one of the older males, unexpectedly came around the corner. Dandy immediately dropped his hands over his penis concealing it from view" (de Waal, *Chimpanzee Politics*, 36–37).

47. Interestingly, Korsgaard acknowledges that the question of whether chimpanzees have the capacity to choose contrary to their dominant desire "is certainly an empirical one. There is nothing unnatural, non-natural, or mystical abut the capacity for normative self-government" (Christine Korsgaard, "Morality and the Distinctiveness of Human Action," in de Waal, *Primates and Philosophers*, 112–13.) While Korsgaard acknowledges that the question of whether a chimpanzee can exercise "normative self-government" (her term for acting contrary to one's desires for one's own or another's good) is an empirical one, she never suggests criteria by which one could determine if chimpanzees have that capacity.

48. *ST* I-II 13.6.

49. *ST* I-II 94.2.

50. *ST* II-II 58.9. As we shall see, it is not at all obvious that "we are not directed immediately to another by the internal passions."

51. See, for example, ST II-II 47.10 ad.3, where Aquinas emphasizes that more so than temperance and courage, practical rationality and justice belong to the "rational faculty."

52. Here it is important to note that by "monkey" de Waal is referring primarily to lesser simians, as opposed to the more advanced ones, especially chimpanzees and bonobos.

53. De Waal, *Primates and Philosophers*, 49.

54. *ST* II-II 58.2. I am indebted to Thomas Hibbs's translations of Aquinas here and in other places, found in Thomas Hibbs, *Aquinas, Ethics, and Philosophy of Religion* (Bloomington: Indiana University Press, 2007), ch. 2.

55. *ST* II-II 57.2; 57.1.

56. *ST* II-II 58.1.

57. See *ST* II-II 117.1. Although Aquinas lists "compassion" under the virtue of charity, it is clear that compassion also is a requirement of Aquinas's understanding of justice. MacIntyre argues that compassion is not only an aspect of charity, but "is recognizably at work in the secular world and the authorities whom Aquinas cites on its nature, and whose disagreements he aspires to resolve, include Sallust and Cicero"

(MacIntyre, *Dependent Rational Animals*, 124). Similarly, while Aquinas's discussion of friendship comes under the virtue of charity, his understanding of justice is unintelligible apart from his understanding of friendship. MacIntyre's extended discussion of "just generosity" as involving compassion (or *misericordia*) is an important resource for a broader understanding of Aquinas on justice (121–135).

58. *ST* II-II 58.5; 47.10.

59. It is worth noting that "altruism" dates back only to the mid-nineteenth century.

60. See MacIntyre, *Dependent Rational Animals*, 160.

61. Ibid. MacIntyre goes on to note, "Self-sacrifice, it follows, is as much of vice, as much of a sign of inadequate moral development, as selfishness."

62. De Waal gives numerous examples from his store of "hundreds of examples" of friendliness among chimpanzees in Frans de Waal, "With a Little Help from a Friend," *PLoS Biology* 5, no. 7 (2007), accessed July 30, 2014, http://www.plosbiology.org/article/info%3Adoi%2F10.1371%2Fjournal.pbio.0050190.

63. De Waal, *Primates and Philosophers*, 31–32.

64. Jakie is the son of Jimmie. Krom is "a female who is inseparable from Jimmie. No other friendship in the [Arnhem Chimpanzee colony] group is as closely knit as theirs"; de Waal, *Chimpanzee Politics*, 69.

65. De Waal, *Primates and Philosophers*, 43.

66. This is, obviously, a conception of justice that requires no court or legal system. For more on that version of justice, see Crane and Gross in this volume.

67. *ST* II-II 30.3.

68. De Waal, *Primates and Philosophers*, 33.

69. *ST* II-II 30.1.

70. *ST* II-II 30.2.

71. *ST* II-II 30.2.

72. *ST* II-II 30.4. Aquinas discusses compassion as a part not of justice but of charity, as he does friendship. See note 57 above for a brief explanation for discussing compassion (and friendship) as parts of justice.

73. *ST* II-II 30.3.

74. De Waal, *Primates and Philosophers*, 170.

75. Ibid., 172.

76. *ST* II-II 108.1.

77. We might mention only two examples of "naughty" chimpanzees or bonobos discussed by de Waal. First is the example of Georgia, the chimpanzee who loves to trick people to come close to her while hiding water in her mouth and then when they are in range, spraying water at them. De Waal notes that when Georgia is "caught" by someone who knows what she is planning to do, she drops her gaze and swallows the water rather than spraying it. Why? According to de Waal, she is clearly being naughty. See de Waal, *Primates and Philosophers*, 59–61. Another example is of a juvenile bonobo playing a trick on the alpha male. The alpha male goes down a chain into a drained moat to explore. While he is down there the juvenile pulls up the chain and stands at the edge making the gestures and sounds of a bonobo that most closely approximate human laughter. The alpha male escapes the moat only when his adult female consort intervenes and lets down the chain. De Waal does not relate whether the juvenile faced any consequences for his prank.

78. De Waal, *Primates and Philosophers*, 170–71.

Twelve Brutal Justice?

ANIMAL LITIGATION AND THE QUESTION OF COUNTERTRADITION

Jonathan K. Crane and Aaron S. Gross

LET US ASSUME THAT SOME kind of moral obligation to animals is beyond doubt; can we say further that animals participate in the moral life to the point of being capable of rebuking humans? Can animals accuse humans or challenge human morality in the way a plaintiff challenges a defendant? There is an obvious sense in which animals of whatever variety are nothing like a plaintiff or prosecuting attorney: no animal speaks the language used in any human court. At the same time, there is an equally undeniable sense in which some animals are very much like human litigants: they can make humans feel accused.[1] The wide-ranging biblical, Jewish, and Islamic texts considered in this chapter interpret this cross-culturally persistent potential for humans to feel accused by animals, and in so doing testify to an enduring impulse found within parts of many religious traditions not only to assert human uniqueness, but also to champion the human potential for what James Serpell has theorized as "zoocentric sympathy"[2]—a spontaneous tendency of human groups to express concern for other forms of animate life.[3] Being objects of moral concern does not require that animals also be moral agents, but it does raise the question of the nature of animal participation in moral life. In this chapter we will consider, in what sense, if at all, some nonhuman animals have the kind of agency, subjectivity, or personhood that allows them not simply to receive moral consideration from humans but to demand it as moral agents in their own right.

The nascent interdisciplinary field of animal studies has pointedly raised this question, and a range of contemporary thinkers, Jacques Derrida noteworthy among them, have presented powerful arguments that bind together, on the one hand, challenges to our contemporary failure to sufficiently consider ethical obligations to animals (in food production, scientific studies, and so on) and, on the other hand, challenges to the Western tradition's denial of reason, soul, language, personhood, friendship, society, responsibility, legal standing, and so on to animals. Some legal scholars, like Steven Wise, are pushing in a similar direction when they argue that animals should have legal standing (that is, one should be able to initiate a lawsuit on the basis of harm done to an animal directly).[4]

Calls for deprivileging human uniqueness in the name of compassion, such as those found in Wise's and Derrida's work,[5] are often viewed as "cutting edge," new ideas associated with relatively recent and relatively nonreligious intellectual movements. However, as this chapter will show, challenges to human cruelty against animals have long been bound up with challenges to human exceptionalism, triumphalist anthropocentrism, and—our primary focus here—the idea that animals cannot be rightful litigants. The texts we consider here are drawn from a wide variety of ancient and medieval religious traditions that depict animals accusing humans—and being heard. While some texts of this kind can reasonably be read as simple allegories about intrahuman affairs, we argue that others—such as the biblical, Jewish, and Islamic stories considered here—cannot. These sources inescapably suggest something about the nature of animality. They also evince theologically based, anti-anthropocentric sentiments that stand in sharp relief to the decidedly more anthropocentric nature of the larger religious textual corpuses and contexts in which they are found. The tension between these textual moments and their larger traditions raises the question of how or why these views were included at all. Are they best viewed as anomalies that prove the rule or, as we will advocate here, could these narratives be better understood as fragments of larger worldviews too persistent to wholly eliminate from the canon—in a word, "countertraditions"?

Derrida has suggested that his own radical challenges to dominant modes of human-animal relationships such as his passionate critiques of industrial farming can be viewed as part of an ancient lineage, one that is old, "as old as man, [as] what he calls his world, his knowledge, his history, and his technology."[6] That these larger and more anthropocentric textual and religious traditions—the Bible, rabbinic midrashim, and medieval Islamic philosophy—incorporate these anti-anthropocentric narratives merits special attention because they perhaps, as per Derrida's suggestion, give voice to long-standing countertraditions still living today that challenge dominant assumptions about animals. Both for reasons of gaining a more robust descriptive picture of the polyphony of views about human and animal nature that characterize biblical, Jewish, and Islamic traditions, on the one hand, and for their potential relevance to contemporary theological and moral reflection, on the other, we offer here a critical reading of these three examples of premodern imaginings of animals' ability to function as legal subjects (rather than merely as objects of legal protection or exploitation).[7] We conclude with some reflection on the question of countertradition; that is, the question of what it might mean to take these texts out of the relative isolation in which we consider them in this chapter and robustly imagine them as part of an ancient thread in the larger weave of particular historical traditions and perhaps human religiosity as such.

THREE CASES

The first of our three cases is from the Hebrew Bible, located amidst the travel narratives of the Israelites as they encountered Gentile nations between Mount Sinai and the Jordan River, and tells the story of a hapless donkey ridden by a Gentile prophet who has been invited to curse the Israelites. Much to the ire of the prophet, the donkey is not fully compliant about following the most direct path. And she is not shy about holding the prophet accountable for his egregious treatment of her.

The second case is one of the earliest exegetical midrashim the rabbis composed to interpret and explain biblical materials, likely third century CE.[8] Granular in detail, it goes nearly word by word through the biblical verse it considers, offering various interpretations. This particular midrash focuses on the opening words of Moses' song at the end of Deuteronomy. Whereas the Bible's protagonist is a singular donkey, this source refers to animals by class. But like the donkey, they too speak up, testifying against wayward (even harmful) humanity.

The third and final case comes from the tenth century Basra (Iraq) encyclopedia, *Rasai'il al-Ikwhan al-Safa*, written by a sect of Shi'i Islam, the Ikhwan al-Safa wa-Khullan al-Wafa (The Brethren of Purity and True Friends).[9] Embedded in the section on natural philosophy is the longest and most well-known epistle, #22: "The Case of the Animals Versus Man Before the King of the Jinn."[10] The Brethren penned the epistle as a court case, a kind of legal thriller that, like some modern ones, includes scrambling plaintiffs and scheming defendants, seething accusations and blundering defenses, conspiracies, character assassinations, an inquisitive judge, and an overpoweringly logical conclusion that meets with a frustratingly surprising denouement.[11]

In various ways, each of these texts has as its explicit theme an examination of human abuses of nonhuman animals. Certainly their hard-hitting critiques of powerful humans abusing animals can also be read as a metaphor for human abuse of fellow humans. So would go anthropocentric interpretations. We favor an approach that takes these texts more literally and less metaphorically. We read the cases with a primary interest in how animals are represented therein and, in a certain sense, how animals represent themselves.

Donkey

Only two animals speak in the Hebrew Bible. The most famous, of course, is the *nachash* (usually translated as serpent or snake) who beguiles Eve to eat of the Tree of the Knowledge of Good and Evil. For the service of opening humankind's eyes to morality the *nachash* receives the multifold curse of belly locomotion, dirty nourishment, and humanity's ire. While much more can be said about the *nachash*, the only other animal that speaks in the Bible is a donkey, and it is this donkey's words that we examine here.[12]

The Moabite King, Balak, was troubled by Israel's nearby encampment so much that he said to his advisors, "This horde will lick clean all that is about us as an ox licks up the grass of the field."[13] Knowing the pagan prophet Balaam's reputation for successful interventions, Balak sought Balaam's assistance to rid his land of this bovine-like infestation. He sent emissaries to escort the prophet to Moab. Balaam requested the emissaries to stay overnight while he received instruction from God. That night God asked Balaam who these people were, to which Balaam arrogantly replied by referring to his own reputation by reminding God that the king, Balak, requested his, Balaam's, assistance![14] [For his failure to respond truthfully to God's question about who those people were, God caused Balaam to become blind in one eye, in addition to already being lame in one foot.][15] God instructed Balaam not to go to Moab to curse the Israelites for they are blessed. Balak again sent more emissaries to Balaam who again invited them to stay overnight while he consulted God. This time God permitted Balaam to go with the escort but with a substantial caveat: "Whatever I say to you, that you shall do."[16]

That morning Balaam arose, saddled his female donkey,[17] and left with the Moabite dignitaries. God was incensed at his going and an angel of God placed itself in the path as an adversary to him. With two servants at her sides and Balaam atop her, the donkey saw the angel of God standing in the way with a drawn sword in its hand.[18] The donkey swerved from the path and went into the field. Balaam hit the donkey to turn her back to the path. The angel of God then stood in the lane between the vineyards, with a fence on either side. The donkey saw the angel of God and pressed herself against the wall and squeezed Balaam's foot against the wall. Balaam beat her in response. Once more the angel of God moved and stood in a place so narrow that there was no room to turn right or left. When the donkey saw the angel of God, she lay down under Balaam; and Balaam was incensed and again hit the donkey with a stick.

God opened the donkey's mouth, and she said to Balaam, "What have I done to you that you have beaten me these three times?" Balaam replied, "You have made a mockery of me! If I had a sword with me, I'd kill you." The donkey replied, "Behold, I am your donkey that you have ridden upon me all along[19] until today. Have I been in the habit of doing this to you?" He answered, "No."

Then God uncovered Balaam's eyes and he saw the angel of God standing in the way with a drawn sword in its hands. He bowed and prostrated himself to his nose.[20] The angel of God said to him, "Why have you beaten your donkey these three times? It is I who came as an adversary, for your way is perverse to me. And when the donkey saw me she turned from me those three times. If she had not turned from me, you are the one I would have killed just now and let her live."[21] Balaam said to the angel of God, "I erred for I did not know you stood in the road to oppose me. Now if you disapprove, I will turn back." But the angel of God said to Balaam, "Go with the men. But you must say nothing except what I tell you to speak." So Balaam went on with Balak's dignitaries.[22]

This story inverts roles and rules. The donkey manifests wisdom by avoiding a collision with the lethally armed angel; Balaam, on the other hand, expresses shortsighted exasperation by whipping her with a meager stick. She steps aside three times in distinct locations, as if each incident occurs in a different kind of society: the wild fields representing pastoral societies; the vineyards, agricultural ones; the narrow lane, urban existence.[23] With each step aside she expresses concern that the humans who ride upon her are on a collision course with the divine will. It is she who sees the folly of setting one's will against the divine, and she labors creatively to bring salvation to the otherwise blind human(s) riding and beating her. She saves, he damns.

Considered within Jewish lore among those things created on the eve of creation's first Sabbath,[24] the donkey's mouth not only magnifies God's voice in a way that Balaam can finally understand, but she also bests him with scathing legal acumen. She first queries what she had done to prompt his cruelty. She does not assume his brutality is for naught; the beating must have some reasonable cause. His embarrassment, he passionately declares, is the proximal cause: for him, insult is an injury and warrants causing injury. She does not interrogate the solidity of his logic. Rather, she lets it hang there, as if to let it drip irony as she moves on to another line of investigation. She wields concepts like history, pattern, expectation, and harm, querying whether she had ever caused Balaam problems before.[25] No, he admits. No historical evidence justifies his repeated assaults. Though he may be violent, he at least can utter the truth. Though this ends the donkey's case—and no other animal speaks again in the Bible[26]— Balaam's trial is far from over.

With Balaam's eyes now opened to the ridiculousness of his brutality upon this beast of burden, God further uncovers his eyes to allow him to observe the angel, which the donkey readily saw. The angel now burdens him with the realization that the donkey saved his life. Existentially indebted to his ass, Balaam can only mutter, "I erred because I did not know you were there." This admission of ignorance completes his humiliation. Whereas at first he was a celebrated prophet renowned for seeing, knowing, and speaking divine things (Numbers 22:38, 23:5, 12, 16), now he can barely see and only belatedly knows what his donkey readily knows. He can speak only as God's ventriloquist mouthpiece in contrast to the donkey, whom God empowers by opening her—the animal's— mouth (Numbers 22:38, 23:5)

The inversion is total: the donkey is the prophet and Balaam is the ass. She is the seer, he the unseeing. She is the supple respondent to divine intervention, he the stubborn beast who must be browbeaten into submission. A rabbinic midrash boils the story down to these pithy comments:

> The Holy One, blessed by God, respects human dignity and knows our needs.
> God shuts the mouths of beasts. For if they could speak it would have been

impossible to put them in service [to humanity] or to stand up against them. Here was this ass, the dullest of beasts, and there was the wisest of men. But no sooner had she opened her mouth than he could not hold his own against her.[27]

According to this midrash, the biblical narrative thus serves as a kind of just-so story: it had to be that animals cannot speak except through divine ventriloquism lest humanity not be able to enjoy exclusively the experiences of prophecy and the benefits of animal exploitation. That animals cannot speak had to be divine intention.[28] Were they to speak as freely as humans, their speech would readily—if not inevitably—reveal the unreasonableness of supposing human superiority and the unjustifiability of human treatment of animals. In this way the midrash expresses the same anxiety manifested in the biblical story itself. Both belie profound wariness about how humans treat nonhuman animals, and both understand animals as rightful agents whose moral stature merits attention.

Testifiers

Other animals in the Jewish textual tradition also testify against humans.[29] The late third-century *Sifre Devarim* §306 comments on a phrase in Moses' final soliloquy: "Give ear, O heavens, let me speak; let the earth hear the words I utter! May my discourse come down as the rain, my speech distill as the dew; like showers on young growth, like droplets on the grass. For the name of Adonai I proclaim; give glory to our God!" (Deuteronomy 32:1–3). The midrash expands upon this exclamation by weaving together interpretations and scriptural verses corroborating those interpretations. R. Meir opens the midrash by saying that when Israel was meritorious, they would give testimony against themselves; that is, they would hold themselves accountable, just as Joshua says (Joshua 24:22). But when Israel erred, they did not hold themselves accountable. Instead, others stepped up to testify against them, as Hosea claims (Hosea 12:1). At first tribes held the people accountable (says Isaiah) (Isaiah 5:3–4), and when those tribes went wrong (according to Malachi 2:11), the prophets testified (as it says in 2 Kings 17:13). This structure—claim and supporting verse—continues. When the people wronged the prophets, the heavens testified; when they wronged the heavens, the earth testified; when they wronged the earth, the roads testified; when they wronged the roads, the Gentiles testified; when they wronged the Gentiles, the mountains testified;

when they wronged the mountains, the oxen testified; when they wronged the oxen, the fowl testified; when they wronged the domesticated beasts, wild beasts, and fowl, the fish testified; and, finally, when they wronged the fish, the ant testified. Finally, R. Simeon b. Eleazar[30] says, "Sad [or humble] indeed is the man who has to learn from an ant. Had he learned and done what he learned, he would have been sad [or humble], but he had to learn from the ant's ways and did not even learn!"[31]

This exquisitely formed midrash views animals—alongside the heavens, earth, roads, mountains, and other humans—as subjects able to testify against humanity. Indeed, the various verses cited in the midrash demonstrate animal knowledge and agency to speak accusingly. As Isaiah says, the oxen can testify because they know their owner, but Israel does not (a.k.a. God) (Isaiah 1:3). In Jeremiah's view, the fowl can testify because they know the seasons, but Israel pays no heed (to natural law) (Jeremiah 8:7). Job holds that the fish can testify because they, like the beasts, birds of the sky, and the earth, know that in God's hands is every living soul and the breath of all humankind (Job 12:7–10). And Proverbs observes that the ant can testify rightfully because even without elected or appointed leaders, it can collaborate to prepare for the future (by storing up food), whereas lazy Israel awaits impoverishment (Proverbs 6:6–8).

Some modern scholars interpret this midrash in a lachrymose manner. In Jacob Neusner's view, "God had called to testify a series of everless honorable witnesses. When Israel had merit, then Israel itself testified to its own failings. But with Israel's decay, a sequence of [increasingly] humble witnesses testified to Israel's failures."[32] Hebert Basser similarly views the midrash as "downgrading" Israel.[33] These interpretations presume that animals are "lesser" beings, whose moral and spiritual compass is "below" humankind's and whose testimonies are petty at best—all of which means that humankind's waywardness must have achieved embarrassingly depraved levels.

While this interpretation is reasonable given R. Simeon ben Eleazar's sorrowful conclusion, it is incomplete. A more optimistic interpretation is also plausible and, in fact, may be more compelling. This midrash can be read as underscoring the notion that animals are bastions of knowledge—knowledge about the natural world, about God and God's plans, and about social cohesion and planning. Animals, this midrash insists, have a sense of both natural morality and revealed morality. Not only are they permitted to testify against wayward humankind, but they are brought forward to do so by none other than God. Differences between species are hardly denied, yet the accent in this source is on the common ground of being creatures of a single God.

The notion that this midrash downgrades humankind is an anthropocentric interpretation: it assumes that the focus of the midrash must be humankind. We hold, however, that this can equally be read as a non-anthropocentric midrash insofar as it folds into the category of rightful testifiers non-Jewish agents (Gentiles) and myriad nonhuman agents (heavens, earth, mountains, even roads, not to mention the many animals). That is, Israel should not be so haughty as to assume that it alone is the sole location of moral, theological, and legal concern or agency. This does not necessarily downgrade Israel as much as it upgrades these other denizens.

Israel is humbled, to be sure, but less because Israel was depraved and more because of the robustness of the moral agents that accompany Israel in creation. The midrash certainly points to human limitation, but the world it invokes is one where the divine will works through almost every part of creation. If humans go off track, yet their course can be corrected by the other agencies about them, must we read this as evidence of human depravity and animal threat? Could the notion of animal testimony not also be a kind of comfort? Instead of reading it as humbling humans to lay us low, could we also read it as a story emphasizing that all creation is collectively bound to the divine will and that we are "in it together"?

The animals—indeed, all entities brought into the proverbial court to testify against wayward Israel—demonstrate this fundamental cohesion and solidarity of creation. This is most evident when their grievances are taken seriously by the court and by one another. When wrongs are committed against one of them by humankind, they are not summarily dismissed. Instead, another creature comes to its aid. In this manner not only does this court recognize each feature/creature/class as a rightful litigant, but each apparently acknowledges this stature of the others. All creatures operate with the assumption that all other creatures are rightful subjects with legitimate interests. We can reach this conclusion counterfactually: if these creatures did not work with this assumption, they would not have come to one another's aid. The exception to this operational feature of the cosmos is humanity, as emphasized in the lachrymose interpretation of the midrash.

Animals in the Court of the King of Jinn

Whereas some ancient sources consider language to be the definitive feature that renders humankind both distinctive and superior to all other species, the "Case of the Animals" assumes differently. Language is not the exclusive tool of humans, since all animals in the case are able to listen, understand, and speak.[34] But unlike the biblical serpent and donkey, who speak only at God's behest,[35] the animals here speak because, as the Brethren explain, they have "put these themes into the mouths of animals, to make the case clearer and more compelling—more striking in the telling, wittier, livelier, more useful to the listener, and more poignant and thought-provoking in its moral."[36] On their own, the animals have neither voice nor speech (Prologue, 13, 84). The animals' articulation of their grievances is thus not some fantasy of animal elocution, some dreamy world in which all creatures necessarily understand each other.[37] Rather, their eloquence is self-consciously understood as a manufactured artifice to persuade the intended audience. However, this artifice is not a deception or play; it is precisely a vehicle for conveying what animals really do "say" to us. The animals are not only metaphors for the actors that really matter; the story line is not an allegory about something other than human-animal relations. Through the Brethren, the animals pronounce in human words what they "really" would say if animals could communicate in this manner. As the Brethren see it, the animals themselves are thus, in the end, the real speakers (not the Brethren, who nonetheless did compose the prose); just as God gives Balaam's ass voice to express the ass's own dismay, so the Brethren make animals talk to make animals heard.

Early humans, the Ikhwan assert, were roaming vegetarians who, in time, became settlers.[38] They eventually captured and enslaved beasts of burden and worked them beyond their strengths (I, 99–100). One of the jinn—ethereal creatures existing in every nook and cranny of the universe—who responded to Mohammad, arose to become king: Biwarasp the Wise, known as Mardan, King Heroic (I, 101).[39] He ruled uncontested among all the jinn and material creatures on an isolated island. A storm wind cast a ship laden with humans upon that island's shores, and they found the island humanly uninhabited but replete with all kinds of animals living peacefully. Soon enough the humans recapitulated their history: they settled and meddled with the animals, forcing them into service, riding and loading them as they did in their former lands. Some animals balked and fled. The humans gave chase, hunted them with all sorts of devices, as they were "convinced that the animals were their runaway and rebellious slaves" (I, 102).

Here the story takes a decisive turn. "When the cattle and beasts learned of this belief, their spokesmen and leaders gathered and came before Biwarasp the Wise, King of the Jinn, to complain of the injustice and wrongs of mankind against them and to protest the human notions about them" (I, 102). These beasts of burden thereby express a two-fold complaint: unreasonable human behavior and unwarranted human assumptions. Both human action *and* human motivation are eligible for interrogation not just by the jinn and other divinities but they can be interrogated by animals themselves. In different terms: the animals question both the humans' claims to their differences in degree (that justify violent action against those with "lesser" qualities) and their differences in kind (that justify assuming that all other creatures are their slaves).[40]

To the king's questions—"What brought you to our island? Why did you come uninvited to our land?" (I, 102)—the humans do not answer truthfully. "We were drawn by all that we have heard of the virtues of the King. . . . We have come before him that he might hear our case and the arguments we shall present, and judge between us and these runaway slaves, who deny our authority" (I, 103). These lies and presumptions open the court hearing in which the humans invoke religious, scientific, and philosophical arguments to justify their twofold claims to excellence and superiority.

Though humans invoke Qur'anic proof texts to buttress their religious arguments, the animals rightfully point out that those sources merely grant humans permission to use animals. The noxious abuses, however, transgress what is permitted. Arguments from (religious) authority thus fail to defend humankind's assumptions or behaviors.

The humans then invoke natural evidence. Their physical form, sophisticated senses, discrimination, and intellect all prove that they are masters and animals are their slaves. Such arguments of rational proof meet with robust animal resistance when they in turn assert that God made each species and animal with the form and capacities best suited for each. The ass, as if channeling Balaam's, speaks up: not only did these humans burden the animals' backs with unbearable loads, "they stood over us, stick in hand to beat us brutally about the face and back in anger." And more: since God's bounties are many and no species can encompass them all, all creatures share in them in greater or lesser proportion (V, 116–17; VI, 123–24). And the ox opines that whoever may be richly divinely endowed should share with those of less fortune (VI, 125). In these and other ways the beasts of burden bellow that arguments of differences of kind are meritless; only differences of degree are intelligible. But even those would fail to support the humans' claims to superiority and excellence, since humans are neither superior nor excellent when compared with various other species.

It is at this impasse that the king adjourns the court so the parties can gather their wits, representatives, and arguments. In their huddle the humans contemplate plausible solutions to the case. The king could rule one of three ways: (1) the humans must *free* the animals; (2) the humans must *sell* the animals for a mandatory settlement; or (3) the humans must *ease* the animals' plight (IX, 146). None is optimal, they argue, but the last is the most reasonable, "for they are flesh and blood like us. They feel and suffer. We have no special merit in God's eyes that he was rewarding when he subjected them to us" (IX, 148). This echoes a biblical sentiment that God chose the Israelites not for any innate quality but merely and solely out of divine love (Deuteronomy 7:7–8). That is, even before the case's arguments were fully fleshed out, these humans admitted to themselves that they have no special merit. Their case is weak, even vain, in their own eyes.

While the humans schemed to fabulate, the animals worried that emotional arguments could not ground the king's judgment. Only reasoned and cogent arguments could persuade the court. They thus secured representatives from every habitat of the animal world to offer arguments defending the animals' grievances.

When the court resumes, human claims to distinctiveness are investigated first. Collective achievements in religion, knowledge, and psychology are put forward by humans to prove their distinctiveness. The jinn, like a commenting chorus, retort that religions delude, knowledge is impure, and temperance is fickle. And the animals chime in, each asserting its own distinctiveness. The frog levels the field with the observation that each creature—human and animal alike—eats and is, ultimately, eaten (XXIII, 228). The food chain is more circular, not linear, and certainly not hierarchical; it does not admit exceptions.

The king interrupts the repartee to direct the investigation with eight rounds of questions on themes much akin to those already rebutted. Humans first offer evidence supporting their claims, and then the animals retort. Regarding *governance and power*, humans are no better than bees. Human *social knowledge* is no different than the intelligence found among ants, locusts, silkworms, and wasps. Human *diet*, while fancy, nonetheless relies upon the toil and flesh of animals, and only humans exhaust themselves haggling over food prices, itself bespeaking a kind of enslavement. Humans may boast of *revelation and theonomy*, the animals concede, but this is only because they need such exogenous instruction; they are themselves already endowed with what they need to know, and they spend their lives praising God without any need for temple or ritual. Human *clothing* does not prove mastery, the animals contend, since it is usually stolen from animals. The abundant *practical knowledge* found across human ranks is no different than the know-how in each species. Humanity argues that their singular *morphology* indicates mastery, whereas animal diversity belongs to servitude. The animals retort that their souls are unified in solidarity with each other and God, and they suffer no malingering doubts, but human religious diversity bespeaks myriad errant confusions. And finally, that God promises *immortality* to humans does not mean that all receive eternal reward; animals, by contrast, accept God's judgment without dread or contrition. While the animals readily claim for themselves souls, they cede to humans both theonomy and immortality. The reasons why humankind needs them both is because otherwise they could not organize themselves aright; they need both carrots and sticks to orient themselves for prosocial, pro-divine, existence.

The king contemplates these arguments and ultimately rules that the animals, despite the persuasiveness of their arguments, are nonetheless to remain subject to the commands and prohibitions of humans until a new age dawns, at which time they will acquire a new fate.[41] This perhaps surprising conclusion may stem from a final human argument that there exist among their depraved ranks a few honest and striving people who "quest after the highest goods, yearn after their Lord, turn to him in all things, and ever hearken to Him" (XLII, 313). These few saints model not what humans are but what they can become; even more, they are not just sources of inspiration but guarantors for all.

Modern scholars wonder at the purpose of this medieval source. Richard Foltz, for one, sees in this premodern epistle the Ikhwan's ecological vision in which animals occupy and speak in distinct niches not because of evolution but because God placed them there. On the other hand, he also reads this source as a postmodern meditation on animal agency: "Non-human animals are presented as subjects of their own experience, not merely as objects observed by humans."[42] The king's decision thus startles all the more:

> This unexpected, abrupt and, from an animal rights perspective, highly un-satisfying conclusion leaves one wondering just what point the Brethren were trying to make. Is their treatise intended to awaken the reader to a non-anthropocentric reality? If so, the ending is clearly unacceptable. But if the intention is to re-assert the view of human uniqueness, why so convincingly make the case on the animals' behalf? Or is the reader's frustration meant to be turned against God, for having established the hierarchy of creation on the basis of such unfair and arbitrary principles?[43]

For Foltz, the case frustrates *any* sensibility or tradition that one holds. No matter what one believes, one cannot help but be disturbed by the fact that it takes seriously nonhuman animal moral stature, grievances, and agency.

The case's destabilizing character stimulates other modern scholars to deploy it as a missive against wanton ecological destruction. The translation by Denys Johnson-Davies provides an ample illustration. His conclusion deviates from the original text to inveigh against human hubris and indifference toward the strains they impose upon beasts and ecosystems alike. Anson Laytner and Dan Bridge similarly offer a creative re-reading of the conclusion, not to erase the Ikhwan's ambiguity or supersede it with certainty, but to spark contemporary reflection on what it means to be a moral creature alongside myriad other creatures that also participate in moral life.

These interpretations raise a question: are, for lack of a better term, pro-animal and ecologically minded interpretations of the Case of the Animals or similar literature so inviting because these texts were crafted (at least in the form they take in their Jewish and Muslim contexts) in consonance with broader countertraditions that intentionally challenged the conventional categorical divisions of humanity and animality in their respective traditions? Further, do these countertraditions, per Derrida's suggestion, persist and recur because they are rooted in the "undeni-able" and ageless possibility of avowing that animals accuse us. As far as canonical Jewish and Muslim texts are concerned, is it only the human face that says, accusingly, "Don't kill me"?[44] Or does that view sit beside long-standing minority traditions, visible in fragments, that insist that nonhuman animals too make this demand? In sum, can scholars speak legitimately of "countertraditions" inside the larger textual corpuses that challenge dominant conceptions of the categorical division between humans and animals?

THE QUESTION OF COUNTERTRADITION

Textual Commonalities

What unites these three stories is the implication that animals can accuse humans in the manner that a plaintiff or prosecutor would in a court of law. These texts suggest, even if indirectly in the case of Balaam's ass, that law, and thus justice too, are not strictly human phenomena. Rather, law and justice are divine and God excludes animals from neither.

By challenging the assumed exclusively human character of legal action, these texts suggest a deep challenge to how the larger Jewish and Islamic traditions of which they are a part imagine religious actors. Namely, they challenge the notion of a categorical distinction between humans and animals that denies animals agency, subjectivity, and personhood. These narratives also are carefully designed to unsettle or surprise the reader who is familiar with the larger corpus and to challenge assumptions about the relationship between humanity and animality before God. Overall, these religious stories of animal participation in law provide a counterpoint to the dominant tradition. Thus these texts can be viewed, we suggest fruitfully, as contributing to countertraditions—textual moments that challenge dominant understandings of humanity and animality too systematically to be anomalies and that thus are best viewed as traditions in their own right. In closing, let us consider further what is at stake in conceptualizing texts such as the three cases considered here as partially constitutive of Jewish and Islamic countertraditions.

Imaging Countertradition

To speak of a tradition assumes that different actors have worked over similar problems over time. We can very straightforwardly speak, for example, of a "tradition" of Jewish biblical exegesis because we can easily show that multiple texts in different strata are all working to interpret the same ancient text, the Hebrew Bible. Jewish biblical exegetes may be separated by great distances in space and time, but they are united in turning their attention to the same object (the biblical text) in similar enough ways to allow recognition of a common project. In the end, the basic work of biblical exegesis in a Jewish context is not radically specific to a particular time and place. We thus speak of both continuity and change in traditions of Jewish biblical exegesis. Can we point to a uniting problematic—something as tangible as interpreting the same biblical passages—that unites these stories of animals as legal actors? We argue that the answer is yes: actual animals, like the biblical text, have demanded responses, and while these responses are shaped by their times and places, this should not stop us from the further observation that these responses are also united as attempts to work through particular human existential questions—in this case questions about the fundamental nature of animals and the human-animal relationship. If we can speak of a tradition of Jewish biblical exegesis made intelligible by a consistent return to the biblical text itself, we can by the same logic speak of a countertradition that leans against dominant views of the human-animal relationship by returning to the now well-documented phenomena of spontaneous empathy for animals, that is, animals' ability to accuse us.[45]

We thus argue that stories like Balaam's ass or *Sifre Devarim*'s animal testifiers or the Ikhwan's myriad species are best interpreted not as essentially independent or isolated human imaginations about what justice we owe animals, but also as humans *responding* to animals—responding, specifically, to (real) animals' responses to human mistreatment of them. In this way of thinking, which seems close to the self-understanding expressed in these texts themselves, animals are coauthors, of sorts, of these very sources. Not merely fictional subjects of the narratives we currently read, they are the subjects that inspire—in a literal sense—the narratives themselves.

Attention to animals as fellow subjects capable exerting a kind of theo-moral-legal agency is important because it suggests that scholars of religion would do well to inquire more seriously about the possibility raised by Derrida: the possibility that the resonances that we have noted among these venerable texts, on the one hand, and the resonances between these ancient texts and what are perceived as "cutting edge" contemporary concerns with animal rights, on the other hand, are intelligible in part because they are part of something we can call a *tradition*. This tradition would be one that is embedded inextricably with the dominant tradition in a dynamic relation, an engagement that subverts the dominant view of animals in which, to employ the vocabulary developed by medievalist Kalman Bland, a "categorical distinction between humans and animals . . . constitutes [an] ideology."[46]

Bland has helpfully named this ideology "Brutism." "Venerable in history," he argues, "Brutism is perhaps the primal template for any ideology that dialectically licenses and restrains both self and the Other."[47] It is a way of thinking that operates with a brutal force, suppressing the noncompliant and ignoring the uncategorizable, among other distortions. "Brutism therefore," Bland continues, "precedes and complements the knot of exclusionary systems. Throughout modernity, for example, Brutism, sexism, racism, and colonialism have worked in tandem, validating and reinforcing one another."[48] We would go perhaps further and suggest that all of these "isms" are best understood as different strands in the same knot. And just as brutism, sexism, and so on function collectively—that is, as interlocking traditions—so do the challenges to brutism that Bland has begun to document in both Jewish and Islamic medieval sources.

Bland notes that while the "modern phase of the revolt against medieval dualism, featuring the comparison *with* animals, is well known,"[49] there has been a tendency to see this revolt as exclusively modern. The medieval phase of the revolt, though robust, has remained "something of a terra incognita in the history of Jewish ideas" and Bland's scholarship is filling that lacuna.[50] This chapter, by suggesting that biblical, rabbinic, and medieval Islamic texts too can be read as containing a certain "revolt" or resistance to more-dominant ways of drawing a line between humans and other animals, raises the issue of whether the modern and medieval "phase of the revolt" are not preceded by even more ancient ones. The "revolt" thus may be best described as an alternative tradition as rooted, ancient, and coherent as the dominant tradition with which it converses.

In closing, let us consider what kind of studies would allow us to more rigorously, precisely, and contextually speak about "countertraditions." A short chapter such as this can hardly demonstrate sufficient grounds to declare the existence of internal countertraditions in Islamic philosophy and rabbinic midrashim except in the most general terms. What kind of evidence would allow scholars to conclude something like "inside [the Bible, rabbinic midrashim, medieval Islamic philosophy, or whatever recognized body of literature or tradition] one can discern a recurrent pattern of ideas and images that challenge dominant anthropocentric ideas—a countertradition that challenges the conventional ideologically invested human/animal divide and prominently elevates regard for animals"? At stake would be the meaning of the word "tradition." Following historian of religions J. Z. Smith, we would be suspicious of the concept of "tradition" in the same way Smith has warned us to be critical of the term "religion."[51] The idea of "tradition," like "religion," is an imagined idea and not a "natural kind." Speaking in broad brushstrokes, the various traditions (Judaism, Islam, and so on) that the study of religion addresses are generally not populations in the social-scientific sense; they are closer to a "collection of oddments left over from human endeavors"[52] (as Levi-Strauss put it) that are unified in some way that serves the purpose of the scholar. For this reason, proving the existence of a countertradition cannot simply be a matter of gathering facts. It is also a matter of the values we scholars, despite our best intentions, bring to bear on the traditions we already (accurately or foolishly) acknowledge and recognize as traditions.

The relationship between a concept like "countertradition" and the data that would demonstrate the existence of a countertradition is thus dialectical: we cannot simply look at the tradition at hand, read its texts, and pronounce the existence or nonexistence of a countertradition therein. We need to actively imagine what might unify a countertradition and thus justify us calling the "collection of oddments" before us a "tradition." This is what Derrida's line of inquiry provides for us. In his hypothesis—and he does present it as only a hypothesis—two streams run through the whole of Abrahamic religion: one stream is made by those who avow being confronted by animals, and the other is made by those who disavow or obfuscate the possibility of being seen by an animal.[53] We do not have time here to elaborate all that is implied in this bifurcation, but what is key for our purposes is that the two streams imagined in tension here pivot around how humans respond to the fundamental reality of sharing existence with nonhuman sentient animals. What separates tradition and countertradition is what "side" sources take on this fundamental issue: do they avow that animals can accuse us or do they deny it? Derrida's criterion for determining which side a particular thinker or text takes—the question of avowing the animals' gaze—works well to capture part of what is more unusual and striking about the three texts reviewed here. All three of our textual exempla can be slotted in Derrida's schema as aligning in the main with those who avow animal gazes, though the Case of the Animals fits less comfortably because of the tension between the bulk of the text and its surprising ending. The unsatisfying ending of the Case of the Animals disavows the force of animal gazes that the first part of the text makes so compelling, complicating the task of situating this text neatly on either side of Derrida's divide: it both avows and disavows animals.

Thus, we suggest that one way to further explore this important question of a countertradition is to pay particular attention to the issue of acknowledging animals as religious subjects, which would be proximate to Derrida's notion of avowing the animal's ability to confront us. We found that what united all the texts looked at here was a relatively rare willingness to view animals as potential testifiers or litigants. We further argued that this amounts to granting animals some kind of religious agency, subjectivity, or personhood. Does this consideration of animals as religious agents, subjects, or persons constitute something like a countertradition? Ultimately, what will decide this question is the infinitely ongoing work of asking it: what else do these texts that grant animals more subjectivity or agency than is usual do? If, as we ask these questions, we find that the division into dominant tradition and countertradition is conceptually helpful—if it would, as we have suggested it might, for example, help us uplift ethically valuable textual insights, stave off overly hegemonic views of tradition, and reveal larger seams within a tradition, then it is productive to speak of a countertradition. Our sense is that the vocabulary of tradition and countertradition will help describe and engage views of animals more fully. It is no longer viable either to simply describe a unified "Jewish" or "Islamic" view of animals (and the implicit links to their views of humanity) or to take texts such as the ones here only as exceptions that prove the rule. We propose, instead, that textual phenomena like the image of the animal testifier or litigant might be best understood and appreciated as part of an ancient stream that deserves the dignity of being called a tradition, even if this tradition has, at least so far, been in the minority.

NOTES

1. In calling this datum "undeniable" we do not intend to suggest that it has not been denied, for it has been. Indeed, few assertions of common sense have been subject to a greater intellectual assault than our ability to say *anything* about animal minds, let alone that animals can accuse us. We insist, however, that those who are honest with themselves can take these arguments at face value; to deny the fact of our ability

to accurately (if very imperfectly) empathize with many animals and the impulse of sympathy that this often elicits is not a disagreement but what Derrida theorizes as a disavowal. One can deny the reality of cross-cultural, cross-temporal sympathetic concern with animals only by failing to be honest with oneself. "Disavowal" is one of the core concepts Derrida employs in his elaborate reflections on animals, and we follow him here. For discussion of his understanding of disavowal in relation to animals, see A. S. Gross, *The Question of the Animal and Religion* (New York: Columbia University Press, 2015), chap. 5.

2. J. Serpell, *In the Company of Animals: A Study of Human-Animal Relationships* (Cambridge: Cambridge University Press, 1996).

3. The cross-cultural phenomena of both empathy and the associated impulse to improve the conditions of animals has long been observed in the study of religion, and seminal thinkers such as Ernst Cassirer and Mircea Eliade have even gone so far as to place this sentiment at the very origin of religion; Gross, *The Question of the Animal and Religion*, 78, 106–108, 230n39.

4. See S. M. Wise, *Rattling the Cage: Toward Legal Rights for Animals* (Cambridge, MA: Perseus Books, 2000).

5. Derrida's most important and comprehensive exploration of animals is *The Question of the Animal* (2008); for a full list of his works dealing with animals in English, see Gross, *The Question of the Animal and Religion*, 214n47. Human uniqueness is not denied by Derrida, but the notion that human beings are "uniquely unique"—different in some way that obviously matters more than what makes, say, dolphins unique—is problematized.

6. J. Derrida, *The Animal That Therefore I Am* (New York: Fordham University Press, 2008), 25.

7. For Buddhist notions of animals as rightful legal subjects, both seen and heard by courts, see Bathgate, chapter 10 in this volume.

8. On dating of this text, see Herbert W. Basser, *Midrashic Interpretations of the Song of Moses* (New York: Peter Lang, 1984), 2; Günter Stemberger, *Introduction to the Talmud and Midrash*, 2nd ed. (Edinburgh: T&T Clark, 1996), 272–73.

9. The Brethren (Ikhwan) found inspiration in many philosophies and traditions beyond the ken of the Qur'an and its interpreters, drawing from Persian, Hellenic, Greek, Hebrew, Indian, Christian, and of course Muslim thought. They produced their epistles collectively and anonymously. Their writings are representative of an impulse to organize all extant human knowledge and their *Rasa'il* divided the world into four domains: (1) the mathematical sciences, (2) the natural sciences, (3) the psychological and rational sciences, and (4) the theological sciences.

10. Considered by some as the most extensive critique of mainstream attitudes toward animals in Muslim literature, "The Case of the Animals Versus Man" pursues two separate yet interlocking goals (Richard C. Foltz, *Animals in Islamic Tradition and Muslim Cultures* [Oxford: Oxford University Press, 2006]), 50). On the one hand, the letter makes explicit the distinctive features of nonhuman animals, and it examines the brutal nature of humanly supposed superiority on the other (Prologue, 1, 65. All citations of the case are from Lenn E. Goodman and Richard McGregor, trans., *The Case of the Animals Versus Man Before the King of the Jinn* [New York: Oxford University Press, 2009]). On the other hand, the epistle opens with a neo-Aristotelian comment: "We will show that the highest animals verge with the lowest rank of human beings; and the highest rank of humans, with the lowest of the angels," suggesting that making hard-and-fast distinctions between human and other animal species is an inherently

fraught if not impossible task (Prologue, 1, 63). (Compare with Aristotle's *Historia Animalium* VIII.1.588b4–11.) Humanity's distinctiveness compared to animals rests upon "reason and discernment" (Prologue, 2, 65). As such, it is a lengthy investigation of difference, both difference of kind and difference of degree.

11. *The Case of the Animals Versus Man Before the King of the Jinn*, though not (as far as we know) influential in legal or theological circles, was popular enough to spur translation into many languages, which further enhanced its popularity. One translation was by Kalonymous ben Kalonymous, a thirteenth-century Provençal philosopher, who translated it from the Arabic into Hebrew at the request of the Catholic king Charles I of Anjou, and his version was then translated into Yiddish and German a few centuries later. Urdu, Latin, Persian, and Turkish versions appeared early on and have since been translated into many other languages, with an English edition emerging in the late nineteenth century, and several more in the past three decades.

12. Genesis 3:1–24. Biblical translations closely follow the *New JPS Tanakh* (Philadelphia: Jewish Publication Society, 1985). For more on the *nachash*, see Jonathan K. Crane, "She Gave Me from the Tree and I Ate: Gender, Eating, and Theology" (unpublished manuscript).

13. Numbers 22:3.

14. Numbers 22:9–11.

15. *Bamidbar Rabbah* 20.6; BT *Sotah* 10a; BT *Sanhedrin* 105a, 106b. This sets the stage for the angel of God "opening" his eyes; Numbers 22:31; see also Numbers 24:4, 16.

16. Numbers 22:20.

17. The reason Balaam rode the donkey is because he put his horse out to pasture—or so he supposedly says. See Rashi, Numbers 22: 30; BT *Avodah Zarah* 4b; BT *Sanhedrin* 106a.

18. Compare Joshua 5:13.

19. This could also be understood as "from your inception," implying that the donkey is much older than Balaam.

20. Compare with Joshua 5:14.

21. This suggests the supine donkey is a divinely dead one, recently killed by the angel's sword.

22. Numbers 22:21–35.

23. The three times could also be a reference to the Israelites' three annual pilgrimages. Or it might be an oblique reference to the people of Israel themselves. See *Bamidbar Rabbah* 20.4.

24. M *Avot* 5.6.

25. Indeed, because of a shared root (*sacan*) with I Kings 1:2, it is imagined that Balaam engaged her sexually. See BT *Avodah Zarah* 4b; BT *Sanhedrin* 105a-b. See other sources in Louis Ginzberg, *The Legends of the Jews*, 6 vols. (Philadelphia: Jewish Publication Society, 1925), 6:128n747.

26. Some rabbinic texts imagine that the donkey dies immediately, lest the heathens worship her or be a cause of continued humiliation for Balaam. See *Bamidbar Rabbah* 20.14. This can also explain the angel's statement in Numbers 22:33 and Rashi, ad loc, s.v. *v'otah hecheyeiti*.

27. *Bamidbar Rabbah* 20.14, end.

28. This donkey narrative also appears in the Christian New Testament. The second letter by Peter mentions Balaam's donkey. Peter proclaims that God "knows how to rescue the godly from trial, and to keep the unrighteous under punishment until

the day of judgment" (2 Peter 2:9, NRSV). Peter speaks of the surrounding heretics as "irrational animals, mere creatures of instinct, born to be caught and killed. They slander what they do not understand, and when those creatures are destroyed, they also will be destroyed, suffering the penalty for doing wrong" (2 Peter 2:12–13a). These hedonistic, insatiable, licentious, and lazy people "have left the straight road and have gone astray, following the road of Balam son of Bosor [Beor], who loved the wages of doing wrong, but was rebuked for his own transgressions; a speechless donkey spoke with a human voice and restrained the prophet's madness" (2 Peter 2:15–16). Peter's presumed mute donkey speaks with a human voice—which does not comport with the Numbers text in which it is God who opens her mouth through which she speaks (Numbers 22:28). On the other hand, that original source does not specify that she speaks with either a divine or a human voice, so Peter could be correct. Either way, the question remains: does the tenor of her voice matter? She speaks, speaks morally sophisticated content at that, and is heard. Perhaps the quality of her voice pales in significance to those facts.

29. *Perek Shirah*, a potentially ancient text about which little is known, also depicts animals speaking. Here, though, they do not testify against humankind but rather praise God. See Nosson Slifkin, *Nature's Song* (New York: Targum/Feldheim, 2001).

30. Elsewhere, R. Yohanan teaches, "Had the Torah not been given, we would have learned modesty from the cat, the prohibition of theft from the ant, the prohibition of forbidden relationships from the dove, and the proper conjugal relations from fowl" (BT *Eruvin* 100b). On this and other moral wisdom drawn from ants, see King, chapter 9 in this volume.

31. *Sifre Devarim* §306, beginning.

32. Jacob Neusner, *Sifre to Deuteronomy: An Analytical Translation* (Atlanta: Scholars Press, 1987), 299.

33. Basser, *Midrashic Interpretations of the Song of Moses*, 6.

34. That all animals had the capacity for speech is an idea upheld in the Judaic tradition as well. See, for example, Philo, *On the Confusion of Languages*, III; Josephus, *Antiquities of the Jews*, 1.1.4; YT *Ta'anit* 8.1; BT *Berachot* 61b.

35. Though the serpent speaks without any explicit divine ventriloquism, the text is clear that it was made (the cleverest of all beasts) by God. Genesis 3:1.

36. Prologue, 1, 65. Again, all citations are from Goodman and McGregor, *The Case of the Animals Versus Man Before the King of the Jinn*, critical edition.

37. Perhaps anticipating Thomas Nagel, "What Is It like to Be a Bat?" *Philosophical Review* 83, no. 4 (October 1974): 435–50, the Ikhwan do not assume they know precisely what animals think, feel, or hope.

38. The epistle opens with a recapitulation of known knowledge about animals. Animal morphology, mortality and striving, their senses, discrimination and training, their endowment with all the organs they need—all are rehearsed as if to remind the audience that animals are but creatures no different than humans, who, like the animals, are made from clay and bidden to procreate (Prologue, 10, 78; see also 68). Such equality of all creatures shifts, however, as the Ikhwan reinforce the long-standing notion of the *Scala Natura*, the Great Chain of Being. The higher are more perfect than the lower, and the lower serve the higher, just as all organs of the body ultimately serve the brain (Prologue, 12, 81–82). The hierarchy embedded in the microcosm of the body reflects and reifies the hierarchy of the cosmos. This ranking is both inexorable and unalterable. Such cosmology bespeaks not just a cosmogony of creation but a particular anthropol-

ogy. Recall, theirs was a two-tiered creation. First was the Intellect *ex nihilo* that then immediately emanated, seriatim, into the present universe.

39. "Biwarasp was a sage, just, and noble king, fair minded and open-handed, hospitable to guests and a refuge to strangers. He had mercy for the afflicted and would not brook injustice but ordained the good and forbade evil, seeking only to please God and be worthy of His favour" (I, 102).

40. See, for example, I, 103–6.

41. Not all printed editions carry this conclusion. Some modern versions radically alter and expand upon the conclusion to meet the proclivities and interests of the authors. See Anson Laytner and Dan Bridge, trans. and adapters, *The Animals' Lawsuit Against Humanity: A Modern Adaptation of an Ancient Animal Rights Tale* (Louisville: Fons Vitae, 2005); Denys Johnson-Davies, *The Island of Animals: Adapted from an Arabic Fable* (Austin: University of Texas Press, 1994).

42. Foltz, *Animals in Islamic Tradition and Muslim Cultures*, 52.

43. Ibid.

44. We allude to Levinas's theorization of "the face"—his name for a non-empirical structure through which we encounter the radical otherness of other humans and are bound in ethical obligation to them—as exclusively human. For discussion, see Gross, *The Question of the Animal and Religion*, 176, 350n104.

45. For an accessible discussion of the state of empathy studies and its findings, see F. de Waal, *The Age of Empathy: Nature's Lessons for a Kinder Society* (New York: Harmony Books, 2009). As de Waal shows, both empathy and the ability to act on that empathy with the intent to improve another animal's condition—including animals of different species—are well documented in both nonhuman primates and humans.

46. K. Bland, "Cain, Abel, and Brutism," in *Scriptural Exegesis, the Shapes of Culture, and the Religious Imagination: Essays in Honour of Michael Fishbane,* ed. D. Green and L. Lieber (Oxford: University of Oxford, 2009): 165.

47. Ibid., 166.

48. Ibid., 167.

49. K. Bland, "Construction of Animals in Medieval Jewish Philosophy," in *New Directions in Jewish Philosophy*, ed. A.W. Hughes and E. R. Wolfson (Bloomington: Indiana University Press, 2010), 190.

50. Ibid.

51. "While there is a staggering amount of data . . . that might be characterized in one culture or another, by one criterion or another, as religious—*there is no data for religion*. Religion is solely the creation of the scholar's study" (J. Z. Smith, *Imagining Religion: From Babylon to Jonestown* [Chicago: University of Chicago Press, 1988], xi).

52. C. Lévi-Strauss, *The Savage Mind* (Chicago and London: University of Chicago Press, 1973), 19.

53. Derrida, *The Animal That Therefore I Am*, 13; for the French, see J. Derrida, "L'animal que donc je suis," in *L'animal autobiographique: autour de Jacques Derrida,* ed. M. L. Mallet (Paris: Galilée, 1999), 264. For discussion, see Gross, *The Question of the Animal and Religion*, 124–25.

Part V **Epilogue**

Thirteen Beastly Morality

UNTANGLING POSSIBILITIES

Jonathan K. Crane, Ani B. Satz,
Lori Marino, and Cynthia Willett

Pulling together the many threads of *Beastly Morality* into some comprehensive or cohesive conclusion is no easy task. Indeed, these arguments, observations, and investigations point toward no specific goal or *telos* but rather open ambiguities and opportunities. They uncover ancient and ongoing philosophical and theological ambivalences that resist easy assuaging or erasure. They discover evidence that challenges long-held assumptions of human superiority and excellence. They displace scholarly narcissism in favor of a new kind of humanism in which the human sits, perhaps uncomfortably, alongside other denizens similarly worthy of contemplation and admiration, even respect.

Yet . . .

So what? What is the significance of the fact that arguments can be made that nonhuman animals are moral agents, too, and not just objects of human moral concern? What implications and applications are entangled here? In which ways might the very questions pursued in this volume lead us even further afield, into ever murkier and knottier ways of thinking, doing, and relating?

Thankfully I am not alone in wondering such things. Matthew Calarco raises similar questions in response to a brilliant Socratic play, *The Death of the Animal: A Dialogue*, by Paola Cavalieri. Calarco asks, "Why do we need to determine the outer limits of moral status beyond animals? What if the logic of deciding inclusion and exclusion within the moral community were itself the problem? And what would be the implications for ethics if we were to abandon the aim of determining the proper limits of moral status altogether?"[1]

To gain insights into such possibilities, I invited three prominent scholars—all of whom are colleagues at Emory University and each of whom is an expert on animal issues, be it in law, psychology, or philosophy—to sit together and reflect on the "so what" of beastly morality, of nonhuman ethical agency, and perhaps forge an epilogue—an additional lecture—on this subject. To be sure, those hours of conversation were some of the most stimulating and illuminating I have ever experienced. The animated and divergent nature of that conversation, however, challenged the very project I suggested. Instead of weaving these scholars' voices into a singular argument, we agreed it would be better to hear their responses to this "so what" question in their own words, using their own disciplinary idioms. What follows is their responses to my invitation to meditate on the "so what" of beastly morality. As anticipated, each scholar interpreted the question slightly differently in her own way.

For Ani B. Satz, a professor of law, *Beastly Morality* inspires reconsidering the legal status of nonhuman animals. Lori Marino, a cetologist and professor of psychology, questions the very link between moral subjectivity and moral agency. And Cynthia Willett, a professor of philosophy, meditates on how animal ethicality troubles our notions of freedom—and this is a good trouble to have.[2]

I agree. The challenges these scholars raise are not to be disparaged because they identify difficulties that are politically unpalatable or pragmatically complex. Rather, they indicate opportunities to understand ourselves afresh, as moral subjects alongside myriad other moral entities who, thankfully, do not look like, smell like, or speak like we do.

ANI B. SATZ

This volume—which examines the capacity of nonhuman animals to be moral agents—raises the significant "so what?" question about the implications of such moral agency. Answering this question is especially difficult, as animals and humans may have different moral codes. And human moral codes may not, as is the default assumption, be superior even under human-constructed notions of moral agency. Nor do we have any way of assessing animal moral codes, much less adherence to those codes, outside our human constructs. Yet, as a general matter, viewing animals as moral agents (however defined) may impose obligations on human and nonhuman animals. While the significance of moral agency must be examined in detail elsewhere, I sketch here a possible consequence and benefit for animals of possessing moral agency: higher legal status.

In order to see how higher legal status might arise, it is necessary to discuss the possible relationship between moral agency and moral status. One consequence of recognizing animal morality may be that it could support animals' moral status, or ability to be wronged.[3] The characteristics that suggest moral agency may overlap with the characteristics used to establish moral status. In fact, moral agency typically is viewed as requiring higher-order characteristics, such as the ability to reason from abstract rules, whereas moral status might be conferred based on the ability to make autonomous choices without such a capacity to reason, for example. Thus, moral agency likely is sufficient to establish moral status, but not the other way around. (Having moral status but not moral agency, incidentally, could prove beneficial for animals, who otherwise might be held accountable for harms they cause.) The characteristics that afford animals moral status could be used in turn to justify granting animals greater legal protection.

Unlike viable fetuses, corporations, and even sailboats—which have been recognized as "persons" under law—animals currently do not possess personhood or another high legal status. Domestic animals are instead a form of living property. As a result, laws covering animals largely protect their interests only when human owner interests and animal interests align, rather than protecting animals in their own right.[4] Animals who are companions enjoy the most protections against abuse and neglect, whereas animals used for experimentation, exhibition, and entertainment may be intensively confined and, depending on their status, worked to the point of exhaustion; have their skin, nails, and tissues removed; or be subjected to painful procedures without anesthesia or pain medication, if it interferes with experimental results. Farm animals have the least protection; the primary federal legal requirement is that they must be rendered insensible prior to slaughter, and they have some protections in transport and if "downed" due to illness. These animals may be immobilized for their entire lives, starved to produce eggs, and have their tails, toes, testicles, part of their posteriors, and beaks removed without anesthesia. The disparate treatment between companion animals and other animals is true even if the animal is the same in each context, for example, a pig. And due to legal exclusions to support human uses of animals, no federal law protects mice, rats, chickens, turkeys, or fish in any of these contexts. Some protections may apply under state anti-cruelty laws to farmed and other animals, though enforcement has proven difficult. Wild animals, who may be protected by government trust, often fare no better, since their protections may wane when human interests in hunting, entertainment, urban expansion, or other activities conflict with protection.

Recognizing higher legal status for animals could change dramatically the manner in which they are confined, raised, worked and otherwise used, and killed. Under the most favorable reading for animals, it might mean that animal interests in such areas as nourishment, hydration, shelter, bodily integrity, avoidance of pain, natural movement, and companionship (and maybe even higher-order interests like mental stimulation or education) would be given equal weight to human interests in the same areas. This could create a presumption against animal use if it interfered with certain interests, and animal users could be held legally liable for compromising these interests. Under a less favorable reading for animals, it could mean that animal interests would be given only some weight against the interests of other individuals with the same or higher legal status, depending on the legal hierarchy of individuals. While it is unclear how a legal hierarchy of individuals would be determined—it might be based on higher-order capacities, "humanness," or other criteria—in this context, human interests in using animals in certain ways may trump animal interests in avoiding even basic deprivations. Animal protections would depend on whether it is viewed as wrong to compromise basic animal needs for human desires. The recent fois gras ban in California reflects this possibility, demonstrating a shift from the view that ducks should suffer through force-feeding for the production of this human food to the view that they should not.

LORI MARINO

This volume raises two quite distinct questions. One of them is the scientific question about whether other animals are moral agents. That is, do members of other species possess a concept of morality in some shape or form? Do they understand "right from wrong" and is their behavior—particularly in a social context—driven, in some part, by concepts of morality? It would be interesting, for instance, to know if chimpanzees evaluate behavior and intentions in other chimpanzees and respond accordingly, by punishing inappropriate behaviors or rewarding valued behaviors like loyalty and fairness. Whatever sense of morality a member of another species possesses, it will, of course, be species specific. So, a member of another species may have very strong notions of "proper" behavior, but those may be entirely different from human concepts of morality. Indeed, differences exist even among humans.

The scientific question of whether other animals possess moral agency fits squarely within the realm of other scientific queries about the characteristics and capabilities of other animals, such as whether they communicate symbolically, grieve their dead, recognize themselves in mirrors, or count to ten. But another dimension to the writings in this volume addresses an orthogonal issue: Is being a moral agent in any way relevant to being a moral subject? Do we have more of a moral responsibility to members of other species who are deemed to be moral agents than to those who are not? I contend that there is little, if any, direct connection between human moral responsibility and nonhuman animal moral agency. In other words, other animals can clearly be moral subjects without being moral agents.

We recognize a moral responsibility to a number of kinds of individuals who are not moral agents. These include infants and young children, individuals with mental disabilities, patients in a coma, etc. There is no question about these being moral subjects. Equally, there is no expectation that they should be moral agents. So, why is it important for other animals to be moral agents in order to be recognized as moral subjects? The answer may lie in the way we frame concepts of morality, mind, and our relationship with the other animals. I argue that the claim that moral agency in other animals requires a moral response from our species is based in the fact that moral agency becomes a proxy for something more general, i.e., psychological complexity. By virtue of its correlation with other sophisticated cognitive traits, such as self-awareness, autonomy, social complexity, etc., the question of moral agency in other animals becomes about whether we have more of a moral responsibility to cognitively and emotionally complex animals than to those who are deemed less so. While this point does not describe the totality of arguments about morality in other animals in this volume or elsewhere, it is worth considering that it is difficult to disentangle moral agency from other characteristics that we view as morally relevant, such as autonomy or self-awareness.

It is well known that we tend to treat animals with whom we are familiar and see as similar to us as more worthy of moral consideration than others.[5] Simply put, our assumption is that highly intelligent animals are more vulnerable to suffering than are less-complex beings and thus

require a more robust moral response from us. Given that we see ourselves as a moral species, we tend to feel greater moral responsibility toward other animals who appear to share some aspects of morality with us
simply by virtue of the fact that they seem more similar to us. Even when
there is no evidence for a hierarchy of sophistication or any meaningful
differences in intelligence between two species, we often impose the belief
that the one we accept as moral subjects is more intelligent than the one
we dismiss as moral subjects. Our treatment of domestic pigs and dogs is
a striking example of disparate moral consideration in the face of a complete lack of evidence for any relevant psychological differences between
the two that would cause one to be more worthy of moral consideration
than the other.[6]

Unfortunately, we are still in the grips of the ancient Scala Naturae
view of the world that places humans and other animals on a hierarchy
of complexity, form, and, most relevantly, value. We apply this model
to considerations of whether other animals possess moral status. Hence,
those "higher up" on the scale are more like us and more worthy of
consideration. But because other animals are not human and do not enjoy "automatic" moral status, they must demonstrate their worthiness
by sharing certain characteristics with us. Thus, it is difficult to argue
that moral agency has any relevance to moral status apart from its connection with the Scala Naturae model of the world. The writings in this
volume strive to articulate our relationship to the other animals in the
moral realm. These thoughts and expressions can only help us to eventually shed ancient views and take a more informed and enlightened stance
toward the other animals.

CYNTHIA WILLETT

"We are heading down a path toward . . . a world without animals,"
Jacques Derrida famously exclaims, exhorting us toward an ethics that is
responsive to radical alterity.[7] His poststructuralist challenge to the threat
of human-induced mass extinction joins with Peter Singer's reason-based
concern for those sentient nonhuman animals consigned carelessly to factory farms, research facilities, and other sites of human abuse and neglect.[8]
Derrida and Singer represent the two major traditions of moral thought—
continental response ethics (also known as alterity ethics and tracing back
to Levinas) and utilitarianism—that have forcefully challenged the view
of animals as lacking moral status. Yet both of these philosophers assume

strong discontinuities between human and nonhuman. Moreover, each conceptualizes the targets of concern primarily in terms of their relative vulnerability or passive suffering. Neither unfolds the rich possibility that our prized human ethical agency is fundamentally continuous with that of other animals across a range of species. Yet, ever more evidence suggests that underlying the spectacular differences among species are the common capacities of creatures who in fact have coevolved in shared habitats and multispecies communities. These continuities give rise to speculations on an impending paradigm shift in moral theory and philosophical ethics. Here I focus on the reverberations of this shift for the meaning of freedom.

In addition to extending moral status and legal protection to nonhuman animals, the essays in this volume, drawing on scientific and phenomenological observations and philosophical and theological arguments, call for philosophical speculation on modes of ethical agency in other species. Otherwise we risk viewing other species too narrowly as passive or amoral creatures vulnerable to pain and suffering but lacking significant subjectivity of their own. In fact, other species may not be at all metaphysically distinct from us or even our moral subordinates and inferiors. Varieties of species develop social codes and mores, communicating to various degrees across species as well as within their own species not only their own interests and concerns, but also modes of ethical agency and social desires that may not be any less sophisticated than our own. The coevolved origins of what we loosely term "morality" offer a basis for understanding both such differences and commonalities within and across species. However, renewed attention to the commonalities among human and nonhuman animals, long underemphasized in Western philosophy, promises a deeper awareness of how humans might engage other species, not as amoral beasts but as creatures who, like us, experience suffering and joy, flourishing through the social connections of camaraderie or community. This social source of flourishing also recalls dimensions of ethics neglected in modern and poststructuralist theory and yet important in our own everyday lives as profoundly social creatures.

Understanding shared animal capacities for ethical agency requires not only enhancing our knowledge of the social behavior and desires of other species and ourselves but also reconceptualizing the nature and significance of morality. Morality as taken up in the abstract formulations of modern moral theory (primarily through Kantian philosophies of rational duty and Singer's tradition of utilitarianism) loses sight of the concrete social codes and mores, the animating desires, and the social emotions that constitute what Hegelians term the "substance of ethical life." Questioning the abstraction of modern moral theories or poststructuralist modes of ethical subjectivity and response, this post-Hegelianism highlights webs of mutual obligation and character development. Abstract moral claims or subjectivities are relatively empty apart from the living world where social bonds attuned through affect give meaning and motivating force. What Hegelians term "ethical substance," or "ethical life," retracts from such modern moral dualisms as individual autonomy vs. dependence or reason vs. emotion toward a larger world of group dynamics and social interdependence, a world indeed shared with other animal species. Nonetheless, few philosophers have yet to trouble the sharp metaphysical divide erected since the time of Plato and Aristotle between human and nonhuman animals.

Singer's assumptions regarding unique human capacities for moral reasoning represent this dominant view of Western philosophy. Singer launched the animal liberation movement in 1975 with the argument that animals no less than humans possess interests and feelings that merit moral consideration; however, he grounds ethics in abstract moral principles that, he continues to insist, provide the sole ground for moral judgment, and that, he also claims, only humans have the capacity to develop. Singer postulates this unique capacity for moral reasoning in humans to shore up the claim that humans, unlike other creatures, have the capacity for impartial moral judgments. This capacity seemingly enables humans to do what no other social animal can do, namely, extend ethical concern to the stranger outside one's own social group (as emphasized in his response to Frans de Waal in *Primates and Philosophers*).[9]

Response ethics also in effect maintains a metaphysical barrier between us and animals in its own attempt to account for the stranger. According to this tradition, ethical concern across the radical differences separating singular individuals challenges the relevance of abstract principles or universals and the reasoning process upon which such abstractions rest. Derrida ventures to ponder the ethical alterity of animals, but leaves standing the traditional assumptions regarding the radical discontinuity between humans and animals. (Sean Meighoo, in chapter 3 of this volume, problematizes this metaphysical claim in Derrida by pluralizing the radical differences across the human-animal divide.)

In distinction from these views, here I invite wonder on the simple possibility that humans may display their ethical agency first and foremost as do some other species through vital needs for cooperative relationships. Common desires for social status and group membership, social emotions such as shame and forgiveness, and social codes and expectations compose the concrete basis for modes of belonging, or an *ethos*, which lies at the too often neglected root meaning of ethics. This ancient Greek word, signifying both disposition and custom, would shift current debates in moral theory or its poststructuralist alternative toward concrete modes of belonging and cultivated dispositions of attuning the self to the other, that, as it turns out, are not only central to human life but also profoundly evident across species. Nonhuman animals, like human animals, participate together in a varying, larger ethos, which can stretch across species and which, despite life's wide variety, can be appreciated, if only inadequately, by our own species apart from any technical discourse weighed down by metaphysical abstractions.

Otherwise oblivious to the ethos and moral codes of other species, humans are tempted to view nonhuman animals largely not through impartial judgment but according to our needs. As a result, we treat them at once as objects of sentimental attachment, frivolous amusement, or indifferent use. Traditional Western and contemporary philosophical perspectives proclaiming a metaphysical abyss between them and us obscure the partially overlapping moral capacities of our and other species, and significantly, the imperfect impartial capacity for humans and nonhumans to respond ethically across group and species lines.

As this volume suggests, and the documentary *Blackfish* dramatizes, animals themselves offer an alternative moral tale. The documentary is based on a whale's struggles in captivity. In the wild, orcas, who have been misnamed as "killer whales," are seen to be a peaceful and nonviolent species with relatively "universal" or "impartial" codes against harming one another and humans. In this way, humans and orcas share a code in which harm to conspecific members and even to members of other species is inhibited. At the same time, Tilikum's murderous rage against his captors in the entertainment industry tells the story of how a toxic mix of abuse, neglect, and frustration narrows the options for ethical response. Yet the documentary also tells the tale of humans—individually and collectively— refusing to see Tilikum's suffering as morally significant. *Blackfish* is a sad tale of a diminished human capacity for ethical response. The kidnapping and captivity of the orca for use in the entertainment industry exhibits a terrifying disregard for the compelling social lives of other creatures. In this case, if the term "beast" signifies wanton disregard for others, as casually postulated of other species by moral philosophers, one is given to wonder: who here is the beast?

Perhaps, if only to free ourselves from being insensitive "beasts," we should reconsider the meaning of freedom. Freedom is commonly understood in modern, liberal democracies and moral theories to signify the right to self-control through choices that we make in our private lives. No doubt freedom should include its modern meaning as autonomy, bearing relevance as it does for other animals as well as ourselves. This can be illustrated in the fact that just as humans suffer myriad psychological and behavioral disorders from struggling to control that which cannot be controlled, so do many animals manifest disorders from similar disability to control their contexts.

However, studies of emotional expression and styles of cooperation among other species suggest a more expansive meaning of freedom via our shared status as social animals. Ironically, studies of other social species' complex needs for freedom prompt more attention to hitherto underemphasized or neglected dimensions of freedom in our own lives. We assume that modern life grants us more freedom than would be possible in premodern, traditional, or indigenous societies because of the privacy and independence that modern life allows. Perhaps it does as measured along the single dimension of autonomy. Yet consider how the exigencies of hyperproductive modern societies often leave us with little more reward than claims to control over an increasingly isolated private life, depriving us of the substantial social bonds and vital affects that we need to thrive. A large part of our lives is dictated by the need to work hard for institutionally defined goals, leaving us disconnected from others in ways that are profoundly removed from ancient human and indigenous lifestyles. In contrast with the community focus of our ancestors and of social primates generally, the fragmentation and atomism of modern individualism combined with sharpening socioeconomic inequalities and hierarchies between wealthy elites and impoverished masses have become the norm, inducing tremendous stress in humans, who are by nature like many of our planet's cohabitants, social creatures, and whose ethicality is performed and embodied in and through social contexts. Is it any wonder that some people, deprived of many features of those social contexts, evidence increasing degrees of depravity?

Perhaps it is within our own interests as humans to pay heed to our lives alongside other social creatures rather than reducing their lives and our own to objects of control on the single axis of freedom measured as autonomy and opposed to dependence. On this scale our social vulnerability is viewed as a weakness rather than as a source of joy and flourishing. The suffering we impose on other animals through the constricted existence of our control-driven lives is a symptom of a deeper malaise. The dramatic reaction of wild animals to their forced removal from their social group or communities when captured eerily echoes the fact that, as mammals, we too thrive in rich social environments. Without that support, social animals suffer characteristically modern ailments such as depression and anxiety, and as Tilikum demonstrates, occasional murderous rampages. The same is true for elephants and other group-housed animals in laboratories and zoos, where transfers of individuals in and out of these often artificially created social groups damage their psyches.[10]

More than self-control and a private life, freedom for social animals requires the connective tissue of a felt life, lived social context, ethos. Understanding this ethos expands beyond any narrow conception of freedom as autonomy to embrace that web of belonging that, after Hegel, has been termed "social freedom." Tilikum's traumatic acting out against his captors is no different from the behavior of most any animal hostage, human or nonhuman. Eons of evolutionary history have spun strands of intra- and interdependence, laying the basis for an ethos of connection and affective response not only within but also across various species. Cooperative societies, predators and prey, and symbiotic groups thrive by learning to sense the potential for alliances as well as threats acutely. To know ourselves as animals, as one species coevolving alongside others, is to recall an expansive existence in this dense biosocial weave. In the process of disconnecting ourselves from one another and the rest of nature, we risk forgetting that other animals are similarly entrenched in a web of social closeness and meaningful interaction. Not surprisingly, we have difficulty learning to respect for others what we no longer appreciate for ourselves. If, on the other hand, we consider the possibilities raised in this book that other species are, like us, agents of ethics, agents in different *ethoi*— we may better appreciate and respect their true natures, if not our own.

NOTES

1. Matthew Calarco, "Toward an Agnostic Animal Ethics," in *The Death of the Animal: A Dialogue*, ed. Paola Cavalieri (New York: Columbia University Press, 2009), 77.

2. For example, see Cynthia Willett, *Interspecies Ethics* (New York: Columbia University Press, 2014).

3. See Dale Jamieson, *Morality's Progress: Essays on Humans, Other Animals, and the Rest of Nature* (New York: Oxford University Press, 2002), 122 (understanding moral status as the ability to be wronged by the actions of others).

4. See Ani B. Satz, "Animals as Vulnerable Subjects: Beyond Interest-Convergence, Hierarchy, and Property," *Animal Law Review* 16 (2009): 65–101.

5. Donald Broom, "Cognitive Ability and Awareness in Domestic Animals and Decisions About Obligations to Animals," *Applied Animal Behavior Science* 126 (2010): 1–11; Hal Herzog and Shelley Galvin, "Common Sense and the Mental Lives of Animals: An Empirical Approach," in *Anthropomorphism, Anecdotes, and Animals*, ed. R. Mitchell, N. Thompson, and H. Miles (Albany: SUNY Press, 1997), 237–53.

6. Lori Marino and C. M. Colvin, "Thinking Pigs: A Comparative Review of Cognition, Emotion, and Personality in *Sus domesticus*," *International Journal of Comparative Psychology* 28 (2015), uclapsych_ijcp_23859.

7. Jacques Derrida, *The Animal That Therefore I Am*, trans. David Wills (New York: Fordham University Press, 2008).

8. Peter Singer, *Animal Liberation: The Definitive Classic of the Animal Movement* (New York: HarperCollins, 2009).

9. Frans de Waal, *Primates and Philosophers: How Morality Evolved*, ed. Stephen Macedo and Josiah Ober (Princeton, NJ: Princeton University Press, 2006).

10. Gay A. Bradshaw, *Elephants on the Edge: What Elephants Teach Us About Humanity* (New Haven, CT: Yale University Press, 2009).

Contributors

MICHAEL BATHGATE is professor of religious studies at Saint Xavier University, where he teaches courses on the religions of Asia and the comparative study of religion. His scholarship addresses the uses and functions of popular literature in medieval Japan and the pedagogical implications of sharing that literature as part of the Catholic liberal arts. He is the author of *The Fox's Craft in Japanese Religion and Folklore*.

MARC BEKOFF is professor emeritus of ecology and evolutionary biology at the University of Colorado, Boulder. He has published numerous scientific and popular essays and book chapters and thirty books, the most recent of which are *Ignoring Nature No More: The Case for Compassionate Conservation*; *Why Dogs Hump and Bees Get Depressed: The Fascinating Science of Animal Intelligence, Emotions, Friendship, and Conservation*; and *Rewilding Our Hearts: Building Pathways of Compassion and Coexistence*. Marc and Jessica Pierce coauthored *Wild Justice: The Moral Lives of Animals*. His home page is marcbekoff.com.

JOHN BERKMAN teaches theological ethics at Regis College, University of Toronto. Over the last twenty-five years he has done pioneering work on ethics and non-human animals in the Catholic Christian tradition. Most recently he has coedited *Searching for a Universal Ethic* and *Nonhuman Animals*. He lectures internationally to many groups, and presented the keynote address for a workshop at the 2013 annual gathering of the United States Conference of Catholic Bishops. Many of his articles on ethics and nonhuman animals can be found at utoronto.academia.edu/JohnBerkman and at researchgate.net.

JONATHAN K. CRANE, the Raymond F. Schinazi Scholar in Bioethics and Jewish Thought at the Emory University Center for Ethics, is the author of *Narratives and Jewish Bioethics*, the coeditor of *The Oxford Handbook of Jewish Ethics and Morality*, coauthor of *Ahimsa: The Way to Peace* on Gandhian philosophy, founder and coeditor of the *Journal of Jewish Ethics*. The past president of the Society of Jewish Ethics, he also serves on the board of advisors for Farm Forward.

DAN DEMETRIOU is an associate professor of philosophy at the University of Minnesota, Morris. He is coeditor of *Perspectives on Modern Honor* (2015) and founder of honorethics.org. His scholarship mainly explores the political, psychological, meta-ethical, applied-ethical, and evolutionary dimensions of agonistic honor, which he sees as an ethical mode in need of rehabilitation.

FRANS B. M. DE WAAL is a Dutch American expert on primate social behavior and cognition. His main areas of interest are the evolution of morality and primate capacities for cooperation, conflict resolution, empathy, and culture. He works with both monkeys (macaques, capuchins) and apes (bonobos, chimpanzees) in group-housed captive settings. De Waal is C. H. Candler Professor in the Psychology Department of Emory University and director of the Living Links Center at the Yerkes National Primate Research Center, in Atlanta, Georgia. He has been elected to the (U.S.) National Academy of Sciences, the American Academy of Arts and Sciences, and the Royal Dutch Academy of Sciences.

MARK GOLDFEDER, ESQ., is senior lecturer at Emory Law School and the Spruill Family Senior Fellow at the Center for the Study of Law and Religion. He is also an adjunct professor of law at Georgia State University College of Law and an adjunct professor in the Department of Religion at Emory University. A former Wexner Fellow for the Rabbinate at Yeshiva University, he received his J.D. from NYU Law and his L.L.M. and doctorate from Emory University.

AARON S. GROSS is the author of *The Question of the Animal and Religion* and coeditor of *Animals and the Human Imagination*, both published by Columbia University Press, and an assistant professor of theology and religious studies at the University of San Diego. He is a former cochair of the Animals and Religion Group of the American Academy of Religion and the founder and CEO of the nonprofit organization Farm Forward.

KENDY M. HESS is the Brake Smith Assistant Professor of Social Philosophy and Ethics at the College of the Holy Cross in Worcester, MA (USA). She has a J.D. from Harvard Law School, an M.A. from Northwestern University, and a Ph.D. in philosophy from the University of Colorado. She practiced corporate environmental law for fifteen years before moving to philosophy, and her current research focuses on the moral agency and obligations of corporations.

HARRISON KING is a doctoral student in religious studies at Northwestern University whose current research explores the theoretical intersections of animal studies, queer theory, and critical race theory through the lens of feminist science fiction. Previous research projects culminated in a master's thesis on religion and the human-animal relationship in the prose and poetry of Ursula K. Le Guin and several conference presentations on the lives of nonhuman animals in a variety of texts and contexts.

LORI MARINO, formerly a senior lecturer at Emory University for nineteen years and faculty affiliate at the Emory Center for Ethics, is the founder and executive director of the Kimmela Center for Animal Advocacy, a nonprofit organization that focuses on scholarship-based advocacy for other animals. She holds a Ph.D. in biopsychology and has published more than one hundred peer-reviewed scientific papers, book chapters, and magazine articles on the evolution of brains and intelligence in cetaceans and primates, as well as human-nonhuman animal relationships and, most particularly, captivity issues. She was recently featured as a *National Geographic* Innovator and appears in several films and television programs, including the influential documentary *Blackfish*, about killer whale captivity. She teaches online courses in animal behavior and evolution.

SEAN MEIGHOO received his Ph.D. from the Graduate Program in Social and Political Thought at York University (Toronto). He is currently an assistant professor in the Department of Comparative Literature at Emory University (Atlanta). His research and teaching interests include twentieth-century continental philosophy and literary theory; race and postcolonial studies; feminism and queer studies; and posthumanism and animal studies. His most recent publication is "Suffering Humanism, or the Suffering Animal," *Journal for Critical Animal Studies* 12, no. 3 (August 2014): 50–74.

ELISABETTA PALAGI has been studying primates—spanning strepsirrhines and haplorrhines, including monkeys, apes, and humans—since 1992. She holds a master's degree in biology and a Ph.D. in evolutionary biology, and has a solid publication record on a wide array of topics bridging sociobiology, psychology, and anthropological sciences. Among others, she has demonstrated individual recognition in lemurs and their use of multimodal signaling. She has also extensively investigated the functions and evolutionary significance of play, conflict management and resolution in social groups, and the behavioral patterns underlying emotional contagion and empathic abilities of human and nonhuman primates. She works at both the Natural History Museum, University of Pisa, and the Unit of Cognitive Primatology and Primate Center, Institute of Cognitive Sciences and Technologies CNR, in Rome, Italy.

ANI B. SATZ is a professor of law at Emory University, with faculty appointments at the Rollins School of Public Health, University Center for Ethics, and Goizueta Business School. Professor Satz holds a J.D. from the University of Michigan and a Ph.D. in philosophy from Monash University in Melbourne, Australia, which she completed while a fellow at Princeton University. Her research focuses on the legal response to vulnerability and governmental obligations to those who are vulnerable, including access to health care, disability discrimination, and the well-being of nonhuman animals. Her work has appeared in books, peer-reviewed journals, and law reviews, among them the *Michigan Law Review; Washington & Lee Law Review; Emory Law Journal; Yale Journal of Health Policy, Law, and Ethics;* and *Washington Law Review.* Professor Satz is chair-elect of the Section on Animal Law; immediate past chair of the Section on Law, Medicine and Health Care; and served as 2009–10 chair of the Section on Disability Law of the Association of American Law Schools.

CYNTHIA WILLETT teaches philosophy at Emory University. Her authored books include *Interspecies Ethics; Irony in the Age of Empire: Comic Perspectives on Freedom and Democracy; The Soul of Justice: Racial Hubris and Social Bonds;* and *Maternal Ethics and Other Slave Moralities.* She has edited the anthology *Theorizing Multiculturalism* and is a coeditor of the *Symposia on Gender, Race, and Philosophy.*

Index